DARE to
DECLARE

DARE to
DECLARE

A Collection *of* Prophetically
Inspired Declarations

DR. MARY FRANCES VARALLO

bush
PUBLISHING
& associates

DARE TO DECLARE: A Collection of Prophetically Inspired Declarations
ISBN: 978-1-944566-08-1
Copyright © 2016 by Dr. Mary Frances Varallo Ministries
4117 Hillsboro Pike, Suite 103–272
Nashville, TN 37215

Published by Bush Publishing & Associates
www.BushPublishing.com
Editor: Deanne Cartagena, San Francisco Bay Area
Hand-drawn antique crown designed by Freepik

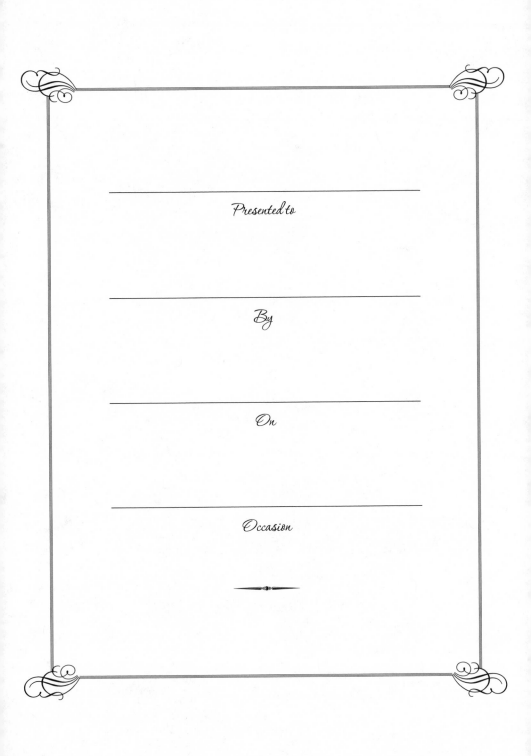

Presented to

By

On

Occasion

DEDICATION

To our daughter, Christina—God brought you to us first;
so petite, so quiet (at first), with such bright eyes,
full of personality and lots of wavy, curly hair.

To our son, Nicholas—God's surprise to us; so big and so loud,
with your intense eyes and determined way, and with no hair!

God our Father blessed our lives with the two of you.
We are family. We have had hard times, and the very best of times.
We have lived through sad moments,
but also the happiest of moments together.
We have cried until we had no more tears,
and have laughed until we cried. But *always* as family.
Our blessed Lord gave us the love of family that we share.
His presence will never leave. Always He will be with you.
No matter what is happening, He is always right there.

The day will come, and I will join your Dad, who stands
amongst the great cloud of witnesses in the heavenlies,
and together we will wait for you to return to us,
and family we shall be for all eternity.

Your Dad and I are so proud of you.
By Jesus Christ you overcome life's difficulties,
and you stand victoriously.

Love,
Momma

ACKNOWLEDGEMENTS

The Holy Spirit places people in your life at different times and seasons. If you will embrace and nurture those divine relationships, eternal fruit will be produced. I would like to acknowledge just a few of the ones who have graced my life, and who have made this book a reality.

My beloved Pastors, Pastor Bill and Linda McRay, who shepherded my heart and schooled me so marvelously in the Word and the Spirit of God.

Reverend Nancy Lowery, gifted and anointed Prayer Director for Mary Frances Varallo Ministries. Highly skilled and proficient in the Word of God, Reverend Lowery rightly interprets the moving of the Holy Spirit, and provides exceptional leadership for the extraordinary men and women who make up the MFVM Prayer Team: Reverend Judy Lee, Nicole Hogue, Pastor Dana Edwards, Bob and Sue McKown, with Bob also serving as MFVM Crusade Director, and Reverend Emje Rolston. Some of these individuals have been with me for 30 years, and all faithfully forge a way for me in the spirit as they see and pray with such great precision and power.

David Flint, MFVM Administrator, who has been with me for more than a decade and a half, and for whom I am deeply grateful. He has served so willingly and with such excellence. Nicole Hogue, whom I have known personally for 25 years, and who joined the MFVM Staff as Administrative Assistant to David Flint in more recent years. She is most necessary to this ministry, and she carries out the many things she does with a servant's heart. Deanne Cartagena, my writer and editor of

14 years, who has captured my words to reach the hearts of the people. Reverend Jen Tringale, who has been such a gift to this ministry.

My precious partners, whose faithfulness and prayers through all these years have been a continual encouragement to this ministry and to my heart.

Thank you to Bush Publishing for the bringing forth of this book.

To the gracious pastors and congregations who make a place for me to walk in the giftings of God the Holy Spirit, and who so inspire me with their hunger and love for our Lord.

To each and every one of you, for the tremendous giftings, anointings and graces you have blessed my life and this ministry with, thank you, I am forever grateful!

First Corinthians 2:4–5, in *The Amplified Bible,* has been the benchmark scripture of my life and ministry. *"And my language and my message were not set forth in persuasive (enticing and plausible) words of wisdom, but they were in demonstration of the Holy Spirit and power.... So that your faith might not rest in the wisdom of men...but in the power of God."*

God the Holy Spirit, the great demonstrator of the works of Jesus Christ, is moving mightily on behalf of the Church in this hour! He confirms His Word most demonstratively through the manifestation of His gifts of revelation, power gifts and prophecy. The gifts of the Spirit working upon and through His servants is marvelous, and through the pages of this book, I want to share with you how He magnificently demonstrates His power, and stir your expectancy for Him to manifest Himself to and through you!

Prophets stand between times, events, dispensations and moves of God and speak of things that were, that are, and that are about to be. One of the greatest graces the office of prophet carries, according to the Word of God, is impartation. So by virtue of these divine impartations, I declare channels of blessing be open unto you, and in Jesus' Name I release unto you the anointings that I carry: grace, favor, prosperity, authority, healings, miracles, seeing and knowing!

It is God your Father's heart, and mine, to build up and encourage you in who you are and *Whose* you are. You are Heaven's most powerful force on Earth! No greater power can one possess than Jesus Christ's indwelling presence through the working of the Holy Spirit. You are God's voice, authority and power in the earth. What you believe and say in faith becomes a royal declaration—and all of Heaven backs you up.

I want to share with you how the Holy Spirit works with me, and help to build your expectation for the workings of God the Holy Spirit through you. As I prayed before a church service where I was ministering, the Holy Spirit began to speak to me about what He was going to show me in the meeting. In great detail He spoke to me about the individuals I would see in the service, including where they would be sitting and what they would be wearing. He described their stature and appearance to me with such precision. He then instructed me to write all of these specifics down, along with the words that He had for these individuals, so that I could show them to the people of the congregation. He also revealed healings that would take place. His workings were so accurate and specific, that when I shared these things with the people, a great expectancy was stirred in the sanctuary for the miraculous.

The Holy Spirit continued to manifest Himself in His wonderful gifts of healings, including the healing of a woman with multiple tumors. In a private setting, the Holy Spirit even chose to confirm future plans for the church that the pastor alone had in his heart. What an encourage-ment the Holy Spirit is to the sons of God!

He who knows all things, knows you, too. It is the Father's heart to open His hand and satisfy the desire of every living thing. I pray that the anointings of this ministry would rest upon your life in great measure as you trust Him to manifest Himself on your behalf. Dare to believe His Word. Set your heart to receive all that He has secured for you through God the Son, Jesus Christ, and by the power of God the Holy Spirit.

Dr. Mary Frances Varallo

The Power of Your Words

At the dawn of creation, the Book of Genesis records that God said, *"Let there be…!"* In an instant, the Holy Spirit, who hovered over the face of the waters, moved in obedience to the command of the Almighty to perform His word, *"…and it was!"*

> *When you give voice to the Word of God in your heart, your faith releases a power that all of Heaven will enforce and none of Hell can stop!*

The Prophet Daniel, knowing that the word of the Lord concerning his beloved nation of Israel had not yet been accomplished, set his face toward the Lord to pray and fast. (See Daniel 9). After 21 days of relentless supplication, Daniel was visited by the angel Gabriel with this message: *"Do not fear, Daniel, for from the first day that you set your heart to understand, and to humble yourself before your God, your words were heard; and I have come because of your words"* (Daniel 10:12, NKJV).

Never underestimate the power of your words. When you give voice to the Word of God in your heart, your faith releases a power that all of Heaven will enforce and none of Hell can stop! I encourage you most earnestly not to be moved by what you see, hear or feel in the sense realm. Do not allow yourself to yield to fear. Keep your mind on Him, and you will be kept in perfect peace. God's Word, hidden in your heart and flowing from your lips, is the sound of faith that pleases your Father and moves Heaven and Earth on your behalf.

DECLARATION: I declare over you that your words are a powerful, creative force that sets God's will in motion on the earth and in your life. You will not underestimate the power of your words. You will hide God's Word in your heart and declare it with your mouth, releasing faith that pleases the Father and it will move Heaven and Earth on your behalf.

The Word and the Spirit

By speaking God's words, you provide substance for the Holy Spirit to hover upon...and to bring forth.

When you worship and glorify Jesus your Lord, God the Holy Spirit inhabits your praises. He comes in and hovers like He did long, long ago. It was the Holy Spirit who hovered over a place in infinity, waiting upon the Creator Almighty to speak. For it is God the Holy Spirit who takes Father's words and gives them form.

As you say what God says concerning your life, the Holy Spirit hovers over those words. He moves in the earth giving form to the words and brings them forth. Know this truth: spiritual law is greater than natural law. Facts are subject to change. Facts—be they financial, medical, relational or academic—everything you can see, feel, taste and touch, came out of the spirit realm and is subject to change according to the words you say.

I encourage you to speak the Word of God regarding the things in your heart and all that concerns you. By speaking God's words, you provide substance for the Holy Spirit to hover upon, give form to and bring forth. What does God say about your situation? Say what God says. Declare it! Decree it! God's Word applied to your situation *will* change it!

👑 **DECLARATION: I declare over you that you will speak words of faith in agreement with the Word of God, which is the will of God. "Hindrances and delays: move out of your way! Circumstances and situations: change and rearrange! Body: be made whole! Provision: be!" I declare and believe the Holy Spirit is moving to bring form to your faith-filled words, and to bring forth the Father's will concerning you.**

New Day

Something wonderful of God has begun! Change is all around you. You have crossed over into a place that is new. If you sense that things are different now, I want to encourage you to keep moving with the Holy Spirit however He is leading you. Stay close to the Word—your daily bread—for the Spirit will never lead you apart from the Word. He who is the Spirit of truth brings revelation upon all of your information.

When God brings a new move to the earth, He does not do away with what we have learned; He builds upon the foundation we have been given just as He has done in every generation.

When God brings a new move to the earth, He does not do away with what you have learned; He builds upon the foundation you have been given just as He has done in every generation. Understand that no one has maneuvered in this new place before, so things can look and feel different and unfamiliar to you. New things are almost always uncomfortable, but the cloud is moving, and if you don't move with Him, you are going to be stuck, and then whatever you have been doing you will have to continue to do. You will be working 24/7 in your own strength to keep things going, and whatever it took to get you there is what it will take to keep you there. Everything changes now. Nothing can remain the same. Why would you want things to be the same?

Pray for your pastor to hear and follow the Holy Spirit into the new, different and exciting plans He has prepared. Be bold to follow the cloud and not the crowd. Embrace what is new and different to you, and be encouraged in these days that God is moving in exciting new ways in preparation for His return!

DECLARATION: I declare over you that you will embrace the new of God for your life this day. His great grace is upon you, preparing and positioning you for divine purpose.

It has Begun

From sea to shining sea. Nation to nation. There will be a decree!

The hand of the Lord comes upon His people and takes them into places of seeing, knowing and revelatory information. You are the sons and daughters who have prayed and believed; those who have waited upon the manifested works of the Spirit of God to be demonstrated in your lives. It has begun! From sea to shining sea. Nation to nation. There will be a decree! It will seem to go from this one to that one, it is moving so fast. The Body of Christ will say, "Oh, my Lord! Look what God just did!" Reports will go throughout the lands. You will go to bed one way and wake up another. There will be those who will go for 20 minutes or more into the heavenlies to see and to know, and who will return with revelatory information to give to this one and that one. It has begun!

Some will say, "I can't believe these things are so. I can't believe these kinds of things."

Oh yes, it has always been that way. Was it not that way for Jesus in His day? There were those who doubted and ridiculed; those who would have killed Him. So do not be surprised if the persecutions of the Church seem to suddenly, severely arise. With such demonstrations and manifestations on display that Heaven would do, starting today. There will also be the naysayers. Did Jesus not say that some will suffer as He did for the things that they would do in His Name? So why be surprised? Because you have come unto the ending of all things, the kingdom of darkness makes its decrees. It will push and it will shove and it will try to be the greater to you, to overwhelm and overcome. But He—Jesus Christ, God the Son—overcame the kingdom of darkness and Satan, its lord.

Now you take Jesus' Name and implement what He so did! Get done what must be done before you are called up and out of here. It is such a time and such a day, and the portions, giftings and anointings were always meant for you. There are those things that were saved in particular for these days. Others could never have carried what you shall carry. For some of you it begins today. You will know the difference when you awake in the morning.

DECLARATION: I declare over you, in the Name of Jesus Christ, that you will receive the graces imparted through the word of the Lord. You are a part of what has begun in the earth and you agree that it has begun for you!

All Things New

Wherever you are today, know that the past is far behind. In fact, if you are born again, your past is no more! The Cross of Christ has made a way for all humanity to step into a place where old things have passed away and all things have become new...and all things are now of God! (See 2 Corinthians 5:17–18, NKJV).

"Therefore, if anyone is in Christ, he is a new creation; old things have passed away; behold, all things have become new. Now all things are of God...."
—*2 Corinthians 5:17–18, NKJV*

The Father knows your life. What has been washed in the blood is not only forgiven, but also forgotten! It is by faith and not by feelings that you can say, *"I have been crucified with Christ; it is no longer I who live, but Christ who lives in me; and the life which I now live in the flesh I live by faith in the Son of God, who loved me and gave Himself for me"* (Galatians 2:20–21).

If old habits, mindsets and patterns of living are hindering you from crossing over into your royal redemption, remember that forgiveness extends to you. Let go of what you have done or left undone, your shortcomings, your pride and your fears. Allow the truth of God's Word to reign, and all things will become new for you.

Our Savior's sacrifice secured a heavenly home for all who will believe, but eternal life isn't reserved just for Heaven: eternal life abides in you today! For when you are born again, all the power you need to overcome—in this life—lives in you through your faith in the Son! *"For whatsoever is born of God overcometh the world: and this is the victory that overcometh the world, even our faith"* (1 John 5:4). May today be a new day for you as you release the past and embrace your new life in Christ!

👑 **DECLARATION: I declare over you that the eternal life abiding in you has canceled out your past and made all things new. Yesterday, today and forever you overcome through the blood of God's victorious Son!**

Feed on His Faithfulness

"Trust in the Lord, and do good; dwell in the land, and feed on His faithfulness."
—*Psalm 37:3, NKJV*

As you cross over into a year and a time that is new, I encourage you to feed on Father God's faithfulness to you. Draw from past victories, recalling how He has blessed, protected and carried you through. Know that whatever you commit to His care is secure. Trust Him completely with your future, for He can be trusted! He is not only Almighty God; He is *your Father,* and He loves you!

Confidence in your Father's faithfulness will hold you steady in the face of doubt, fear or lying symptoms that would try to steal from you. Submit yourself to God's words and ways, resist the thief, and he will flee from you.

It is a great time of change in the earth. The seasons and times will continue to change ever-so rapidly now. Stay steady and hold fast the profession of your faith without wavering, for your faithful Father does not change!

DECLARATION: I declare over you that today you will put yourself in remembrance of your Father's faithfulness. The One who knows the past, present and future is your God, and in Him you remain stable, steady and fixed in the face of change.

Choose to Forgive

The Scriptures show that Jesus often encouraged His disciples and others who came to Him for various needs, to forgive.

"For if you forgive people their trespasses, their reckless and willful sins, leaving them, letting them go, and giving up resentment, your heavenly Father will also forgive you."
—Matthew 6:14, AMP

"And whenever you stand praying, if you have anything against anyone, forgive him and let it drop (leave it, let it go), in order that your Father Who is in heaven may also forgive you your own failings and shortcomings and let them drop.

"But if you do not forgive, neither will your Father in heaven forgive your failings and shortcomings."

—Mark 11:25–26, AMP

My, how the Holy Spirit wants you to be clear of all offenses. It is only by His grace and through an act of your own volition that you are truly able to forgive. Disappointments with others, yourselves—even God— are not yours to hold on to, so "let them drop, leave them, and let them go." Forgive that one whom you have carried ought against. Forgive yourself where you have fallen short. Go to God the Father in the Name of the Son, and in His justice, His righteousness, and His great love, He shall forgive you. Choose to forgive before this year continues; don't let any sin be found in you.

👑 **DECLARATION: I declare over you that today you will choose to release hurts and offenses you have carried toward God, others or yourself. Refuse to carry the sin, disappointments, failings and shortcomings of anyone. Turn every offense over to your Lord Jesus Christ and walk forward by faith, forgiven and free!**

A Planting of the Lord

"...Behold, I make all things new...."
—Revelation 21:5

God, by His Holy Spirit, is working in you both *to will and to do* of His good pleasure! (See Philippians 2:13). That means whatever He is rooting out and bringing to a close is for your good and for His glory. The Father desires to restore you to wholeness, and to prepare your heart to begin a planting of the Lord in you.

Believe that God is a good Father who can be trusted to lead you into all truth. What you may not have seen accurately or clearly before, He is defining and illuminating with such precision now. He is healing you… making you brand new…in soul and body, too! He wants you whole and complete not in your own strength, but in Him and by His magnificent grace.

Know that His Word concerning you is true: He really does make all things new! *He gives unto you beauty for ashes, the oil of joy for mourning, the garment of praise for the spirit of heaviness; that you may be called trees of righteousness, the planting of the Lord, that He may be glorified.* (See Isaiah 61:3).

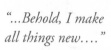 **DECLARATION: I declare over you that God's Word concerning you is true, and all that He wills to do in and for you is complete! He heals you and makes you new—spirit, soul and body! You are a tree of righteousness, a planting of the Lord, and you shall glorify your Father in all you say and do.**

The Time of Manifestation

So much is unfolding for the Church, for nations, for leaders, for you and for me. My heart is full of anticipation for you, as I know the Father's heart is, because I believe it is a time of manifestation of what you have believed. What is it that you have contended

"Now faith is the substance of things hoped for...."
—Hebrews 11:1

for concerning your life, your family, your health, your finances, your ministry, your job, your relationships? There comes a fullness of time for those things that you have truly believed to come to fruition, and it seems to me you have moved into that time.

Have confidence that the Word you have spoken will not return void, but will accomplish what it was sent forth to do! God's Holy Spirit is moving even now to bring forth the fruit of the faith-filled Word you have declared and decreed. It is that day, where you will see what you say.

The glory is poured out upon God's sons and daughters in demonstrations of power and displays of love beyond what you have dreamed! Then, the Father sends you and me forth in His wisdom, His compassion and His power to give people hope. He extends this hope to you first, for you cannot give what you have not received. *"Now faith is the substance of things hoped for...the evidence of things not seen"* (Hebrews 11:1).

Be encouraged and do not lose hope concerning the things you have seen by the Spirit of God; those things He has imprinted upon your heart of hearts. They really do come to pass!

👑 **DECLARATION: I declare over you that it is time for what you have seen, believed and declared by the Spirit of God to manifest in your life. What you have hoped for becomes the tangible substance of faith, and what you have believed in your heart you now see. God brings to pass His will for you!**

Filled With the Knowledge of His Will

...You must be able to interpret the moment with God the Holy Spirit....

Dear one, I believe the year before you is one of great decision. You must have sure answers to the many questions pressing on your heart and mind. Have confidence in this truth: The Father's plan for you is already settled in Heaven! His desire is that you be filled with the knowledge of His will in all wisdom and spiritual understanding. (See Colossians 1:9). He extends to you His heavenly wisdom that will only come out of your fellowship with the Holy Spirit. As you give Him your time, God will speak deep within you by His Spirit, He who is your revelator of the truth! In those moments with Him, illumination and understanding will come upon the knowings inside of you, so that you will see, hear and know ever-so clearly, what to do.

If you will quiet yourself and listen with spiritual ears you will discern and interpret most accurately the workings of the Holy Spirit. *In this time we have come into, you must be able to interpret the moment with God the Holy Spirit, for He will save your life!* God is going to envelop you—literally clothe you—in His manifested glory! Yes, He is going to dress His earthen vessels with Heaven's magnificent presence! You will wear the glory of God in such a way that people will run to you because you are going to handle situations notably differently, and they will want to know why. Believe this. Receive this. Keep your heart open to the supernatural, miraculous life the Spirit of God has destined for you, and He will demonstrate His power in and through you. What was recorded in Daniel so long ago is true concerning you today: *"...The people who know their God shall be strong, and carry out great exploits."* (See Daniel 11:32b).

♛ **DECLARATION: I declare over you that you will have intimate fellowship with the Holy Spirit. It is what prepares you to rightly interpret each and every moment. His wisdom floods your heart. His understanding illuminates your mind. You will see clearly where to go and what to do, because you have spent time with Him.**

A Year of Acceleration

You have crossed over into a new year, and are moving ever-forward through the corridor of the time of the end. What the Holy Spirit speaks to you in this hour is of utmost importance. You must take the time to fine-tune your

There is an acceleration in the manifestations of what you have believed.

hearing of Him so that you will know what to do, how to do it and when. God the Holy Spirit is your personal guide and helper, sent by the Father at Jesus' request, to lead you victoriously through all things.

Utterances from Heaven have come forth so clearly—such sounds I did hear concerning the year. I share with you what I believe I heard the Holy Spirit say, to encourage your heart and stir your faith to believe and receive these knowings from Him.

"It is a year of acceleration!" Acceleration is a term used in physics. It denotes the rate of change of velocity with time. Because of the time you have come into, there is an acceleration in the manifestations of what you have believed. Yes, the awakening of the Church comes quickly now, and with it a propelling of believers into their destinies with exceptional provision. A divine acceleration in prosperity comes upon you! The Gospel moves at such speed in demonstrations; all for the purpose of winning the lost! Acceleration in revelation comes upon the world's information that brings discoveries and advances in medicine and other sciences. Even reports of angelic activity and visitations of the Christ Himself will increase. As you move closer to Heaven, Heaven moves closer to you! Changes in the names and faces of leaders both spiritually and governmentally worldwide are at hand. Sounds of false peace and, not war, but the sounds of warrings, abound. There is a knowing of something wonderful and something terrible trying to be, but remember, *the light always overtakes the darkness,* and you are of those who overcome! Be encouraged by the Holy Spirit's securing of you for this time; look and listen earnestly for the sounds of acceleration in this brand new year!

👑 **DECLARATION: I declare over you that acceleration in provision comes upon your life, positioning you for increase spiritually and naturally. Revelation from Heaven comes upon your information. A great awakening comes upon you, and in Jesus' Name, you overcome the darkness.**

The Hope of Glory

The root of the righteous cannot be moved.

You have come into a wonderful time! Before your very eyes the forces of darkness loom over the earth, and deep darkness blankets the people. But for you—His glorious Church—your righteousness goes forth as brightness, and your salvation as a burning lamp, beckoning the world and its kings to come to the light emanating from your life. (See Isaiah 60:2, 3; 62:1). Christ *in you*, the glorious hope of all humanity!

What is of the world is crumbling all around, for those of the world have built their lives on the sand. Only what is a planting of the Lord, founded on the Rock, will stand. All who have made God's law their meditation day and night shall be like trees planted by the rivers of water, bringing forth fruit in their season, their leaf also shall not wither; and whatever they do shall prosper. (See Psalm 1:2, 3).

Son and daughter of God, this is your season! You who are rooted and grounded in love, with rivers of living water flowing in and out from you, arise now as lights in the darkness, drawing the lost to your Savior. When the bodies, minds, marriages, careers and lives of the world fail and fall, they will know there is a difference in you. Not that the storms of life don't come to you, but the storms will not take you down or out, for *"the root of the righteous cannot be moved."* (See Proverbs 12:3).

"Be ready always to give an answer to every man that asketh you a reason of the hope that is in you," (1 Peter 3:15). I have a great expectancy for the wondrous encounters approaching for you, and a great confidence in the God whose heart desires that all men be saved and come to the knowledge of the truth!

👑 **DECLARATION: I declare over you that you are a beacon of God's glorious light! Open doors and opportunities abound to you to tell of Christ in you—the hope of glory!**

Abide in Him

At the start of a year, when things are fresh and new, so many ponder, "What does this new year hold for me?" I would ask you, "What is in your heart of hearts? What is it that you desire?" For if you are abiding in God, and His words are abiding in you, as John 15:7 describes, then you carry the Father's heart, and His desires already stir within your heart.

"If you abide in Me, and My words abide in you, you will ask what you desire, and it shall be done for you." —John 15:7, NKJV

In the quiet moments of intimacy and fellowship with God the Holy Spirit, He will speak to you very specifically about *you* and the things that concern your life. He will speak to you of what is to come, what to pray, how to prepare, where to be and where not to be and when. In this time it is necessary that you learn to listen and follow the Holy Spirit in the seemingly little things. The better you know Him, the better you can trust His promptings and your ability to hear them.

It is your Father's heart to open His hand and satisfy the desire of every living thing. Stay in a place of fellowship with the Father, and you will be positioned for the plans He has destined for you!

DECLARATION: I declare over you that you will abide in your Almighty God. His Word lives in you. His desires well up from the inside of you, and His Spirit leads you into His glorious plans for your life. You will walk in wisdom, favor, prosperity and extraordinary divine connections in Jesus' Name!

Eternity in You

How marvelous of God to bring you to this place in time—this Kairos—a moment where destiny, events and timings of things come together!

You have come on through a new door, dear one, and for this time you were created to be and to bring forth on behalf of the beloved Son! How marvelous of God to bring you to this place in time—this Kairos—a moment where destiny, events and timings of things come together! From Heaven comes such revelation to the sons and daughters of the Most High. It is necessary that you be ever-cognizant of who you are and of Whose you are, for it will make all the difference now in the time you have come into.

The Kingdom of God in you is operating in divine order, but the system of the world is not. In fact, the world's system is decaying. But you who are of God's Kingdom are becoming greater, for the Kingdom of God is within you! (See Luke 17:21.) Yes, God's Kingdom surrounds you—it is everywhere around and about you—but the Kingdom resides *inside you*. Understand that eternity isn't a place you are trying to get to, eternity is the person that you are! God is eternity and God is in you. God—eternity—inhabits you! *"Do you not know that your body is the temple, the very sanctuary, of the Holy Spirit Who lives within you, Whom you have received as a Gift from God?"* (1 Corinthians 6:19, AMP). God doesn't want another edifice. He doesn't desire another cathedral. He doesn't long for another synagogue. *You are His abiding place, and He is eternity.* The Kingdom of Heaven is a destination—a physical place. The Kingdom of God is position—authority, dominion and power in you. Do you see the difference? I believe you will.

Learn to draw out of God's Kingdom. It's not difficult. You have but to speak what He would say to draw out. Eternity He is, and so are you. For you are spirit, not speaking of your body—earth suit—but speaking of the real you, spirit person, and God inhabits you.

DECLARATION: I declare over you that your God is an eternal Spirit and dwells in you; therefore, you are of the eternal One, for eternity dwells in you! From God's Kingdom you declare and decree what will be, for this is your position of dominion, power and authority!

Divine Impartations

It is your Father's heart that you possess and walk in every good thing Jesus Christ purchased for you. He poured out His life to secure your eternity, and by His divine power—through an intimate knowledge of Him—He bestowed upon you all things that are necessary for life and godliness (See 2 Peter 1:3, AMP).

"For I am yearning to see you, that I may impart and share with you some spiritual gift to strengthen and establish you...."
—Romans 1:11, AMP

How marvelous of Him to make such perfect provision to establish you in your giftings, your callings and in your spheres of influence in this earth! Everything the Holy Spirit has made available to you is good, and you receive His wondrous supply by faith. The Apostle Paul understood that what he received of the Lord was for others too, and so to the believers he longed to impart—give, grant and convey—these divine equippings.

Whatever it is you require to stabilize, strengthen and secure you concerning your life, family, ministry, business and decisions to be made, I encourage you to place a demand on Heaven. May light illuminate you now, bringing revelation upon your information. I decree that given unto you is great wisdom so you know what to do! Impartations be made in one and all—everything you need to fulfill your call!

DECLARATION: I declare over you that in Jesus' Name you walk in the wisdom, revelation, grace, favor, prosperity, authority, healings, miracles and divine connections granted unto you!

Seeings and Knowings

If you can see it, you can possess it!

Wat is God the Holy Spirit speaking to your heart today? What is He showing you? Take this moment to be still and listen. Quiet your soul and the thoughts that so often race and press upon your mind. Our beloved Lord said in John 16:13, that when the Holy Spirit—the Spirit of truth—was sent to Earth, He would *speak* what He heard and would *show* us things to come.

Seeings and *knowings* are the language of the Holy Spirit. He comes to you in dreams and visions, illuminating and declaring the great plans the Father has for all humanity and for your individual life, too. "Plans for me?" you ask. "Oh, but what I have seen is so big!" The Holy Spirit would say to you, *"Look and see the invisible with the eye of faith, and the God of the impossible will manifest what you saw. If you can see it, you can possess it!"*

I pray that God, who is the Spirit of wisdom and revelation, would open the eyes of your understanding this day, so that you would see and know what the hope of His calling is for you. Then, once you see, you will believe and do!

DECLARATION: I declare over you that you have been granted the Spirit of wisdom and revelation by your God. He opens the eyes of your understanding so that you see and know the hope of His calling for your life. You see it, believe it and do it!

The Greater Awaits

Your God is faithful. His Word is alive and full of power! With thanksgiving, open your heart to receive the promises of God for your life and expect a bountiful harvest to overtake you.

Expect things to change—in you, around you and for you—this year. It is your Father's heart concerning you. What has been so hard concerning you will suddenly, miraculously give way as you begin to thank and praise the One

"You crown the year with a bountiful harvest; even the hard pathways overflow with abundance. The wilderness becomes a lush pasture, and the hillsides blossom with joy." —Psalm 66:11–12, NLT

who has made the way for you. Worship Jesus in all that you do, for the greater in Him awaits you!

 DECLARATION: I declare over you that the greatness of God is reserved for you—greater ability, greater provision, greater joy. You will be productive and abounding in every area of your life because you put your confidence in Almighty God and Jesus, your Savior. Obstacles now move out of the way because you choose to praise and worship Jesus Christ.

Faith and Fellowship

The strength of your faith is related to the quality of your fellowship with the Spirit of God.

Today I believe the Holy Spirit would have me encourage you in your faith and in your fellowship with Him. I have often said, "Truth is greater than fact; facts are subject to change, but truth is eternal." God's Word is truth, and I exhort you to keep yourself in agreement with His Word concerning you.

Jesus said, *"For verily I say unto you, that whosoever shall say unto this mountain, be thou removed, and be thou cast into the sea; and shall not doubt in his heart, but shall believe that those things which he saith shall come to pass; he shall have whatsoever he saith"* (Mark 11:23).

All the blessings of God flow out of fellowship with Him. The strength of your faith is related to the quality of your fellowship with the Spirit of God. The Scriptures tell us when the angel of the Lord visited Mary, her reply to his message was, *"Behold the handmaid of the Lord; be it unto me according to thy word"* (Luke 1:38). Mary agreed with the Word of the Lord for her life, and destiny was fulfilled. From a deep place of fellowship you can say the same. When you agree with what God says, your faith is activated to receive.

I believe the Spirit of God desires to move mightily on your behalf this year. There is so much He wants to reveal and manifest in your life. Through fellowship, you will know those things clearly and distinctly, and you will agree with Him to bring them to pass.

DECLARATION: I declare over you that you will set your heart to agree with God and press into a deeper place of fellowship with the Holy Spirit. Your faith is strengthened today as you fellowship your relationship with the Spirit of truth.

Stay Christ-Minded

In prayer one day, I believe I heard the Holy Spirit say, "Keep your affections on God in all you are believing for. Stay Christ-minded."

Keep your affections on God in all you are believing for.

The Holy Spirit will never lead you apart from God's Word, and God's Word confirms in Matthew 6:33, *"But seek ye first the kingdom of God, and his righteousness; and all these things shall be added unto you."* "These things" refer to material goods.

A season of supernatural prosperity has come upon you, dear one! In this time of wealth and increase, it is vital that you stay fixed and steady in the source of the increase and remain mindful of Jesus, your first love. He is so wonderful! It was Jesus' blood that sealed the new covenant on your behalf. It is because of Jesus that you enjoy all the benefits of redemption, including prosperity.

In the Scriptures, your beloved Lord instructs you to be about Kingdom business and the prosperity will follow. I believe that, and I have experienced it for myself. The spirit of prosperity that rests upon this ministry comes out of a close fellowship with the Holy Spirit and out of obedience to God. I believe when you are obedient to the promptings of the Holy Spirit concerning your giving, you are truly seeking God's Kingdom. You have done as your Lord said, so expect prosperity, because Jesus said it would be added unto you!

DECLARATION: I declare over you that your heart and affections are set on Jesus Christ, your beloved Savior and Lord. His Spirit leads, guides and instructs you in your finances and giving. Obey His promptings, for He adds prosperity unto you!

Generation of Destiny

Each and every believer has an important supply to give into God's Kingdom.

What a time in which you live! Before the foundation of the earth, God ordained your very existence for such a time as this. I believe this is a generation of great destiny!

You have a special part to play in God's plan for these last days. Each and every believer has an important supply to give into God's Kingdom. Ephesians 4:16, *The Amplified Bible,* declares, *"For because of Him the whole body (the church, in all its various parts), closely joined and firmly knit together by the joints and ligaments with which it is supplied, when each part with power adapted to its need is working properly in all its functions, grows to full maturity, building itself up in love."*

As every believer contributes his or her supply, another part of God's plan is fulfilled. I watch in awe as the Holy Spirit divinely connects believers together, like pieces of a puzzle, to carry out His wonderful plans. In the process of building His Kingdom, you are blessed by the working of the Spirit in and through you, and by the fellowship of the brethren. It is magnificent to partake of His giftings and to participate in His plans. Be assured that you are precious and valuable to your Father, and dare to discover your divine supply and offer it to God's Kingdom in this most exciting time of destiny!

👑 **DECLARATION: I declare over you that your destiny shall be fulfilled. He has anointed and appointed you to be on Earth for such a time as this! You are graced to give of your supply to His Kingdom, and fulfill all that He has destined for you!**

Do it Now!

Do it NOW! Whatever it is that the Spirit of God is showing you to do, I encourage you to begin right away. It may seem a very small thing, but it is a building block to fulfilling your destiny. It may simply be to write down on paper what is in your heart to do. Maybe it is to awaken earlier in the morning to spend more time fellowshipping and studying with Him. Perhaps it is helping with the children's ministry at your church, or befriending a new neighbor, or going on a mission trip, *or....*

Once you act on what God has already placed in your heart, then He will impart a greater understanding of His plan for your life.

With God the Holy Spirit, there is always a progressive order to things. Once you act on what God has already placed in your heart, then He will impart a greater understanding of His plan for your life. The time is passing so very quickly, and I urge you to take the next steps in fulfilling your destiny NOW!

DECLARATION: I declare over you that you respond to the nudging of the Holy Spirit to step out in faith and move with Him in God's calling for your life. Acknowledge Him in every way; know that He is directing your steps. As you take the first step, He will show you another. By faith you will act on what is in your heart and greater understanding will open unto you this day.

Spirit of Prayer

The Holy Spirit is visiting the peoples of the earth, searching for those who will come aside with Him to pray.

Prayer is so very vital to you for the time you have come into on Earth. I have often said, "Prayer is the track you run on; no prayer—no track—you're stuck." Your prayers bring forth the plan of God in the earth, both for the Body of Christ as a whole, and for your life personally.

There is a great urgency now concerning prayer. The Holy Spirit is visiting the peoples of the earth, searching for those who will come aside with Him to pray. *"And he that searcheth the hearts knoweth what is the mind of the Spirit, because he maketh intercession for the saints according to the will of God"* (Romans 8:27).

The Holy Spirit is your helper in so many ways, in particular, in the place of prayer. His promptings, leadings, seeings and knowings are accessible and available for you any time you step into that place of intercession with Him. "But prayer is so hard," some might say. No, God makes prayer easy; we make it hard. If prayer becomes rote with formality and ritual then it is hard, but when you catch a spirit of prayer; my, oh my, it's like Heaven on Earth! This ministry carries a spirit of prayer. By your association, the spirit of prayer is available to you. Receive of it now in Jesus' Name! Heaven has so much to be prayed out, and if you will learn to follow and flow with God the Holy Spirit in prayer, He will take you on marvelous adventures with Him!

👑 **DECLARATION: I declare over you that you will receive and partake of the spirit of prayer. The same Holy Spirit that raised Christ from the dead leads you and guides you in the place of prayer, giving you great unction and utterance to pray out the will and plans of God on the earth and for your life!**

Use Your Authority

As a son or daughter of Almighty God, your place in Him is one of authority. *"Even when we were dead in sins, (God) hath quickened us together with Christ... And hath raised us up together, and made us sit together in heavenly places in Christ Jesus"* (Ephesians 2:5–6).

When you command and decree what shall be according to the eternal Word and in the Name of the Son, all of Heaven backs you up!

It's a time of great positioning in the earth: positioning of nations, leaders of nations and of individuals, too. Of utmost importance now is an understanding of your place and position, because with it comes a great responsibility to use the authority secured for you through the work of Jesus Christ. When you command and decree what shall be according to the eternal Word and in the Name of the Son, all of Heaven backs you up! Don't ever be afraid to use the authority purchased for you, and don't ever take your God-given authority for granted.

From the office in which I stand, I take my authority over the enemy who would try to rob from you. I speak provision, protection and prosperity over you and all that concerns you in the Name of Jesus Christ.

👑 **DECLARATION: I declare over you that in Christ you have authority over principalities, powers and the rulers of the darkness of this world. Sit in your heavenly seat and declare and decree what will be from your place of authority.**

Do Not Fear

...Be not moved by what you see and hear; dear one, do not fear!

It is a defining hour for you, the believer, for the nations and your nation in particular. It is a time to anchor yourself in the Word of God as never before, for His Word is truth that does not change. By the Spirit of God I am stirred to remind you that *God did not give you the spirit of fear. Do not partake of what can make a nation shake. Garner His peace, which is on the inside of you, and be not moved by what you see and hear; dear one, do not fear!*

The Holy Spirit expressly said of the events unfolding *in the world*, "Do not partake." Know that there is a difference between the Church and the world. Just as the children of Israel, in the land of Goshen, were separated or set apart from Egypt and were not subject to the plagues poured out upon the Egyptians, a line of demarcation has been drawn between the Church and the world. You are *in* this world, but you are not *of it*. You are a citizen of Heaven, ruled and governed by the King of kings, Jesus Christ. Rest in the truth that He is faithful and will never leave nor forsake you. In the midst of adversity all around you, in Him you are safe, secure and set on high. *"The name of the Lord is a strong tower; the righteous run to it and are safe"* (Proverbs 18:10).

I encourage you to be vigilant to keep your heart and mind stayed on Him, for He will keep you in perfect peace. As you fellowship with the Holy Spirit at the start of your day, you will receive His mind and will concerning your life. Be sure not to oppose yourself, but to agree with Him by aligning your words to His. Pray in the spirit much, for in your heavenly language you commune with the Father and turn mysteries into revelation, thwart the plans of the enemy and make tremendous power available, dynamic in its working!

DECLARATION: I declare over you that you will resist fear in every form and refuse to partake of what can make a nation shake. The peace of God on the inside steadies you in the midst of adversity in the world, which you are *in* but *not of*. Jesus Christ—your strong tower—keeps you, a righteous one, safe, secure and set on high.

Suit up, Church!

I am so impressed with governments: governments in the Body of Christ, in this nation and in the nations beyond. The peoples of the congregations in the cities of nations are awakening now, for there is a sound. A resounding sound is coming down to the Body of Christ. Governments, both apostolic and prophetic, are coming forth. The prophets will speak, and they will say and give the direction, and things will happen in a day. Then the apostles will pick it up, and they will say, "This is how it needs to be," and they will begin to go, and they will begin to do, and so will their people across the nation from city to city like an army arrayed. Arrayed! Suit up, Church! Suit up!

"I have set watchmen upon thy walls...."
—Isaiah 62:6

Don't go to prayer after this day without suiting up; put on your armor! Put on the whole armor of God. The governments stand at the gates in the spirit and in the natural, too. Pray-er, you are the watcher. What comes into the city is up to you. Get up on the walls of your cities. Do it today! Like an army marching from city to city. It's that kind of day. It's that time. Use your authority in prayer, and you will clear the air.

The atmosphere changes now. The watchers are up on the walls of their cities in prayer. They can see afar off, further than they have ever seen before. For after today the vista, the view, will be greater than ever before for you. You will know what to do about this and that, for the Spirit of the Lord visits you and gives you great discernment. You will no longer wonder, *What will I do? What will I do?* After today, believe and you will know, and you will see, and you will be able to say accurately.

👑 **DECLARATION: I declare over you that you will suit up to pray, and on the walls of your city you will stand and stay. You will decree what you see most accurately, and in the spirit the atmosphere changes today. (See Ephesians 6:10–18).**

Watchers on the Wall

A nation can be no greater than the Church within her.

Be encouraged today to take your place in prayer concerning your beloved America. I have high hopes for the U.S.A., because I have high hopes for the Church! In my 30 plus years of ministry, I have been in over 35 nations, and I have come to understand that a nation can be no greater than the Church within her. When the Church begins to fail, every aspect of that nation begins to fail, too.

What is the answer for your nation? The Church, the Body of Christ, must come back into order with the Head, Jesus Christ. The Church must not deny the Christ or the Spirit of God and His ways. It is vital for you who carry prayer to step up into your place with ears to hear what the Spirit is saying. Only through times of fellowship with the Father will you, the pray-er, hear more correctly. For in this hour you will literally become a "watcher on the walls," standing in the gap, for not only your family, community, city and state, but you will now move into a national position in prayer in your seeings and knowings.

It is your Father's heart to show you things to come by the Spirit of truth, that you might join your voice as one sound that arises from Earth to Heaven and declare His will in all matters. Concerning your sweet land of liberty, what you—the Church—declare and decree according to His will, shall be! Ask for your city, pray for your leaders and those in authority, and intercede on their behalf. Just as Noah sealed the ark with pitch; pitch this nation inside and out through your prayers.

DECLARATION: I declare over you that you will heed the call to pray for your nation, for your leaders and for those God has placed in authority. You will watch in the spirit, stand in the gap and make up the hedge in your place of prayer.

Perfect Protection

There is, in God, a place of perfect protection and impenetrable refuge. For all who dwell in the secret place—that abiding place of intimate fellowship with the Creator Almighty—there is both a promised preservation of your way and divine protection to live out the fullness of your days. Regardless of what is raging around you, you can confidently remain stable and fixed *in Him*, where you are hidden away from harm, danger, destruction and the fear they bring.

> *"He who dwells in the secret place of the Most High, shall abide under the shadow of the Almighty."*
> —Psalm 91:1, NKJV

My, what a promise you have in Him! Heaven came to Earth to abide with and in you, an earthen vessel, ensuring your safety, security and favor. His divine cover, angelic assistance, peace and supernatural provision belong to you! How wonderful!

If you will take hold of it, there is right now for you a supernatural, divine protection. In this place of refuge no weapon can touch you, and those who would seek to bring you harm, cannot enter. Even as in the cities of refuge of old, where once a person had entered its gates, no enemy in pursuit could penetrate its walls. *"God is known in her palaces as a refuge."* (See Psalm 48:3). For whatever would seek to bring you fear and terror shall not come near you.

DECLARATION: I declare over you that divine protection covers you! Angels come to your aid and maneuver you into places of safety. Today you will take hold of His Word by faith for you and your family. God is ever-watching over you and you are now in the secret, impenetrable place of refuge where you shall dwell in safety.

A Higher Authority

Regardless of the forces that array themselves against you to seal your destruction, if you believe, God is able to deliver you!

Your God is able to save to the uttermost! He is your refuge and strength, your strong tower and deliverer! In Daniel Chapter 6, we read of the miraculous deliverance of one of God's servants from the mouths of lions and the plans of wicked men. To ensnare Daniel, a decree was made that anyone who petitioned any god or man other than the king would be thrown into a den of lions.

Knowing well the plot devised against him, Daniel knelt to pray and give thanks to God, *"as was his custom."* So great was God's favor upon him, that even as a stone sealed the mouth of the lions' den where Daniel had been cast, the king called to him: *"Your God, whom you serve continually, He will deliver you."*

The law concerning Daniel could not be changed even by the ruling authority in the land…but Daniel served a higher authority! He was found innocent before God and the king, and the next morning he was taken out of the lions' den alive with no injury on him, *"…because he believed in his God."*

Regardless of the forces that array themselves against you to seal your destruction, if you believe, God is able to deliver you!

♛ DECLARATION: I declare over you that you will set your love upon the Father, He will deliver you; He will set you on high, because you have known His name. Call upon Him and He will answer you; He will be with you in trouble; He will deliver and honor you. With long life He will satisfy you and show you His salvation.

Obeying God's Ways

The things of God are miraculous! You need His supernatural intervention in your life. Since that is the case, when it comes to the things of God, you ought to be going about them God's way. If you love someone enough, you want to know his or her ways.

Your obedience is the power to bring the return unto you.

When God lays down the ways for you, it is always best for you to cooperate with Him. What God is trying to do right now is to cause the Body of Christ to become the lender and not the borrower, and so you must cooperate with Him, even in your finances. Be led of Him in all your giving, and be obedient to the ways set forth in His Word regarding tithes and offerings. Your obedience is the power to bring the return unto you.

I pray as you obey and follow the leading of the Holy Spirit in all of your giving, there will be a notable *shift* in the monies coming to you. May you be blessed through your obedience to the supernatural laws of a very supernatural God, who is your Father!

DECLARATION: I declare over you that God's plans position you for blessing and increase. His thoughts and ways are so much higher. You yield to His ways and flow with His Spirit in your giving, for He brings supernatural return to you.

With Revelation Comes Motivation

Given unto you is great wisdom, so you will know what to do!

It is God the Holy Spirit who brings revelation to the Body of Christ. As you step over into the time of the end, the Holy Spirit now sweeps through to bring revelation upon all of your information.

What is it that has been gathered unto you by the Spirit of God? What are your meditations that have brought forth information for the Spirit to open unto you? If you have given Him something to work with, He can bring revelation upon it and make a way for divine motivation to ignite what has been revealed. With revelation comes motivation! What you see, you now have divine power to do!

DECLARATION: I declare over you an increased clarity as divine revelation comes upon your information. Understanding is opened unto you, giving you the motivation to do what is in your heart to do!

Expect Good to Come

I want to encourage you today that *something* is coming! I stand before you as a flagman on the road of your life to signal to you that something is coming up ahead, and I tell you with certainty and with authority that something *good* is coming on your behalf.

"Every good gift and every perfect gift is from above...."
—*James 1:17, NKJV*

When John the Baptist came on the scene, it was to tell the world that Jesus was coming! Life was about to change as they knew it, and they needed to hear, know and prepare so they would be ready to receive the good of God that had been sent just for them. *"There was a man sent from God, whose name was John. The same came for a witness, to bear witness of the Light, that all men through him might believe. He was not that Light, but was sent to bear witness of that Light. That was the true Light, which lighteth every man that cometh into the world"* (John 1:6–9).

The winds of change are blowing, and the Holy Spirit needs your attention. Something miraculous of God is aloft. Can you sense the stirrings of it when you visit with God the Holy Spirit throughout the day? He is doing something in each and every heart in preparation for what is on the way. Listen, watch, wait...believe, expect and pray! *"Every good gift and every perfect gift is from above, and comes down from the Father of lights, with whom there is no variation or shadow of turning,"* (James 1:17, NKJV).

👑 **DECLARATION: I declare over you that something *good* of God is on the way for you! The Holy Spirit prepares your heart to receive all that God has purposed to be, and through fellowship with your Father, you are made ready.**

Revelation of God's Love

God loves you the same way He loves Jesus!

Hebrews 12:29 describes God as a *consuming fire!* What an awesome and powerful truth! One thing the Father is consumed with is love for *you!* If you knew and could comprehend the Father's limitless love for you, I believe it would change you in a remarkable way. You would more readily accept and forgive yourself for your shortcomings and for the times you miss the mark. You would most certainly have a different view of the world and those who make up your world.

Jesus loved people the way the Father did because He had a revelation of God's love for Him. He knew and proclaimed that He and the Father were *one.* Beautifully depicted in John 17, is both an expression of the Father and the Son as *one heart.* Your beloved Savior prayed that you would be included in that same place of intimacy.

> **"Neither pray I for these** *(His disciples)* **alone, but for them** *(you and me)* **also which shall believe on me through their word;**
> **"That they all may be one; as thou, Father, art in me, and I in thee, that they also may be one in us: that the world may believe that thou hast sent me.**
> **"And the glory which thou gavest me I have given them; that they may be one, even as we are one:**
> **"I in them, and thou in me, that they may be made perfect in one; and that the world may know that thou hast sent me, and hast loved them, as thou hast loved me."**
> **—John 17:20–23,** *(added emphasis mine)*

My prayer for you today is that you, *"May be able to comprehend with all saints what is the breadth, and length, and depth, and height; And to know the love of Christ, which passeth knowledge, that ye might be filled with all the fullness of God"* (Ephesians 3:18–19).

👑 **DECLARATION: I declare over you that God loves you the same way He loves Jesus! Receive His all-consuming love for you. The Holy Spirit floods you with a renewed passion for your Savior. His love transforms you with a supernatural compassion for souls.**

The Goodness of God

The goodness of God your Father is a wondrous thing! He cares intimately and personally about the things that concern you each and every day, even that you have the provision of food, drink and clothing.

Knowing intimately the Father, Son and Holy Spirit and building God's Kingdom must be first place in your life.

By the unction of the Holy Spirit, Matthew penned, *"Do not worry about your life, what you will eat or what you will drink; nor about your body, what you will put on...For your heavenly Father knows that you need all these things,"* (Matthew 6:25; 32). *He* feeds the birds, *He* adorns the field lilies, *He* clothes the grass...and *you* are more valuable to Him than any of these. *"But seek first the kingdom of God and His righteousness, and all these things shall be added to you"* (Matthew 6:33, NKJV).

Knowing intimately the Father, Son and Holy Spirit and building God's Kingdom must be first place in your life. When you embrace God's ways and divine order *then* all you have need of will be at your disposal, provided for you by the King Himself!

I pray that as you make Kingdom business and the fellowship of your Father first place that you will be filled to overflowing and abounding in every good thing.

👑 **DECLARATION: I declare over you that you will make the fellowship of your Father and Kingdom business your priority each day. You are filled and overflowing with an abundance of every good thing.**

Places Everyone

Begin to put your hand to what is in your heart to do.

God the Holy Spirit is moving His Body into position all over the earth. Like the cast members in a play just before the curtain is raised, the director calls, "Places everyone, places…" and each one swiftly moves into his or her slot. *There's about to be a performance!* The great demonstrator of the works of Jesus Christ will display His grand and glorious power *to* and *in* and *through* you, *if* you are in your place. For when you are in your place, God's grace flows, His anointing manifests and His glory is revealed.

God is a God of order, and nothing about the way He works is random. From the dawn of creation the voice of His Word set matter and elements in their places to govern and rule and operate according to His divine plan. You, who He so fearfully and wonderfully formed, were made in His image to know Him, to love Him, to reflect His nature and to move in His power. By being in your place, doing what you were created to do, you bring the Father glory and honor, and you experience a joy, grace and peace that come no other way than by doing His will His way.

Whatever adjustments you might need to make or steps you might need to take to come in line with His divine plan for you, obey those promptings now, because the Holy Spirit says, *"There's about to be a performance!"* In your heart let Him rule and let things be done His way and not your own. Begin to put your hand to what is in your heart to do. God longs to satisfy your heart with the desires He has placed there. Jesus opens a way for you now, and the Holy Spirit will show you how.

👑 **DECLARATION: I declare over you that you will move with the Holy Spirit into your God-ordained place and position. God's grace flows, His anointing manifests and His glory is revealed through you because you are divinely aligned with God's plans.**

Trust Me

The Spirit of God brings a visitation to you saying, *"TRUST ME."* No matter what you hear, feel, see or do not see, believe that He is faithful to bring to pass what you have spoken, believed and committed to His care. *"Commit your way to the Lord, trust also in Him, and He shall bring it to pass"* (Psalm 37:5, NKJV).

He is a miracle-working God and in your trust of Him He will manifest what is impossible for you!

What is *trust?* Trust is confidence demonstrated when you rely and rest your mind on the integrity, veracity, justice and friendship of another. When you are confident in the truth of God's Word, you will not confound yourself with *how* His plan will come to pass for you. You will never figure things out in your mind. The Holy Spirit says, "STOP!" Is this *thing* greater than God? Is it greater than the blood of His Son?"

Remember that God is truth, God is in you, and truth is always greater than fact. Eventually fact will bend under the weight of truth. Your part is to believe and speak His truth, then begin to thank Him for what has already been done by God the Son. I know the struggle it can be. In the hardest of times trusting Him can be the hardest thing to do; but He is a miracle-working God, and in your trust of Him, He will manifest what is impossible for you!

👑 **DECLARATION: I declare over you that God is greater than your situation. Facts are bending under the truth of God's Word this very moment. Choose to trust Him and commit your way to His care. God is manifesting the impossible for you!**

End-Time Events

Be calmed and at peace that all of God's purposes will be fulfilled!

Glory to the Father, to the Holy Spirit, and to His Son—the risen One! I want you to be encouraged—emboldened and inspired with hope today—that the God of compassion and power desires to manifest Himself in and through you!

Your intimate fellowship with God the Holy Spirit has brought you to the place you have come into in the spirit, and I believe He has been talking to you about specific plans in order to prepare and position you for events now in motion. LISTEN to what the Holy Spirit says to you in these times of intimacy, and pray most earnestly in the spirit. He is sharing the Father's heart with you! It is the Father's deep desire to guide, lead, protect and comfort you through the purposes, plans and events unfolding for you personally, nationally and worldwide.

Be calmed and at peace that *all* of God's purposes will be fulfilled. There are leaders of nations, men and women, and events that must be for end-time positioning. These things you cannot change. Then there are other things you must prepare for as the Spirit of God instructs you, just as He did Noah. Understand the difference and you will be at peace when others are fretful and fearful about what they see and hear. God is in control, and you can trust Him to bring His purposes to pass in His most excellent way and in His perfect time. For then the glory will be His and His alone. The best is yet to come!

DECLARATION: I declare over you that you will take time today to listen and hear what the Spirit would say. Receive His instructions of how to prepare and pray. In the midst of unfolding events you shall stay in a place of supernatural peace and rest because your Father holds the times and seasons in His hand.

Time of Transition

The Body of Christ is experiencing a time of great transition. Transition is a time of change. It seems to me that believers everywhere, in some way or other, are experiencing change.

...Remain steadfast to the vision God has placed in your heart.

The Holy Spirit reminded me of a time when I was a visitor on a Navy battleship. When my husband and I were first married, he was in the Navy. We were based with a clinic in Norfolk, Virginia. The Navy offered a "dependent's cruise" to the officers and their families.

When we boarded the ship, it was calmly floating in the harbor; but then the time came to go out to deeper water, into the open sea. As we began to move, the huge metal ship made sounds, almost like groans. The noise became louder and louder as we moved along. The battleship was turned, ever-so carefully, as it left the harbor and headed out to sea. Once we were in the deep water the groaning ceased, and the ship moved about with ease.

I believe we are moving into deeper places in God. I encourage you to remain steadfast to the vision God has placed in your heart. As you go with Him into the deeper places, like the battleship, you experience a time of transition. Once you reach the deeper water, you will move about, fulfilling your purpose with ease.

👑 **DECLARATION: I declare over you that you will have a clear understanding of the time of transition you have come into. As the Holy Spirit maneuvers you into the fulfillment of God's plans, everything becomes easier; in the deep places you move with God effortlessly!**

Imparting the Difference

You must draw the line and take your stand concerning your life, your family and your city, understanding that this is your realm of authority.

Heaven is calling, dear one! Will you answer and arise to your place of authority in this hour? We have come into a season of great change, and so to the grace you carry, *I impart to you the difference you need* to walk in your authority in this time.

I believe spiritual forces and entities of times yet to come are bleeding on through to this time—*before their time*—as described in Matthew 8:29. *"And suddenly they cried out, saying, 'What have we to do with You, Jesus, You Son of God? Have You come here to torment us before the time?'"*

You must draw the line and take your stand concerning your life, your family and your city, understanding that this is *your realm* of authority. Your seat is in the heavenlies with Jesus Christ! Here you are positioned far above all principalities and power and might and dominion and every name that is named. (See Ephesians 1:21). Know that the battle is not against flesh and blood, *"...but against principalities, against powers, against the rulers of the darkness of this world, against spiritual wickedness in high places"* (Ephesians 6:11–12). All things come first out of the realm of the spirit, and then they manifest in the earth; therefore, things must be dealt with *first* in the spirit realm.

How mighty is this authority you possess! You are the one who speaks the words of Heaven to people everywhere you go, encouraging and giving them hope in Jesus Christ. It is your destiny to implement the works of His righteousness in the earth, and in His power and might, you take dominion over your domain and stand against the "wiles" or strategies of Hell. Where the Kingdom of God reigns, laws change! His Kingdom reigns in you, dear one. *You* are the representation of God's Kingdom in the earth!

DECLARATION: I declare over you that God's Kingdom reigns in you! Take your place of authority in the spirit and declare and decree the way things are to be. Receive impartations now to implement the works of righteousness in this hour.

The Name of Jesus

There is no name like the Name of Jesus! *"Wherefore God also hath highly exalted Him, and given Him a name which is above every name: that at the name of Jesus every knee should bow, of things in heaven, and things in earth, and things under the earth; and that every tongue should confess that Jesus Christ is Lord, to the glory of God the Father"* (Philippians 2:9–11).

Whatever you can name, Jesus Christ is above it…!

You have the awesome privilege of sharing the Name of Jesus with a world in desperate need of a Savior. His very name means, "He will save." *He will save, deliver, protect, heal, preserve, cause you to do well, He will make you whole!* What a wonderful and all-encompassing salvation. This is the Gospel that we preach and demonstrate, and it is Good News to the lost, the bound, the sick and the broken-hearted. The Name of Jesus crosses all barriers, for He is truly Lord of all.

Meditate on all that He is, for He is all those things *in you!* Praise and worship Him for all He has done, for He has done all these things *for you!* Whatever you can name, Jesus Christ is above it, and so are you, for you are seated with Him in the heavenlies!

DECLARATION: I declare over you that there is no other name under Heaven by which men might be saved. The Name of Jesus is above cancer, depression, confusion and fear; every name you can name! Everything that would try to exalt itself against the knowledge of God must bow to Him and to you, for you are seated with Jesus in the heavenlies!

Know Him and Make Him Known

Jesus wants you to be a witness with demonstration and with power.

"And my language and my message were not set forth in persuasive (enticing and plausible) words of wisdom, but they were in demonstration of the Holy Spirit and power, a proof by the Spirit and power of God, operating on me and stirring in the minds of my hearers the most holy emotions and thus persuading them,

"So that your faith might not rest in the wisdom of men (human philosophy), but in the power of God."

—1 Corinthians 2:4–5, AMP

Man has not the wisdom that we must have in this hour. Jesus Christ has been made wisdom unto you and me (1 Corinthians 1:30). Don't ever forget that. Say it aloud to yourself throughout the day. You must know it. *"But we have the mind of Christ and do hold the thoughts (feelings and purposes) of His heart"* (1 Corinthians 2:16b, AMP).

A witness presents evidence. Jesus wants you to be witnesses with demonstration and with power. A great compassion comes forth from the passionate love you have for the Lord Jesus, and that makes you want to know the Holy Spirit in His gifts and His demonstrations. It makes you want to be so comfortable and so sure of Him, that should He ask you to turn to this one or that one and share the love of Christ, you will do it. Keep pursuing Him with all your heart so that you will know Him and become confident in making Him known.

DECLARATION: I declare over you that Jesus Christ has been made wisdom unto you. His compassion flows through you in demonstrations of power! With all your heart, pursue His presence that you might know Him and make Him known.

Jesus is Coming!

Something wonderful is happening right now. It is as if time has speeded up in the realm of the spirit. For in the natural, time is time, but in the spirit, time is flexible. What you thought you would do at the end of the year, the increase has come, so prepare right now, for it is about to get done!

What you thought you would do at the end of the year, the increase has come, so prepare right now, for it is about to get done!

This increase and momentum is coming from God. By His Spirit you are stepping up and crossing a threshold into a very wide, deep, high place in the greatness of Him. It seems to me the things that must be are coming to pass quickly, because Jesus is coming quickly! He is coming sooner than we all thought. A knowing like I never had before came upon me recently...*Jesus, you really are coming back!* I release to you this knowing and resolve concerning you and the Christ! By the Almighty One you see and you know and understand which way to go.

So much of God is upon you for this time. His greatness is being revealed to and through *you*—His Body in the earth. Jesus is coming; Jesus is coming quickly!

👑 **DECLARATION: I declare over you that the Spirit of seeing and knowing is released unto you! Receive increase in momentum, increase in understanding and increase in grace to do all He desires for you in preparation for the coming of Jesus Christ!**

Places in God

Something wonderful of God is happening right now for you!

The glory, the power, the grace of God in a place. Abba, Papa takes you up into that place with Him. You are flying high. Eagles, each and every one how they see. You can see far and wide by the Almighty One. No matter the fierceness of the storm, the strength of the winds that blow; like eagles lock wings and soar, in the spirit you go. You see further out and wider yet than ever before. You have eyes to see and ears to hear. You know what to do by the wisdom of Him.

By His design in a place: addictions go, minds are clear, broken hearts are mended, demons must leave. The anointing has destroyed the yoke and all is well. The understanding of destinies is made very clear. Momentum and increase come to propel you over the threshold of where you've been. Cross over into a place of greatness prepared for you. What a place in God you have come into! Blessed, blessed Holy Spirit; I thank You, Sir. You do everything to help the people and to glorify the Son!

DECLARATION: I declare over you that by the Spirit of wisdom and revelation you see and know. In this place with God, the atmosphere is clear; all is well and you can hear. Heavenly momentum and increase propels you over, through and into a place of greatness prepared by Him.

Become What You Believe

I came upon a scripture in *The Message Translation* of the Bible that I just love! It comes from a passage in Matthew chapter 9, where two blind men were crying out to Jesus to heal them. The word *cry* in this context literally

If you see it, you can be it!

means, "scream." These men were desperate for their circumstances to change, and would not simply sit back quietly while their miracle passed them by.

"Mercy, Son of David! Mercy on us!" they shouted after Jesus (v. 27).

What did Jesus do?

Nothing.

So, the men groped along and followed Him into a house. Finally, Jesus turned to face them and posed the question, *"Do you really believe I can do this?"* (v. 28).

Emphatically, they answered, *"Why, yes, Master!"* (v. 28).

Jesus touched their eyes and said, *"Become what you believe"* (v. 29).

Oh, I like that! *"Become what you believe!"* What do you believe? What do you really believe? Jesus says to you, "Become it!" See yourself well. See your circumstances changing. See your body recovered, healed and whole. See first in the spirit with the eyes of faith; if you see it, you can be it!

Believe what God's Word says of you, and become what He sees and says of you today!

DECLARATION: I declare over you that from this day forward you will see yourself another way: with eyes of faith. You say only what God would say. Things are different starting today—you become what you believe!

Hear and Be Healed

"But so much the more went there a fame abroad of him: and great multitudes came together to hear, and to be healed by him of their infirmities."
—Luke 5:15

Jesus, wonderful Jesus! He is your Savior, your Lord and your Healer! When He walked the earth He, *"...went about doing good, and healing all that were oppressed of the devil..."* (Acts 10:38).

With every word, every command, every touch of His hand, Jesus demonstrated the will of His Father. *"And Jesus went about all Galilee, teaching in their synagogues, and preaching the gospel of the kingdom, and healing all manner of sickness and all manner of disease among the people"* (Matthew 4:23).

News of Jesus traveled far and fast. *"A fame of him went abroad,"* Luke tells us, *"...and great multitudes came together to hear, and to be healed by him..."* (Luke 5:15, NKJV).

Jesus spoke and the Holy Spirit confirmed the Word through healing miracles for all who asked. He is no respecter of persons! As we gather around the Name of Jesus in crusades and church services throughout the nations and in our beloved America too, the Spirit moves most demonstratively in the area of healings. A gentleman attending one of our *Holy Spirit Healing Services* shared this testimony with us. "I was stationed in the lobby as part of the Crusade Helps team, when I heard Dr. Varallo say from the auditorium, 'The Holy Spirit is healing ears. Raise your hand if you need a healing in your ear.' So I raised my hand and then, *snap, crackle, pop!* After 36 years of being deaf in my right ear I was completely healed!" Praise God for His goodness and mercy! Jesus is the same yesterday, today and forever!

Do you need healing in your body? Reach out for it today! Healing is yours because of the price Jesus paid. Hear the Word of the Lord and be healed!

DECLARATION: I declare over you that you will stretch forth your hand with expectancy to receive the healing Jesus purchased for you. No sickness, disease, infirmity or pain can remain in Jesus' Name! Hear His Word. It is medicine to you; it heals you and makes you whole.

Born of Love

O f all the things Jesus could have instructed us to do under the new covenant, He gave us one commandment: *love*. *"This is my commandment, that ye love one another, as I have loved you. Greater love hath no man than this, that a man lay down his life for his friends"* (John 15:12–13). "Thou shalt love" is all-encompassing of the "thou shalt nots" recorded in the Old Testament, greater than faith and hope, and the only force in the universe that cannot fail. God is love, and whatsoever is born of God— born of *love*—overcomes the world. (See 1 John 5:4).

...Love spawns the miraculous!

Jesus walked in the power that He did because He operated in the greatest power in existence—the power of love. Is it any wonder that His earthly ministry was marked by the miraculous? We pray for the day when healings and miracles of every sort are commonplace. We long for the power of God to flow through us in this most spectacular of ways. But I challenge you: if you want to see the miraculous, I want to see you love someone! *Love spawns the miraculous!*

Let the divine nature of God flow out of you to that lost one, to that hurting one, toward that one who has treated you wrongly. Lay down your life and let the life of God—the life of love—dominate all that you think, say and do. May you walk in the greater of God today as you choose the more excellent way of love.

DECLARATION: I declare over you that you will walk in love, for it is the greater way. Expect to see miracle-power manifest to you and through you to the glory of God!

A Move of Love

"And on some have compassion, making a difference."
—Jude 22

Nothing affects the hearts of humanity like love—divine love, demonstrated through forgiveness, mercy and compassion. I believe we are beginning to see a move of God's great love like we have never known before. Love has begun to flood this land and the nations beyond, turning people to repentance, washing away the stain of sin and affecting all that has been troubled.

Love is a tangible, faith-filled force that carries the power of possibility. For what is impossible with men, is possible with God! God is love, and wrapped up in Him is all that you could ever want or need. God's love brings healing, restoration, wholeness and the unity of the spirit. Love mends and binds hearts together where division has driven wedges and caused rifts in God-ordained relationships. His love brings light and truth to dispel darkness and deception. The wind of His Spirit is blowing, lifting clouds of depression, reviving and breathing the breath of life into His Creation.

Remember that *you* are a demonstration of Christ's compassion in the earth, and *you* are making an eternal difference in the lives of everyone you touch with His divine love.

DECLARATION: I declare over you that your expression of divine love will bring change to the destinies of those around you. Walk in the divine love abiding in you, for it fuels your faith and is the power of possibility!

Plans and Purposes

"But the path of the uncompromisingly just and righteous is like the light of dawn, that shines more and more (brighter and clearer) until it reaches its full strength and glory in the perfect day to be prepared."

Everything the Father does, He does with purpose.

—**Proverbs 4:18, AMP**

Everything the Father does has purpose. He has plans for you that He prepared from the foundations of the earth! It seems to be the great desire of every human being to know what he or she was created to do and to fulfill what the Father has destined.

Your ultimate purpose is to know Jesus as Savior and Lord and to have fellowship with the Godhead. From that vital relationship will flow your love and compassion to those around you. You have an assignment: to give every person an opportunity to hear the Name of God's beloved Son. When you are about the Father's plan, the specific plans He has for you will unfold. They will shine "brighter and clearer" as the perfect day approaches.

DECLARATION: I declare over you that God has prepared a wonderful path for you to walk. You have great purpose! Your future is bright, for you carry the Light of the world, and He illuminates your path!

That You May Know Him

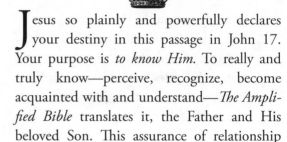

"And this is eternal life, that they may know You, the only true God, and Jesus Christ whom You have sent."
—*John 17:3, NKJV*

Jesus so plainly and powerfully declares your destiny in this passage in John 17. Your purpose is *to know Him*. To really and truly know—perceive, recognize, become acquainted with and understand—*The Amplified Bible* translates it, the Father and His beloved Son. This assurance of relationship is your hope; sealed with the promised Holy Spirit, the earnest or guarantee of your eternal inheritance.

What a promise! What a tremendous gift of grace Father God has bestowed upon you if only you believe on His Name and make your life a pursuit of knowing Him personally and intimately. Love Him because He first loved you. It is your love for Him that moves you to tell of and demonstrate His love to humanity. My prayer for you this day is that you continue to fellowship your relationship with your Creator and make it your quest and great aim to follow on *to know* Him!

👑 **DECLARATION: I declare over you that the eyes of your understanding are open to comprehend God's love for you today. Through His Word you are becoming more and more sure of this love, and it moves you to be compassionate toward others. Know Him just as you are known by Him.**

Of the I Am

God has destined for you to walk as Jesus walked on the earth. You are *not* God, but you were created in His image and you are *like* Him. As His son or daughter, you are *of Him*. You represent the Christ and have been given the right and responsibility to operate in all of the power and authority that the Name of Jesus holds.

Walk as Jesus walked: in love, in authority and in the miraculous power He has destined for you!

Just as the enemy came to challenge Jesus' identity while He walked this earth, he will also come to challenge you in this same manner, saying, "Who do you think you are casting out devils and healing the sick?"

You tell him, "I am of the I AM!"

"What? Who are you?"

"I am of the I AM!"

This is not pride nor arrogance, but a boldness that comes from knowing the God you serve and having an assurance of who you are *in Him*. Walk as Jesus walked: in love, in authority and in the miraculous power He has destined for you!

👑 **DECLARATION: I declare over you that you will receive a revelation of who you are and Who illuminates your heart and understanding. Resurrection power resides in you! It is your right and responsibility to operate in His Name and authority. You are of the I AM.**

Keepers of the Keys

With your keys— your authority— whatever you bind on Earth is bound in Heaven, and whatever you loose on Earth is loosed in Heaven.

"And I will give you the keys of the kingdom of heaven, and whatever you bind on earth will be bound in heaven, and whatever you loose on earth will be loosed in heaven."

—Matthew 16:19, NKJV

Your confession of faith in Jesus Christ translated you into a new Kingdom! By the blood of the Son, the stain and pain of your sin has been washed away, and you now stand righteous before God your Father. To you, the righteous ones, who walk amongst humanity throughout the earth, the Father has granted authority in the Name of the Son. *You, oh righteous one, are a keeper of the keys of the kingdom!* No one has access to these keys unless he or she be of the Kingdom of God. For the Kingdom of God is *in* you! With your keys—your authority— whatever you bind on Earth is bound in Heaven, and whatever you loose on Earth is loosed in Heaven.

Yes, you are in this world, but you are not of it. Satan knows this, and he will try to take your keys from you. However, he cannot take your authority from you; you have to give it to him. Don't give him anything! You are the keeper of this authority granted to you by the King of the Kingdom. Remember this and remember to use your keys.

DECLARATION: I declare over you that you will stand in your place as a righteous one in Christ Jesus and give neither place nor authority to the enemy. Enforce your authority as a keeper of the keys of the Kingdom of God, and whatever you bind is bound; whatever you loose is loosed. Earth comes in line with the will of Heaven when you use the keys of God's Kingdom.

The Battle Around Your Miracle

You are living in a time of great destiny! It is a time of destiny for the Body of Christ corporately, for the sons and daughters of God individually and for those who do not yet know your Lord.

There is war in the natural and there is war in the spirit, too, because destinies are at stake!

What happens in the natural takes place first in the spirit realm. So in the spirit is where the battle is fought and the victory is won. *"God disarmed the principalities and powers that were ranged against us and made a bold display and public example of them, in triumphing over them in Him and in it, the cross"* (Colossians 2:15, AMP). Now you, the Church, must enforce the victory that Jesus fought and won.

Just before something magnificent of Heaven bursts forth, all of Hell tries to run interference, swallow it up and stop it. The enemy works tirelessly to move you out of a position of receiving from God both naturally and spiritually. Where destiny is concerned, the impact reaches beyond just your own life. Know this: *there will always be a battle around your miracle and war around your destiny.* There is war in the natural and there is war in the spirit, too, because destinies are at stake! So don't be surprised when you have to contend with determination and resolve around the things you are believing for that are miracle-size.

The Holy Spirit would bring to your remembrance that you have the authority in the Name of Jesus Christ to press through; you win because He won! Miraculous intervention is coming upon the destiny you possess. Don't concede the victory that is already yours through the work of Jesus Christ. Remind the enemy and yourself that the battle has been won, and the miracle is yours!

DECLARATION: I declare over you that you will stand firm on the finished work of Jesus Christ. Put yourself in remembrance that the battle around your miracle and the war around your destiny have already been fought and won by Jesus Christ, God's victorious Son!

Praying for the Lost

Intercession is the sound of His infinite love....

I am stirred to cry out for God's harvest—the precious fruit of the earth for which He is so patiently waiting. *"Be patient therefore, brethren, unto the coming of the Lord. Behold, the husbandman waiteth for the precious fruit of the earth, and hath long patience for it, until he receive the early and latter rain. Be ye also patient; stablish your hearts: for the coming of the Lord draweth nigh"* (James 5:7–8).

The Bible says in Genesis 8:22, *"While the earth remains, seedtime and harvest...shall not cease,"* and so continue to plant and water and trust the Father to bring the increase—the precious fruit of the earth.

As you speak out the Father's heart in prayer, give voice to His mercy, which triumphs over judgment. Intercession is the sound of His infinite love; for the blood of God's Son still speaks, saying, "I love you...you are forgiven!"

Stand with me in the gap for that lost one, for the one whom you've contended, for those you do not know. Your prayers make a way for love to turn their captivity in Jesus' Name!

👑 DECLARATION: I declare over you that you will take authority over principalities, powers and rulers of the darkness of this world; blinding spirits that are keeping God's precious harvest from seeing the light of the glorious Gospel. You will send laborers to those who are ripe and ready to receive. You will pray for minds to be loosed, and understanding to be opened! You will thank your Father for the blood of His Son, and ask Him to forgive those who have opposed Him. You will cry *mercy* over each and every one in Jesus' Name.

The Power of Prayer

Now, in the fullness of this time, give yourself to praying the Word and praying in the Spirit, *for it is your prayer life that stimulates your sensitivity toward the Holy Spirit and enables you to hear Him.* Praying in a heavenly language from God Almighty Himself will help you surpass all of your information and take you into the corridor of revelation. In this time you have come into, in order to have more than what you know in your intellect; you have to know from the Holy Spirit!

...It is your prayer life that stimulates your sensitivity toward the Holy Spirit and enables you to hear Him.

I would suggest you pray in the spirit an hour every day. Do you know what can happen in that hour in the presence of the Third Person of the Trinity, praying through you—declaring and decreeing in a language you don't even know—up into the heavenlies? What you have sought the answer to in your life will *suddenly* come to you by the Holy Spirit!

DECLARATION: I declare over you in Jesus' Name that doors of opportunity *open*, promotions *arise*, provisions *come*, favor *abounds!* For the Lord has need of these to come upon His sons and daughters, of which you are one. You will pray in the spirit and in your understanding, and receive the revelation that comes now upon your information. Mighty demonstrations of His love are happening—not going to be—but are *right now* upon you!

The Promise of the Father

When you pray in your heavenly language, you speak divine secrets unto your Father and turn mysteries into revelation!

"And, being assembled together with them, commanded them that they should not depart from Jerusalem, but wait for the promise of the Father, which, saith he, ye have heard of me.

"For John truly baptized with water; but ye shall be baptized with the Holy Ghost not many days hence."

—Acts 1:4–5

What a gift you have been given in the Person of the Holy Spirit! He is the long-awaited promise poured out by the Father at Jesus' request. His indwelling, enduement from on High provides you power to be a witness of the Christ. Through His fiery baptism described in Acts chapter 2, you give voice to the utterances the Holy Spirit gives. When you pray in your heavenly language, you speak divine secrets unto your Father and turn mysteries into revelation! At the same time, you strengthen your own spirit and find that the grand plan God has placed inside you begins to unfold!

By tapping into the power on the inside, you are connecting directly to an eternal source of strength and supply that will build up your spirit like nothing else can or will. *"But you, beloved, building yourselves up on your most holy faith, praying in the Holy Spirit…"* (Jude 20, NKJV).

Take time today to yield yourself to God the Holy Spirit and pray in the spirit. You will see and know what you didn't before, and in the spirit you will soar!

👑 **DECLARATION: I declare over you that you will yield yourself to the Holy Spirit and pray in your heavenly language. Mysteries become revelation! All is clear; you see and hear. Your spirit is infused with strength as you build yourself up today, partaking of your Father's powerful promise.**

Respond to His Spirit

As I travel to the nations and throughout the United States to minister to the peoples of the congregations, again and again I am privileged to watch Heaven reach down and touch Earth. The supernatural presence of God comes in demonstration upon the people, and they respond. All over the world, people

Draw out when the Spirit of God comes, and partake of His marvelous presence!

are born again into Father's Kingdom; they are delivered from oppression and miraculously healed and baptized in the Holy Spirit.

The Word is preached, and the Holy Spirit comes in power and in presence to confirm the Word. It is marvelous! But, things don't happen for you simply because God comes; you must *do* something. You must *respond to His Spirit*. God manifests Himself, and you draw out and partake of His marvelous presence! By faith you believe and reach out to receive whatever it is that you need. It's not hard. God makes it easy for you.

I believe the Father is moving on your behalf even now. You are divinely positioned to receive all that you desire and require. Respond to His Spirit, dear one. Draw out now and partake.

DECLARATION: I declare over you, by faith, that you will draw out of the reservoir of grace, power, provision and healing that the Holy Spirit provides. You will receive all that you need from His supernatural presence in Jesus' Name!

The Workings of God the Holy Spirit

Know that where God opens up revelation there is a promised manifestation; and what you have believed of Him, He now demonstrates for you!

It is God the Holy Spirit who gathers you together to partake of His glorious presence. It is God the Holy Spirit who visits you most magnificently when you come together corporately. What an indescribable gift God lavished upon you through the precious Holy Spirit! The Holy breath of God comes to you as your sound of worship goes up to Him. My, oh my, how His Holy presence changes you, opens your understanding, answers questions and flows freely in healings of all sorts, removing pain in your heart, soul and body! How wonderful of Him!

In His wisdom, the Holy Spirit reminds you of the necessity to pray much in the spirit. For as you meet with Him and pray in your heavenly language, He will reveal the hidden things you need to know concerning your life. In His light, which is His revelation, mysteries are opened unto you. He speaks to you most clearly of the authority and dominion that is yours to enforce, and reminds you that the declarations and decrees of faith from your lips will order the day rather than the day and its circumstances dictating to you what will be.

I believe the impartations He makes are life-changing and eternal. His glory shines forth from you, and revelation comes. Know that where God opens up revelation there is a promised manifestation; and what you have believed of Him, He now demonstrates for you!

Let the glory of God that has taken up permanent residence in you arise now in every arena of your life, and in His Name, walk in this power from on High. The world is waiting and listening for *your voice!*

DECLARATION: I declare over you that you will give voice to the Word of God in all matters concerning your life. Everything must align and obey God's will and way. Circumstances don't dictate what will be; in agreement with God you make your decree, and in Jesus' Name, His will shall be for you!

The Suddenlies of God

The *"suddenlies" of God* are coming to you! I know that I know that when tremendous things of God are about to be for you, the devil tries to get in your space and bombard you with his thoughts, his lies, his doubts and his fears. But *suddenly*…God!

I declare and decree a suddenly…a manifestation of the coming to pass of your dreams!

Just as the Psalmist wrote in Psalm 126:1, *"When the Lord turned again the captivity of Zion, we were like them that dream."* When your miracle—that promise you have been standing and waiting for—comes, it can seem like a dream.

As a messenger commissioned by God, I declare and decree a suddenly; a manifestation of the coming to pass of your dreams! I carry that impartation just as I carry prosperity, a spirit of prayer, a spirit of favor and of supernatural connections. If it's a miracle you need, I release this miracle life that I carry to you now in Jesus' Name!

DECLARATION: I declare over you that you will receive the "suddenlies" of God upon your life! No plan of the enemy can hinder, delay or extinguish the dreams God has given to you; they come to pass…*suddenly!*

Your Place of Authority

Always remember that you are a carrier of the Christ, and wherever God sends you, that is your place of authority.

Just as the Holy Spirit hovered over the face of the deep awaiting the sound of the Creator's voice commanding light to be, God the Holy Spirit is always waiting, poised and ready to perform the words and works you declare in Jesus' Name!

Jesus was commissioned by God Almighty and sent to Earth to demonstrate the will of the Father. He spoke to wind, waves, trees, bodies, diseases, death and demons. *All things* were subject to Him: they obeyed His command and responded to the touch of His hand.

Dear one, the Holy Spirit is ever-present with you wherever you go. Where has the Father sent you? *Always remember that you are a carrier of the Christ, and wherever God sends you, that is your place of authority.* In your workplace, at your school, in your city, in your ministry and among those He has destined you to meet, *there* you have authority! *Whatever your sphere of influence, He has divinely positioned you there for purpose!* As you speak His Word into and over situations and circumstances, things will shift, change and move…*suddenly!* For those who operate in their dominion and authority, who are encompassed with favor and grace, a way is made to demonstrate God's will wherever they are sent.

DECLARATION: I declare over you that you are a sent one, commissioned by the Head of the Church to "Go." Wherever the Holy Spirit sends you, you have dominion and authority. As you speak His Word over situations and circumstances, things shift, change and rearrange in Jesus' Name!

The Spirit of the Lord is Upon You

"The Spirit of the Lord is upon me, because he hath anointed me to preach the gospel to the poor; he hath sent me to heal the brokenhearted, to preach deliverance to the captives, and recovering of sight to the blind, to set at liberty them that are bruised,

Be ever-mindful of this truth: the Spirit of the Lord is upon you!

"To preach the acceptable year of the Lord."

—Luke 4:18–19

The Spirit of the Lord is upon *you!* He has anointed *you* to preach the Gospel to the poor; He has sent *you* to heal the brokenhearted!

I am sent of God the Holy Spirit to demonstrate His power and compassion to people in healings and deliverances, but that is God on *you,* too! Answers to the problems people face every day will not be found in human wisdom: the wisdom of man will never fix the problems of the world. God sends you and me forth in His wisdom, His compassion and His power to give people hope.

Be ever-mindful of His presence upon you, and expect the Holy Spirit to demonstrate His love to someone through you today! This is *His* time and you were born for it!

👑 **DECLARATION: I declare over you that the Spirit of the Lord is upon you! You have something to give to the people you meet. The anointing of God upon you heals the broken-hearted, delivers the captives and sets people free—spirit, soul and body!**

Not Life as Usual

Speak to situations and circumstances in your life and expect a change!

I have often said, "It's not life as usual, anymore!" The time has come to live the life of faith that you have been taught. God always makes provision for you, and that provision is received by faith. I encourage you to begin exercising your faith in ways where you haven't before, or in areas where perhaps you have grown weary. Speak to situations and circumstances in your life and expect a change!

In John 14:12, Jesus said, *"He that believeth on me, the works that I do shall he do also; and greater works than these shall he do...."*

Some of the works that Jesus did include: healing the sick, raising the dead, calming the weather, multiplying food to feed multitudes and knowing where to find money. Jesus said we, as believers, would do greater works! Life with God the Holy Spirit is an adventure, and when you make a conscious decision to walk with God, it will not be life as usual anymore!

DECLARATION: I declare over you that you will live a life of adventure with God the Holy Spirit. It's a life of faith, a life of love, a life of healing and a life of power! Situations and circumstances change; in Jesus' Name you can't remain the same. It is not life as usual for you anymore!

Understanding of the Times

Great grace be upon you for this day and hour! It is my heart to share with you words of edification, exhortation and comfort, to settle, strengthen and steady you in the time you have come into.

When you view world events and the events in your own life in the light of Christ's return ... it will change you!

You can be just like *"the sons of Issachar,"* written of in First Chronicles 12:32, *"who had understanding of the times, to know what Israel ought to do."*

When light—understanding—comes, you can see; and therefore, you will know what to do even in the most uncertain of times. As you follow world events and the changing faces of the leaders of nations, be encouraged that these "times" have already been recorded in the Scriptures. Begin to see each event unfolding in the light of Christ's Second Coming. As you do, your understanding will be opened. Instead of the fear and dread the world would have you embrace, you will be encouraged by the truthfulness of God's Word. When you view world events and the events in your own life in the light of Christ's return, it will change what you think on, what you say, what you do…it will change *you!*

👑 **DECLARATION: I declare over you that you will filter every end-time event through your understanding of Christ's return. You will see clearly and know distinctly what to do, how to do it and when. God's Word is truth that edifies, exhorts and comforts you to stand strong and steady in Him.**

Those in Authority

Praying scripturally for those at the head creates an opening in the spirit for others... even yourself.

"Therefore I exhort first of all that supplications, prayers, intercessions, and giving of thanks be made for all men,

"For kings and all who are in authority, that we may lead a quiet and peaceable life in all godliness and reverence.

"For this is good and acceptable in the sight of God our Savior, who desires all men to be saved and to come to the knowledge of the truth."

—1 Timothy 2:1–4, NKJV

A great shifting is taking place in the spirit realm so that all things might come into divine alignment according to God's order. If you watch and listen to the events unfolding in the earth without keeping your focus on the Author and Finisher of your faith, it will be troubling to you. But, if you are rooted and grounded in God and His Word, your foundation is sure. Though you may *feel* the shaking, you will not be moved.

The faces of leaders of nations are shifting and changing, too, and so in this time it is great on my heart to pray as God's Word says according to the above passage in First Timothy. In this way you are praying scripturally for those at the head, and it creates an opening in the spirit for others and even yourself.

It is time for hearts on Earth to be aligned with Heaven. Your prayers of supplication, intercession and thanks for leaders and all men will make a way for true heart changes. Give voice to the Word of God for leaders in this hour, for it is the Father's first line of request in prayer. The leaders in position and power will directly affect all that concerns you.

DECLARATION: I declare over you that your prayers for the leaders of the land, whose hearts are in God's hand, effect change and turn each leader's heart to the Father's will and plan. Their eyes are open to see and know which way to choose. Wisdom from the counsel rooms of Heaven flows now through the leaders He has placed and positioned for end-time purpose.

Praying for Leaders

It is in the turning aside to look and listen when God asks you to "give Him but a moment," that He will speak to you of things to come; of things concerning His Son. Through these intimate times His voice will become ever-so familiar to you.

Praying for leaders opens a door for you; for it is God's divine order.

In the season you have come into, you must hear His voice and know which way to go. Leaders are front and center now, and so you must make praying for leaders a priority. You carry leaders because the Scriptures direct you to pray this way in First Timothy chapter 2. Praying for leaders and those in authority opens a door for you; for it is God's divine order. As you give voice according to the Father's will, you receive direction for your nation, knowledge of unfolding events and wisdom to know what to do.

Come aside with God the Holy Spirit today. Take a moment to listen and pray. Give voice to the Father's heart concerning leaders in place and those about to arise. Your agreement and sound make all the difference!

DECLARATION: I declare over you that you will thank God for the leaders He has placed—spiritual leaders and heads of state, too, leaders of nations, states, cities and families—cover them in the blood of the Son. Speak to their eyes to see and their ears to hear, for their minds to be clear and their hearts to obey and go God's way.

Pray for Laborers

"The harvest truly is great, but the laborers are few; therefore pray the Lord of the harvest to send out laborers into His harvest."
—*Luke 10:2, NKJV*

Momentum is building; a call from Heaven is echoing in the earth. The call is for the harvest! The Father is sending forth reapers as never before. As one of those sent ones, there is such urgency in me to declare Jesus to the people. Everything stands still at the mention of His Name.

The beloved Lord said, *"The harvest truly is great, but the laborers are few; therefore pray the Lord of the harvest to send out laborers into His harvest"* (Luke 10:2, NKJV).

The Scriptures give you such clarity of what to pray! You have assurance when you pray according to the Word of God that you are praying the will of God—you are praying God's heart. Jesus said you can ask the Father in the Name of the Son to send laborers into His harvest. An anointing comes upon you when you are sent to declare and decree with such authority in the place where you are destined to be. A grace—God's supernatural ability—keeps you too, where you would not otherwise be able to stand.

Laborer, I call you forth! Assignments from Heaven are coming down to direct and carry you to places and faces you know and those you don't. To you who have already thrust in your sickle, I release equipment from Heaven in Jesus' Name! Greater grace to stand in your place in the land, and ask for the harvest where you have been sent!

👑 **DECLARATION: I declare over you that you will ask your Father to send laborers into the harvest! Grace and anointing are released unto you now to go, and to stand, to declare and decree in the place the Father has sent you.**

Bold Witness

Boldness is a sign of New Testament believers! When the promised Holy Spirit was poured out on the Day of Pentecost, Jesus' followers were filled with a power that propelled them out of hiding in the Upper Room to testifying in the streets of Jerusalem! This glorious infilling of the Holy Spirit endues you with power from on High to be a witness for Jesus Christ and a conduit of His healing-miracles!

The glorious infilling of the Holy Spirit endues you with power from on High to be a witness for Jesus Christ and a conduit of His healing-miracles!

The Father did not leave you an orphan, but gave unto you "another Comforter," who is with you everywhere, at all times. You need only yield to this precious Person who lives on the inside and envelops the outside so that you say and do what He says and shows. You walk in the power of Heaven when you walk with this eternal One who knows all things and reveals to you His wisdom in this most unusual of times.

Draw on this reserve of power on the inside, for through you—His Body—His Kingdom comes in great glory, revealing His love, saving grace, compassion and healing for all humanity. It is an exciting time to be moving in the power of Heaven on Earth!

DECLARATION: I declare over you that you don't underestimate the power that lies within you and in the Person of the Holy Spirit! You are filled with the power to pray and praise. You have the power to produce and prosper, and you persevere under any pressure. You have the power to be a bold witness of the saving grace of the Lord Jesus Christ!

Financial Crisis Prophesied

Only through the Lord Jesus Christ, and your knowledge of Him through time spent in His presence, will you succeed and overcome.

I look and see from a place so high. In the next three years, so it seems to me, financially it will be very difficult except for the supernatural intervention of the Lord. As a righteous one, you hear and know which way to go, which is with the Word and Spirit. You implement the victory that was won. Never will you see yourself trying to obtain; you have a knowing inside of you that you have already obtained! From your place of victory you obtain. Never see yourself trying to get the victory; victorious you already *are*. Say so and implement so.

You must not look at what you can see in the natural. For the greater is in the unseen, and it is making its way toward you. Do not oppose God or yourself with words, deeds or actions. Say only what God would say and prepare for the season at hand. You must prepare in the natural. Do what the Holy Spirit directs you to do. Others will seek you out and have need of your water or your food. Be prepared to share. Regardless of what you hear and see, do not look for the answers in an elected official. Keep your eyes set on Jesus; for no man will solve this crisis for you or for your nation. Only through the Lord Jesus Christ and your knowledge of Him, through time spent in His presence, will you succeed and overcome. You overcome by the blood, the Word and the Spirit.

The glory will only get greater upon you and through you. Be quick to pray, to declare and decree what God has said. Take time to worship the Lord God Almighty. Things are moving very fast now. Days will seem shorter, but they are still 24 hours. Change, change, tremendous change has come. Nations align like on a great chessboard moving into position. Righteous one, all is well for you. Believe and receive and you will see it. You cannot look at how it appears; you must look in the spirit and in the Word or you will be deceived, confounded and confused and make wrong decisions right and left. The end is glorious for you, righteous one! The end is glorious for you!

👑 **DECLARATION: I declare over you that you will believe and receive the word of the Lord that prepares and steadies you. Believe the end is glorious for you.**

Cities of Our God

There is a sound! Through the congregations of the cities of nations a sound has
come down from Heaven to you. The prayers
you have prayed have been heard and here
comes the angelic host! Your prayers have
opened the gates to the portals above, for you
asked that the gates would be opened and the
gates are opening today!

There will be those cities in this nation and other nations, too, which will be known as cities of God.

I heard the Spirit say, "Once upon a time the word would be, 'Steady, Church!' But today it is, 'Steady, cities of our God!' To those in power— mighty ones—who meet to make decisions, 'Steady now!'"

There will be those cities in this nation and other nations, too, which will be known as cities of God. For a great work will begin in this city and that, and it is as though a great wind of the Holy Spirit does blow upon the fire that He began. Embers from the fires spread from this city to that city, and city to city in this nation and NATIONS! Something wonderful has begun in city to city across the nation. Such a sound abounds throughout the land; it penetrates the hearts of man. So grand is this Holy sound from this land and from others, too. The Church, she arises, for she hears the heavenly sound. In adoration and worship from household to household she arises, and the air is full of a wonderful sound!

👑 **DECLARATION: I declare over you that your Heavenly Father makes a way for you! I declare and decree that your city will be a city of God! Arise now in His grace and glory and march to His heavenly sound.**

God is Coming!

Some events you can change; some you can affect; some you can only prepare for.

God is a good God! He extends His tender mercies to the uttermost that all men might know the depths of His love. In the wake of events and tragedies in your land and nations beyond, you are often riveted by the devastation of cities, structures and lives. But know this: It is not the Father's will that any should perish; therefore, He always goes before such events and makes a way for the people. God is always talking, but sometimes you are not listening, or in some instances, not understanding what you are hearing.

The events unfolding before you have been moved into position very carefully. There are some events for which you are instructed by the Holy Spirit to pray over to change and others you can only prepare for. You prepare in prayer. Your prayers—following the leadership of the Holy Spirit—cover the people who don't know your Lord or who have strayed away. Prayers of intercession make a way of escape or open a door of opportunity for people to choose Jesus Christ.

Be comforted in knowing that your prayers do make a difference in the lives and eternities of others. Rise up in your crying out for the souls of this nation now, for it is time. God is coming! He will sweep across this nation with His great glory, His love, His healing, His compassion and His joy. He will turn the mourning into dancing in the very streets once trodden with sin and iniquity.

DECLARATION: I declare over you that you will cry out for souls in your nation! Your prayers open for them a door of salvation! You walk in great discernment concerning events unfolding worldwide, and by the Holy Spirit you hear and understand how to pray to change, affect or prepare for them.

Governments

Pray and agree, declare and decree for a knowledge of God to flood the minds of leaders....

It is always my desire to encourage you with words of edification, exhortation and comfort. It is a time of great uncertainty for the world; a time of fear and even dread for all who have put their trust in riches and joined themselves to this world's system. But for you who belong to the Father, it is a glorious time; when His tangible glory will shine forth as light to those in darkness!

Watch now as governments on every level come to the forefront. From leaders of nations in the political arena, to heads of monetary establishments in the financial realm, to the very personal level of family—governing bodies are front and center. Those of you who stand in positions of authority and influence, who make decisions on behalf of others, are highlighted in the spirit, and the decisions you make determine your intended direction and position either in the Kingdom of Light or the kingdom of darkness. You, who are of God's Kingdom, pray and agree, declare and decree with me for a knowledge of God to flood the minds of leaders, bringing a reservoir of hope and healing to all under their influence.

Though the world may be facing famine financially speaking, as a citizen of Heaven and a partaker of God's system of seedtime and harvest, IT IS HARVEST TIME! Harvest is not just financial or economic; *harvest is souls—the precious fruit of the earth!* God promised, *"I will give you the treasures of darkness and hidden riches of secret places..."* (Isaiah 45:3, NKJV).

You have God's Word, you have His Spirit and you have all of Heaven's resources at your disposal to manifest the supernatural...the spectacular...to usher in a harvest of souls from the kingdom of darkness to the Kingdom of God!

👑 **DECLARATION: I declare over you, leaders in God's Kingdom, an increase in the influence you carry, and a yielding of yourself to pray for those in authority. Your prayers make a way for minds and hearts to be flooded with light and turned to Christ.**

Christ *in* You!

A mystery concealed is now revealed to you who are righteous....

For decades the Church has been saturated with tremendous teaching of God's Word. It has been wonderful; for you have been afforded time and rich resources to build an immovable foundation of faith, rooted and grounded in Love Himself.

Much emphasis has been placed on understanding *"who you are"* and *"what you have"* in Christ, and rightfully so. But it is a new time, and a new *"sound"* has come—one that has been drawn in by the Holy Spirit to give revelation knowledge of what has not yet been captured by the Church. It speaks not of *us in Him,* though that be true, but of *Him in us!* According to Colossians 1:26–27, NKJV, *"The mystery which has been hidden from ages and from generations, but now has been revealed to His saints. To them God willed to make known what are the riches of the glory of this mystery among the Gentiles: which is Christ in you, the hope of glory."*

Christ in you! A mystery concealed is now revealed to you who are righteous in the earth! Such a moment occurred when you received Jesus into your heart. Two became one and now you are a son or daughter of God! Is there anything too difficult for Him? Nothing! And if Christ be in you, there is nothing, nothing you cannot do! I want to encourage you to believe in the amazing person you became when Jesus came into your life. Let Him consume you so that you walk, talk, heal, forgive and love as Christ does.

DECLARATION: I declare over you that the mystery of *Christ in you* is opened unto you now. You have revelation knowledge of Him and the power of His resurrection at work in you. See yourself the way God sees you: He sees *Christ in you!* Carry this glorious hope on the inside of you everywhere you go!

Clothed in His Glory

You have come into a wonderful time in the earth with God the Holy Spirit. His glory is coming upon the sons and daughters of God in demonstrations of power and displays of love beyond what you have dreamed. It's the glory that will make blind eyes see, cause body parts to be and bring the lost into divine relationship with Jesus the Christ!

"...The Lord shall arise upon thee, and his glory shall be seen upon thee."
—Isaiah 60:1–2

Isaiah prophesied of this glory to come: *"Arise, shine; for thy light is come, and the glory of the Lord is risen upon thee. For, behold, the darkness shall cover the earth, and gross darkness the people: but the Lord shall arise upon thee, and his glory shall be seen upon thee"* (Isaiah 60:1–2).

It is a day of darkness upon the earth, but the bright light of the Lord's glory will shine forth from you for all to see. You are part of an extraordinary generation, not just for what you do, but also for *who you are!* You are a son or daughter of the Most High, clothed in His glory and prepared to walk as Jesus walked on the earth.

👑 DECLARATION: I declare over you that you will arise and shine with the glory of God. Like the rising of the sun in the morning that brightens and dresses the day, you are clothed in this supernatural manifestation of His power and presence to draw all men unto Jesus Christ!

Pressing Through in Prayer

...It is given unto the Body of Christ to see, to know and to have understanding of things supernaturally on behalf of your cities and nation.

Dear one, you must have divine direction in this hour! By the leadership of God the Holy Spirit you will know which way to go and will show the way for others to follow. It seems to me that utterances attempting to make their way through from the third heaven to the first are being distorted, hindered and delayed, just as they were in Daniel's day. *"But the prince of the kingdom of Persia withstood me for twenty-one days. Then Michael, one of the chief of the celestial princes, came to help me, for I remained there with the kings of Persia. Now I have come to make you understand what is to befall your people in the latter days, for the vision is for many days yet to come"* (Daniel 10:13–14, AMP).

If you sense that Heaven is trying to move information through, but you cannot hear well enough, then keep pressing for the watchmen and intercessors to bring those utterances on through so that the prophets can speak rightly, and the leaders and the Body of Christ will know what to do.

It was given unto the sons of Issachar to have *understanding of the times* as a security for their nation, Israel. So it is given unto you as the Body of Christ to see, to know and to have understanding of things supernaturally on behalf of your cities and nations. If you want change in your nation, then church government must first be set in order, and the divine order in the church will overflow into the nation. *A nation can be no greater in its government or its military than the Body of Christ within it.*

👑 **DECLARATION: I declare over you that you are part of the most powerful force on Earth—the Church of the Lord Jesus Christ! The gates of Hell shall not prevail against you. Through prayer you make the way for utterances to come through from the heavenlies, and by the Holy Spirit you see and decree on behalf of your nation and city.**

Who are You?

It is a time of great preparation and transition for the Body of Christ and for all the earth. All things are coming full circle now, slipping into their slots in preparation for a glorious harvest of Earth's precious fruit.

"I am the voice of one crying in the wilderness: make straight the way of the Lord."—John 1:23, NKJV

In the Scriptures, the Prophet Isaiah foretold of one who would prepare the way for the Messiah. The gospels eloquently echo the prophetic picture of our Lord's forerunner; Jesus' beloved cousin, John. *"And he went into all the region around the Jordan, preaching a baptism of repentance for the remission of sins, as it is written in the book of the words of Isaiah the prophet, saying: 'The voice of one crying in the wilderness: Prepare the way of the Lord; Make His paths straight. Every valley shall be filled and every mountain and hill brought low; the crooked places shall be made straight and the rough ways smooth; and all flesh shall see the salvation of God'"* (Luke 3:3-6).

John heralded a baptism of repentance and forgiveness of sins in preparation for the Lord's first coming. When questioned by the religious leaders of his day, his testimony was sure. John knew who he was, and he knew who he wasn't. He confessed that he was not the Christ, not Elijah nor the Prophet. *"Who are you?"* they persisted, *...that we may give an answer to those who sent us? What do you say about yourself?"* (v. 22). John's identity and purpose were clear. Without hesitation he answered, *"I am the voice of one crying in the wilderness: make straight the way of the Lord"* (v. 23).

Who are you? What do you say about yourself? Just as John declared with great certainty, you answer these questions with the Word of truth! Your purpose and calling are the same as John's—to prepare the way for the coming of the Lord and to make His paths straight!

👑 **DECLARATION: I declare over you that you are a child of the Most High! You are the redeemed of the Lord! You have an unction from the Holy One and know all things. You stand as a forerunner to the return of the Lord, and you lift your voice as a righteous one in your generation to cry out in prayer, in preaching, in declaring and decreeing: "Jesus is coming, prepare your heart for His glorious return!"**

Members Individually

Whatever your specific place, you are a forerunner, preparing the way for your Lord.

You are precious to God! I want to encourage you in your specific place in Christ's Body. There is no room for "Big I" and "Little you" thinking in the Body of Christ; it is only "Big God" and His "sons and daughters." What Father God has purposed for me might look very different from what He has prepared for you, and that's OK. We are all individual members of the same blessed Body. *"...Now you are the body of Christ, and members individually"* (1 Corinthians 12:27).

God has set each one of you in the Body as it pleases *Him,* and it pleased Him to set you in this exciting time in history! Whatever your specific place, you are a forerunner, preparing the way for your Lord. God' didn't say it would necessarily be easy to pave the way, He just said, "Make His paths straight." That means you might have to lay some things down that are your ideas. You might have to pick some things up that are His ideas. Submitting to His way is always best. The end result will be exceedingly, abundantly above all you could have asked or thought!

DECLARATION: I declare over you that you are in the right place at the right time, fulfilling God's purpose for you. Your heart and will are submitted to Him and you take the place He prepared for you.

Positioned by God

Something wonderful of Heaven is coming upon the sons and daughters of God!

"You have heard these things foretold, now you see this fulfillment. And you will not bear witness to it? I show you specified new things from this time forth, even hidden things kept in reserve, which you have not known. They are created now (called into being by the prophetic word), and not long ago; and before today you have never heard of them, lest you should say, Behold, I knew them!" (Isaiah 48:6–7, AMP).

The position in which you find yourself must be all God, or it will be nothing at all.

Though the Prophet Isaiah addressed Israel with these words, you, as a New Testament believer, are a type of Israel in the spirit. Your ears are now opened to the spiritual sound and words from the heavenlies that are coming down from your Father God, the Lord Jesus Christ and by the leadings of the Holy Spirit.

You have come into such a time now that you must hear concerning your life, business, finances, ministry and family. The position in which you find yourself must be all God, or it will be nothing at all. His instructions and not your own ideas are what will carry you to the finish line. You now see and know what you didn't before, for these specified new things were hidden away, reserved and preserved for this day!

👑 **DECLARATION: I declare over you that you will possess a holy determination to follow your Lord. Your ears are opened to His sound and you now hear, see and know what you didn't before. He positions you perfectly in His plan as it pleases Him. See the fulfillment of the things in your heart, for it satisfies you and honors your Father.**

Places and Purposes

Now is not the time to retreat, stand still or quit.

It is a most decisive moment in history. With this new and vastly different season you have entered into, comes a convergence of place and purpose. A culmination and breaking forth of Heaven's purposes are propelling you, while the forces of Hell seem to be arrayed against you. But oh, how great is He that is in you; far greater than he that is in the world!

The Holy Spirit takes hold together with you and carries you on through into the place He has prepared for you. Even this time of seemingly greater resistance is part of the preparation for your place. Through the fiery trials He protects you, preserves you and helps you to press on through to possess your place.

Now is not the time to retreat, stand still or quit. When opposition comes, you don't give up, you suit up in the armor of God—in truth, righteousness, peace and faith—declaring God's Word, praying with all manner of prayer and giving praise and thanks to the One to whom the battle truly belongs!

DECLARATION: I declare over you that you will stand firm and resolute in your place of victory in Christ! His purposes for you are fixed and sure. No weapon formed against you can prosper. The greater One in you overcomes the forces of opposition. Press through to possess the place He has prepared for you!

Your Words

My, oh my; you are in such a time on the earth! The decisions of leaders, directions of nations and destinies of mankind are greatly affected as events quickly unfold now. In everything that is making its way through to manifest in the earth and in your life personally, *your words* carry great weight. It is ever-so

...Words release power and authority over all that is and all that is yet to be.

critical now to set a watch over your words, for words release power and authority over all that is and all that is yet to be.

The Holy Spirit, the great manifestor of God's power in the earth, waits for your sound. In Genesis He moved instantly to perform the Father's command, "Light, be!" In eager anticipation He listens for the words you voice in agreement with God's. When you speak what you believe, things begin to form! Something new comes into being, manifests, moves or changes. What wasn't there before, now is! What once stood as a barrier is now removed...*suddenly, supernaturally*...because you believed and agreed and chose to say what God says is true.

Don't let your words oppose you! Let not circumstances dictate and have their way. You declare and decree what will be each day!

👑 **DECLARATION: I declare over you that your words are a creative force that carry the power to produce! Set a watch over your mouth and boldly give voice only to what the Father says about the situations circling you. Agree with the Father in the Name of the Son, and by the mighty Holy Spirit, God's plans will be done!**

With all Boldness!

"And now, Lord, behold their threatenings: and grant unto thy servants, that with all boldness they may speak thy word."
—Acts 4:29, NKJV

Be bold! Don't just speak God's Word in your life; boldly declare it by faith! According to Acts 4:29, the disciples prayed and asked to speak God's Word *with all boldness.* *"And now, Lord, behold their threatenings: and grant unto thy servants, that with all boldness they may speak thy word..."*

Immediately following their request, Acts 4:31 records that the place where they were praying was shaken, they were filled with the Holy Spirit, and a spirit of boldness came upon them! *"And when they had prayed, the place was shaken where they were assembled together; and they were all filled with the Holy Ghost, and they spake the word of God with boldness."*

The Scriptures go on to say that the multitude of the believers was of one heart, that great power and great grace came upon them, and none among them lacked anything! (See Acts 4:31–34). By moving in boldness to declare God's Word, you see that strife was eliminated, and signs, wonders, miracles, grace and prosperity were released in the lives of the disciples.

DECLARATION: I declare over you that you will ask for and receive a spirit of boldness right now in Jesus' Name! With God's Word coming out of your mouth and Holy-Ghost boldness upon you, you will shake nations with the power and demonstrations of the Spirit of God!

The Corporate Anointing

The atmosphere in a corporate anointing is rich with the Spirit of God. When hearts are full of expectation, your prayers, praise and worship come together as one voice that opens a portal of seeing and knowing concerning God Almighty's keeping of your beloved nations, cities and congregations. What the Lord keeps is kept! Glory to God!

...Your prayers, praise and worship come together as one voice that opens a portal of seeing and knowing....

His great love, compassion and tender mercies are ever-flowing toward you. What magnificent power bursts forth in His presence through His utterance gifts and His power gifts to bring healings. The anointing destroys every yoke, bringing deliverance to you...all in a *moment* of time! Oh, the suddenlies of God are grand and glorious!

DECLARATION: I declare over you that when you gather corporately with the Body of Christ, that you come with great expectation! Your faith and supply prepare a platform for the Holy Spirit to manifest and pour out upon the congregation. Seeings and knowings open unto you when you minister to the Lord corporately.

Warriors—Every One!

They are those who won't back down or back off.

Everything the Holy Spirit does is to glorify Jesus Christ, Savior and Lord of all. It is always my heart to follow Him and give voice to what I believe He says and shows, so that you will be encouraged, edified and comforted by the Spirit of grace and truth.

Concerning the youth of our land, the Holy Spirit spoke. I prophesy this to you so that you may take a stand and declare this to be true.

A mighty sound I did hear as we worshipped the Christ. And of the youth the Spirit of God revealed: "They are warriors—every one! They are those who won't back down or back off. Just as in the military; no one is left behind. These faithful ones leave no one behind."

What a sound did abound from the heavenlies to us here below, and it was in the music that these words of prophecy did flow. The Holy Spirit highlights the youth! Receive this and declare it is so!

DECLARATION: I declare that the youth of Almighty God will arise in this time! Agree with the word of the Lord, "Calling forth the warriors of God's glory to finish His work and get the job done!"

Opened Unto You

...Vistas of wisdom and revelation, reserved for this time, are opened unto you....

One of the most tangible ways you can express your love and gratitude for someone is to pray for him or her. Agreeing with God in the place of prayer makes tremendous power available, dynamic in its working. Just as the Apostle Paul prayed for the believers he encouraged along his missionary journey, you can pray for others and yourself today.

"I do not cease to give thanks for you, making mention of you in my prayers.

"For I always pray to the God of our Lord Jesus Christ, the Father of glory, that He may grant you a spirit of wisdom and revelation, of insight into mysteries and secrets in the deep and intimate knowledge of Him,

"By having the eyes of your heart flooded with light, so that you can know and understand the hope to which He has called you, and how rich is His glorious inheritance in the saints (His set-apart ones),

"And so that you can know and understand what is the immeasurable and unlimited and surpassing greatness of His power in and for us who believe, as demonstrated in the working of His mighty strength,

"Which He exerted in Christ when He raised Him from the dead and seated Him at His own right hand in the heavenly places,

"Far above all rule and authority and power and dominion and every name that is named above every title that can be conferred, not only in this age and in this world, but also in the age and the world which are to come,

"And He has put all things under His feet and has appointed Him the universal and supreme Head of the church a headship exercised throughout the church,

"Which is His body, the fullness of Him Who fills all in all for in that body lives the full measure of Him Who makes everything complete, and Who fills everything everywhere with Himself."

—Ephesians 1:16–23, AMP

I believe and speak these eternal words over you who are destiny! May vistas of wisdom and revelation, reserved for this time, be opened unto you now through the avenues of God's Word, prayer, dreams, visions and fellowship with your Father.

DECLARATION: I declare over you that vistas of revelation are opened unto you! By the power of the Word and Spirit you know and see. The Spirit of wisdom and revelation has been granted, flooding the eyes of your heart with light, and opening unto you the great mystery of knowing Jesus Christ.

In Presence and Power

God's presence stills you; His power stirs you!

What a multi-faceted God you serve! The Holy Spirit moves upon the earth in power *and* in presence; and you must understand the difference between the two so you will be aware of Him and know how to move with Him. God's manifested presence *is* His power. So often you equate God's presence to what you *feel*, but just because you don't feel His power, doesn't mean God is not present.

God's presence affects your heart. In the stillness of Him, when a holy hush prevails, God settles you, causing you just to "be." Then, in His mighty power—His manifested presence—your soul and body are riveted to action to do what the Holy Spirit desires. God's presence stills you; His power stirs you!

I pray God's presence will rest upon you in a greater measure in the coming days, empowering you to stand, to overcome, to press on in your pursuit of Him, and to be all that He has destined you to be.

👑 DECLARATION: I declare over you that you are becoming well acquainted with the presence of God the Holy Spirit. He calms your heart and settles your spirit. Understand how to move with Him in power, to listen, to yield, to obey and to follow His promptings. Greater is His presence upon you, and greater is His power that flows through you.

Your Faith

I am stirred to share with you words to build up and strengthen your faith.

Your *faith* is the substance of things hoped for, the evidence of things not seen.

Your *faith* is the victory that overcomes the world.

Faith is the hand that reaches out and receives what God has provided....

Your *faith* is what you believe in your heart about Jesus the Christ, and release through your words concerning all that pertains to this life and the life to come.

What you believe in your heart and give voice to in accordance with God's Holy Word, will cause His power to move mightily for you and through you to others. Everything the Father has secured for mankind by His Spirit and through the finished work of His beloved Son is delivered through the avenue of faith. *By faith* you were saved, *believing* you have received, *your faith* makes you whole. Faith is the hand that reaches out and receives what God has provided: life, wholeness, strength, provisions, peace of mind, answers and mended relationships. Be bold to speak His Word; God's spoken Word breathes life into every situation. Fueled by love itself, your active faith is a conductive force that cannot be stopped!

If you have been pressed on all sides and seem to have grown weary in the waiting, I speak *strength* to you today. I take hold together with you for what you are believing and thanking God to manifest. In due season you shall reap if you faint not!

👑 **DECLARATION: I declare over you that your faith is a tangible substance. Plant your faith with your words and it will take root and grow. Your faith is working out every situation and circumstance for the glory of God. Your faith overcomes this world. Your faith is the avenue that receives all your Father has procured and secured through Jesus Christ.**

Strong in Faith

Now is not the time to waver, doubt or wonder; it is time to give God the glory....

It is my great pleasure to encourage you with words of life. As I listen to my Father's heart, it is as if I hear a sighing on behalf of Christ's Body in the earth. It seems a weariness has come upon so many, and I hear them saying, *"It feels like I've come to an impasse and cannot move forward."*

What stirs in my heart for those who seem "stuck," are words of strength and hope from the faithful, who, contrary to hope, in hope believed! (See Romans 4:18). The truth of *"faith comes by hearing and hearing by the Word of God"* stands, but what you do between the believing and the receiving of the promise makes all the difference.

Dear one, we all have opportunities to waver, doubt and wonder, which only weakens our faith and defers our hope. You want to strengthen, gird, buoy and build up your faith. How? Romans 4:19–21, NKJV, says: *"And not being weak in faith, he did not consider his own body, already dead (since he was about a hundred years old), and the deadness of Sarah's womb. He did not waver at the promise of God through unbelief, but was strengthened in faith, giving glory to God, and being fully convinced that what He had promised He was also able to perform."*

Abraham was strengthened in faith giving glory to God! Now is not the time to waver, doubt or wonder; it is time to give God the glory because you believe that what He promised He is also able to perform! You don't have to know the *how,* just *the One* who gives life to the dead, and begin calling those things which do not exist as though they did! (See Romans 4:17).

Be refreshed and strengthened in faith and in your inner man as you give glory to God for His plans, purposes and promises coming to pass in your life!

👑 **DECLARATION: I declare over you that you will give your Father all glory. If you do, your faith will be strengthened. Praise and thank God now for what He works out on your behalf. He has a plan, you have a purpose. Glorify Him for bringing it to pass.**

Blessings of Obedience

In Deuteronomy, the Lord speaks of the blessings of obedience and the curse of disobedience. As you obey the Lord your God, you have many blessings promised to you. *"The Lord will bless everything you do and will fill your storehouses with grain. The Lord your God will bless you in the land He is giving you. The Lord will send rain at the proper time from his rich treasury in the heavens to bless all the work you do"* (Deuteronomy 28:8; 12a, NLT).

Now is not the time to draw back, but to press out of your humanity into His divinity!

I encourage you to stay focused on your end-time destiny. Things are lining up with the plan of God. With God all things are possible! As you stay true to what God has placed within you to do, you will experience supernatural living. Proclaim what the Holy Spirit has spoken to your heart. Release your faith and receive it as yours, for it belongs to you! There is much for you to do, and it is by your relationship with Him that you will be encouraged to believe all that He has so lovingly promised you.

If God has placed desires in your heart, they will undoubtedly bring increase and blessings into your life as they are accomplished. It is God's plan for you to operate out of His divine overflow. He freely gives you all things that you need to fulfill what He has put in your heart to do. Now is not the time to draw back, but to press out of your humanity and into His divinity! God the Holy Spirit dwells within you with resurrection power to cause the impossible to be possible for you! Expect change. Expect things to rearrange. Continue to prophesy your destiny by the Word and Spirit of God. Get ready for the demonstrations of God in your life and family. He has equipped you for the work of the ministry of Jesus Christ!

DECLARATION: I declare over you that you will choose to be obedient to God in everything you think, say and do. Press into God as you never have before and resurrection power will be released. Things change! They rearrange—supernaturally—in Jesus' Name!

Life to the Full

God's Words are the very substance that restores you to health.

Jesus came that you might enjoy life; and have it in abundance (to the full, till it overflows). (See John 10:10b, AMP). Life in abundance encompasses wholeness for every part of your being: spirit, soul and body. That means salvation of your eternal spirit, soundness of mind, healing and walking in divine health have been made available to you through the redemptive work of Jesus Christ! He is the living Word—the Word made flesh! His words are *spirit* and they are *life*; they are the very substance that restores you to health.

Proverbs 4:20–22 admonishes: *"My son, attend to my words; incline thine ear unto my sayings. Let them not depart from thine eyes; keep them in the midst of thine heart. For they are life unto those that find them, and health to all their flesh."*

Dear one, healing, health and wholeness are yours—right now! This is the Father's will for you! You have only to receive what He has provided. Feed diligently on God's life-giving Word, keep it in the center of your heart, and let what is spirit impart healing to your physical body. Life in abundance is the Father's will for everyone, and He demonstrates this love in such glorious fashion as bodies are healed and lives are made whole.

DECLARATION: I declare over you that you will find God's words and let them fill you until you overflow with life and health. Abundant life floods your soul, spirit and body, too; you are healed, whole, strong and sound.

Perfect Soundness

My confidence is great in the God we serve. His Word is the foundation you must place your trust in and govern your life by. What you believe about God and His love and care for you will determine what you are able to receive from Him.

What you believe about God and His love and care for you will determine what you are able to receive from Him.

In reference to the man who was healed at the Beautiful Gate, Acts chapter 3 says that he was lame from birth and was laid in the same place day after day hoping for a handout for his very existence. But one day, when Peter and John passed by on their way to the temple, something happened. The man looked up at them, *"...expecting to receive something from them"* (v. 5). Expectancy was the man's faith! He may not have been believing for healing or restoration for his body, but his expectancy for *"something"* made a way for the miraculous power of God to flow!

Acts 3:6 goes on to say that Peter and John gave what they had—what they had freely been given. In the Name of Jesus, what was weak became strong, and what was lame became healed! Unable to walk his whole life, the man received more than what he was expecting that day; he leaped and danced all the way to the temple praising God! (See verse 8).

"And His name, through faith in His name, has made this man strong, whom you see and know. Yes, the faith which comes through Him has given him this perfect soundness in the presence of you all" (Acts 3:16).

Only your expectant faith to receive from Jesus, the Word made flesh, will bring perfect soundness: wholeness for your spirit, soul and body!

👑 **DECLARATION: I declare over you that expectancy is your faith in action. Look up with expectant faith to your Father and believe that you receive perfect soundness, wholeness, healing and restoration— spirit, soul and body—through faith in His wonderful Name.**

Things to Come

The Holy Spirit will announce and declare to you the things that are to come.

I encourage you to fellowship your relationship with God the Holy Spirit. He will reveal the wisdom of God to your understanding and direct your steps into the fulfillment of your God-ordained destiny. John 16:13, *The Amplified Bible*, says, *"But when He, the Spirit of Truth comes, He will guide you into all the Truth (the whole, full Truth.) For He will not speak His own message (on His own authority); but He will tell whatever He hears (from the Father; He will give the message that has been given to Him), and He will announce and declare to you the things that are to come (that will happen in the future)."*

Through spending time with the Holy Spirit, you will become comfortable with His presence all day, every day. He will show you what you need to see in advance. He prepares the way for you, and prepares you for the way. The Father always makes a way for you, and His provision to communicate His plans is through the Person of God the Holy Spirit. What you must know for your life, He will show, tell, announce and declare to you!

DECLARATION: I declare over you that the Spirit of truth will lead you today. Know His voice and follow Him. Be prepared and ready naturally and spiritually for all He has announced, declared and shown to you.

Divinely Positioned for Increase

Such a time and place God the Holy Spirit has brought you to in history! The Father has taken great care to make spiritual deposits and impartations into your life to prepare you for this time you have come into. He is always preparing for the future, and He plants in you

God is always preparing for the future...!

what you will need at just the right time so that it will spring forth when you need it!

Genesis 8:22, NKJV, tells us, *"While the earth remains, seedtime and harvest, cold and heat, winter and summer, and day and night shall not cease."* Seedtime and harvest is a law that applies to every part of your life: your time, attention, prayer, bodily exercise, the investment of study, finances and the sowing of the very heart of you. *"...God is not mocked; for whatever a man sows, that he will also reap"* (Galatians 6:7, NKJV). *"Give, and it will be given to you: good measure, pressed down, shaken together, and running over will be put into your bosom. For with the same measure that you use, it will be measured back to you"* (Luke 6:38, NKJV). God honors the law He set in motion, but the operation of the principle comes through the avenue of people.

I believe the Father is moving on your behalf even now. You are divinely positioned to receive a harvest from the seeds you have planted. I encourage you to be expectant of Him for the increase that He brings to your life.

DECLARATION: I declare over you that you will operate in the law of seedtime and harvest. Whatever you sow is exactly what you will reap. You will sow godly words, give of your heart, your time and your goods, and God brings great increase to every part of your life.

The Force of Favor

Favor is a divine force from Heaven that envelops your life and draws blessing to you.

The ministry the Father has entrusted to me is rich with the graces and giftings of the Holy Spirit. One of those giftings is favor. Favor is a divine force from Heaven that envelops your life and draws blessing to you. The favor comes from God, but it is demonstrated through men. God says that He is able to make *"...every favor and earthly blessing come to you in abundance."* (See 2 Corinthians 9:8, AMP).

God's grace is unmerited favor, meaning there is nothing you did to deserve it. You can't work for favor, but there is a way to activate favor in your life. Your expectation can be set for a flow of favor and released through the words you speak. The blessings of the Lord are already yours, but you engage your faith and open the way for God's blessings to come to you through what you believe and declare concerning your life.

DECLARATION: I declare over you that you are highly favored of the Lord! Favor flows to you in abundance with your family, at work and in your business dealings. Increase, bonuses, jobs, ideas and opportunities flow to you from your Heavenly Father who does exceedingly, abundantly above all you can ask or think!

Carriers of Christ's Compassion

A great release of God's mighty power is upon you to demonstrate the works of Jesus Christ. I want to encourage you to be mindful of the truth that *you* are a carrier of the compassion of the Christ! In you dwells the One who conquered every enemy; the One who lives and was dead; and is alive forevermore, Amen; and has the keys of Hell and of death (Revelation 1:18, paraphrased).

As His compassion consumes you, His Spirit will compel you to press past yourself to a place of complete surrender to Christ in you....

With all boldness you speak God's Word, by stretching forth your hand to heal, that signs and wonders may be done through the Name of God's Holy Child Jesus. (See Acts 4:29–30). As His compassion consumes you, His Spirit will compel you to press past yourself to a place of complete surrender to Christ *in you*—the hope of glory.

Destinies and eternities—including your own—are transformed through Christ's magnificent life-changing grace that flows to and through you! As you extend your hands in Jesus' Name, and speak His Word over every situation, you will see His love in demonstration be manifested everywhere you go.

👑 **DECLARATION: I declare over you that you are consumed with compassion from your Savior and Lord. It transforms you, compels you and thrusts you out of your comfort zone. Press past yourself, past fear and past doubt. Everywhere you go Christ's compassion flows out!**

You are a Son

"For as many as are led by the Spirit of God, these are the sons of God."
—Romans 8:14

Each and every day you have the opportunity to fellowship with your Father and follow the Holy Spirit in your every endeavor. In all you say and do you can be divinely led by the Spirit of God who has taken up residence in your born-again spirit.

Being led by the Holy Spirit is a right, privilege and responsibility given to you as a believer in the Christ. Through intimate fellowship you learn to hear His voice, understand His promptings and discover how He leads you individually and personally.

In the time you have come into, you must be able to hear from God for yourself. The sons of God are led by the Spirit of God. *You are a son or daughter of God if you are a believer in Jesus Christ as your Savior.*

Being led by God the Holy Spirit will be of great significance to you in the days, weeks, months and years ahead. Become ever-so keen now on knowing His voice—*His sheep know His voice* (John 10:4)—obeying His promptings to move this way or that, to stay put, to invest, or to hold. The Holy Spirit knows *all* things, and He wants to make a way for you, to secure you, to protect you and to position you as any good father would do.

👑 **DECLARATION: I declare over you that you are a child of God! You have ears to hear what the Spirit is saying. You know His voice and obey His promptings. He leads you specifically and accurately to position and protect. Thank your Father for making you His child!**

Privileges of Sonship

It is a blessed privilege to stand in your place as a son or daughter of the Most High God! Particularly in this time of great change in the earth, the revelation of your sonship provides you supernatural peace, comfort and assurance of the Father's steadfast promises.

Holy Spirit asks, "Give Me a moment. Turn aside in this moment with Me, please."

So many are in need of instructions for their lives, and I believe the Holy Spirit says to you, *"For those things that lay ahead of you this year, you are going to have to be able to follow Me ever-so accurately and do what I show you. That is where you will find success."*

Dear one, the ability to follow God the Holy Spirit with great precision will be developed through time spent with Him. You are going to have to turn aside as Moses did to gaze at the burning bush, and give God your time. This year—in the middle of all that is unfolding—the Holy Spirit asks, *"Give Me a moment. Turn aside in this moment with Me, please."* As you give Him your time, His voice will become so familiar to you. He will give you instructions, guidance and knowledge of what to do; it will help you and those around you, too.

I encourage you to turn aside and give Him enough of your time. Begin this day. You will walk in greater wisdom and understanding and in the victory He desires for you this year.

♛ **DECLARATION: I declare over you that you will set aside time to fellowship with God. Thank Him for this moment. Open up to wisdom from Heaven and His understanding, too. Hear, listen and do all He has purposed in His heart.**

Fear Not

"For God has not given you a spirit of fear, but of power and of love and of a sound mind."
—2 Timothy 1:7

I want you to know with great assurance today that you are loved! Before the Father formed you in your mother's womb, He knew you, and destined you for divine purpose. The care your Creator took to give you life has not changed; He continually cares passionately about you and all that concerns you. When you truly know and comprehend God's love for you, nothing can hold you back, because in love there is no fear.

Second Timothy 1:7, says that God did not give you a spirit of fear. Based on the authority of the Scriptures, you know that: 1) fear is a spirit, and 2) God didn't give it! Fear is an entity that wants to track you, get on you and work through you. When you are afraid, a spirit of fear is behind that, and the master of fear is death.

God has given you a spirit of power, love and a sound mind! A sound mind is a mind founded in truth, not broken or bruised; firm and strong; and one that cannot be overthrown or refuted. If you don't feel like you have soundness of mind, resist that "feeling"—that spirit—yield to the Holy Spirit, who is your helper and the Spirit of truth, and declare that God gave you a sound mind. Then be transformed through the renewing of your mind. Meditate on the Gospels, Epistles and Acts. Step into Psalm 91 and make it your own.

Be encouraged that when you are confounded with life, which so often can be the way of things, you can always rely on the simplicity of God's Word. The Holy Spirit has stirred me to address your fears and those things that would come upon you, because He loves you, and He sees you victorious in the Son. Draw from the reservoir of the Word you have built inside of you, and the Holy Spirit will give you the revelation of the Word that you must have for your life's sake in this hour. Fear not, my friend, but be consumed by His perfect love for you, which swallows up every fear.

DECLARATION: I declare over you that God's perfect love for you casts out all fear. Love abounds, so fear can't stay. Anything that confuses or confounds must get out of the way. Spirit of fear be bound and be done. Death, the master of you, be gone too. This battle has already been fought and won by Jesus Christ, God's victorious Son! His victory is yours!

Under Your Feet

The Father has put *all things* under the feet of the Son. Given into His hand are all rule, power, dominion and authority as the Head of the Church. In His Name, we—His Body—now exercise the authority granted to our Lord. Because you are seated with Jesus, *all things* are under your feet too: all sickness, disease, depression, poverty and pain…*every name* you can name.

> *"And hath put all things under his feet, and gave him to be the head over all things to the church…"*
> —*Ephesians 1:22*

From my place of authority I want to speak to *all things* that are not aligned with the Father's will. In Jesus' Name I command them to obey. Even as you read these words, expect to receive, because right now God's infinite power is present to heal. A tangible healing anointing is released on your behalf by faith.

I know there are those who have been given no hope: medical science has done all it can do. But I declare and decree, "*Creative miracles* for you!" In Jesus' Name, "*All things* become new!" Restoration, BE, for your mind and your body! Tissues and organs now function fully. I say to pain, "Be relieved!" For Jesus carried it away and it cannot remain. He sent His Word and healed you!

Whatever your situation, *all things* are under your feet and must bow to the authority of the Name. May all things become new for you…never the same in Jesus' Name!

I stand with you in faith concerning those you hold close to your heart. Healing and wholeness for the Body of Christ!

👑 **DECLARATION: I declare over you, from my heavenly seat of authority, that these things are true concerning you. With the Word of God, both written and prophetically decreed, you will agree: *"all things new"* it shall now be.**

In Him

Every provision is in Christ....

Easter is a blessed time for you and your family to gather in celebration around the finished work of your Lord and Savior, Jesus Christ!

All that God has accomplished is sealed by Jesus' blood and delivered to you through His Holy Spirit. Such provision the Father has made available to you: wisdom, understanding, wholeness, healing—spirit, soul and body—and abundance in every realm!

Every one of these provisions is *in Christ, "in whom are hid all the treasures of wisdom and knowledge"* (Colossians 2:3). *"In him was life; and the life was the light of men"* (John 1:4). *"For in him we live, and move and have our being..."* (Acts 17:28). "Apart from *Him* we can do nothing" (John 15:5, paraphrased).

Because of who Jesus is, because of what Jesus has done, you can partake of the promises secured through His life, death and resurrection! You can extend His life and love to others in His Name, by the power of His might and for His glory.

May you see yourself *in Him* this day, and live your life ever-mindful of your place in His heart.

DECLARATION: I declare over you that you will be thankful that God prepared a place for you in Him! By revelation you receive greater understanding that you have been accepted in the beloved and not rejected. Your Father wanted you for His own; through Jesus Christ He brought you home.

Fellowship With the Father

The Apostle John writes of the intimate fellowship he shared with the Father and with fellow believers. That kind of fellowship is born out of a relationship with your Savior, and it is one of the privileges that belongs to you as a son or daughter of God.

It is the fellowship of knowing Him that will get you through the responsibilities of life...

"That which we have seen and heard declare we unto you, that ye also may have fellowship with us: and truly our fellowship is with the Father, and with his Son Jesus Christ. And these things write we unto you, that your joy may be full" (1 John 1:3–4).

Wonderful times of fellowship are destined to be had by you with God the Father, God the Son and God the Holy Spirit. There are places in Him that you have not yet gone, simply because you have not taken the time, or perhaps because you were too timid to go.

I encourage you to spend time with your Creator today. Set a special time aside, just for you and Him. It is the fellowship of knowing Him that will get you through the responsibilities of life, and it is His heart to help you *through.*

May your joy be filled to overflowing as you fellowship the relationship that belongs to you in Jesus Christ!

👑 **DECLARATION: I declare over you that the Holy Spirit will take you to places with Him where you have never been. He will open up the written Word to you as never before. He will teach you to follow and flow wherever and however He wants to go. The times of fellowship with Him will always carry you through.**

Rooted and Grounded

What is of God endures forever!

The Kingdom of God has come unto you as a believer in Jesus Christ! In His love you are rooted and grounded, so that you may remain stable, fixed and established in the midst of anything that would try to move you. What is of God endures *forever!* What is not of God, will—in His timing—fall, fail and be consumed.

Know that *you* are a planting of the Lord. Through you, God's Kingdom is established in the earth. Wherever you have been sent to occupy, the work of God has taken root, is growing and is springing forth now. Jesus had authority in the earth because the Father sent Him here for a purpose.

Wherever God sends you, that is your place of authority. Coming upon you for your place is grace in such great measure it will astound those to whom you have been sent. Giftings and anointings from Heaven are given to equip you for service in this hour. God upon man—just like Jesus! And with God, nothing shall be impossible for you!

DECLARATION: I declare over you that you are flourishing where God planted you. In His love you are established, and fruit is springing forth from your life. Great grace abounds toward you! Walk in your authority. All God has purposed for you from the foundations of the earth is coming to pass!

Prophetic Prayer

I look through the city and I look through the state. I look through the region and I look through the nation. From the office in which I stand, I extend my voice, my authority and my hand, too, and I speak to forces that roam the streets that try to steal from the families. I speak to the forces that roam the corridors of the Senate and the Congress of Washington, D.C.

Look for the souls of men around and about you. Help them to know the Christ before their end does come.

I say, "Be exposed each and every one! You would use the flesh of man to confer even with the President of the United States and with other leaders of nations, too. Be exposed! Be made known! Those of you who would be so used by such demonic forces: Be made known! Not only in the places of leadership of nations, but in the pulpits, too. Be exposed! Be made known…all of you!"

The time has come and surely is where all things change by the leadership of the Holy Spirit. The Body of Christ worldwide is taken into another dimension of the Christ and of the Spirit, and they will go without manipulation and control. The wars will never cease in the spirit and in the earth until there is a new Heaven and a new Earth. Until there is the millennial reign, there will be war in man, with man and in the spirit, too.

Pray that the souls of man worldwide will bow their knee and receive of the Christ before the end does come. Do not look for peace; for when it is touted and cried out, know that it will be a false peace. There is no peace; there is only war. Do not look for the peace. Look for the souls of men around and about you. Help them to know the Christ before their end does come. Lord God Almighty, let your purpose of heart become a passion in the people of the congregations of the cities of all nations. In the Name of Jesus Christ I am heard and it is done. And everyone said, "Amen." So be it.

👑 **DECLARATION: I declare over you that you will agree with your Father, with this utterance from Him. Speak to these forces and entities to be exposed! Pray according to His Word for minds to be enlightened, souls to be loosed and hearts to be open so they might choose His Son before the end comes.**

Authority in Prayer

Always stay with the Word of God and follow the Spirit of God in prayer.

I believe our nation is on the verge of a visitation of unprecedented magnitude. The Spirit of God is trying to come in! Whatever happens in this natural arena must first take place in the spirit realm, and so many of those who pray are experiencing an intense wrestling or contending in prayer.

"For we wrestle not against flesh and blood, but against principalities, against powers, against the rulers of the darkness of this world, against spiritual wickedness in high places" (Ephesians 6:12).

Be not surprised when you encounter demonic opposition to the plans of God in the place of prayer. Though your flesh may "feel" the need to retaliate with the same aggression, stay in the spirit. Do as Jesus did when Satan tempted Him in the wilderness: simply speak the Word of God. Use your authority in Jesus' Name, and tell whatever is opposing the Holy Spirit to move out of the way.

Always stay with the Word of God and follow the Spirit of God in prayer. Your prayers will be in line with God's Word, resulting in His will being done on Earth as it is in Heaven.

DECLARATION: I declare over you that you will stay with the Word of God and follow the Spirit of God in prayer. Tell the principalities, powers and rulers of the darkness of this world to stand down in Jesus' Name. All things on Earth and in the heavenlies hear and obey the command, and align to the will of God Almighty.

Changing a Nation

"Elijah was a man with a nature like ours, and he prayed earnestly that it would not rain; and it did not rain on the land for three years and six months.

"And he prayed again, and the heaven gave rain, and the earth produced its fruit."

—James 5:17–18, NKJV

Never underestimate the power of your prayers to change a situation, meet a need, turn a heart and even a nation for God's glory!

In the midst of great drought and famine in the land, Elijah declared and decreed what the Lord said would be: *"...Go up, eat and drink; for there is the sound of an abundance of rain"* (1 Kings 18:41). God wanted to touch the people who, under the rule of wicked King Ahab, no longer followed God. You see an interesting progression unfold through the leaders on behalf of the people, and prayer was at the heart of God's plan.

Through the prayer and obedience of one man, God turned the people's hearts back to Him. God demonstrated His power in a display of falling fire that consumed the sacrifice and even the altar on which it lay. Immediately, He "cleaned house," wiping out all the false prophets. Once the land was purged of corruption, it was time for the promised rain to come. Yet before one drop of rain fell or even a wisp of cloud formed in the sky, Elijah said he *heard the sound of an abundance of rain.* God said rain was coming, Elijah heard it in the spirit, and *then* he went to pray. *"And Elijah went up to the top of Carmel; then he bowed down on the ground, and put his face between his knees"* (1 Kings 18:42). One man of faith, who bowed between Heaven and Earth in the posture of prayer, changed an entire nation!

The opening passage says Elijah was a man with a nature like ours! How much more can you as a born-again, washed in Jesus' blood, baptized in the Holy Ghost and fire believer do? Never underestimate the power of your prayers to change a situation, meet a need, turn a heart and even a nation for God's glory!

DECLARATION: I declare over you that your voice in prayer carries great power and authority! I declare supernatural provision and protection over all that concerns you and your family. Divine positioning maneuvers you to be a miracle for another. A spirit of intercession falls upon you to stand in the gap and help prepare the way for hearts to turn to the Lord. Believe for the fire, the rain and the power of Almighty God to fall *now* over your land so the earth can produce her fruit!

Revived Hunger

"After two days will he revive us: in the third day he will raise us up, and we shall live in his sight." —Hosea 6:2

I am so thankful for you, precious one. You are the apple of your Father's eye! A wondrous work of God is unfolding in the earth. He, the Person of the Holy Spirit, is moving upon the hearts of people in a very personal way, drawing you into a new depth of relationship with your beloved Savior, Jesus.

God the Holy Spirit is the demonstrator and manifestor of the works of Jesus Christ. He is the anointing and power of the Godhead. He is the Author of God's Word: the Spirit who inspired the scribes. He is the Third Person of the Trinity. He is with you, in you and upon you. Everything the Holy Spirit does blesses you and glorifies God's only begotten Son.

My cry is that this Person—this magnificent Spirit of grace and glory—would breathe upon you this day and revive you in your passion for Jesus Christ.

DECLARATION: I declare over you that your world, your land and each and every heart needs revival. Holy Spirit visits you! He revives you! He pours out upon you. He breathes on you and revives you in your hunger for your Lord! Ask Him to visit the nations, your nation, your state, your city, your church and your heart in Jesus' Name.

Worldwide Awakening

The time has come for you and me to be about doing the works of Jesus Christ. Oh, it has always been time to do the greater works—but you have come into something marvelous of God the Holy Spirit, and I believe there is a greater awareness of His efforts to move on your behalf. *Yes, I believe a glorious, worldwide awakening is upon us!*

We have come into something marvelous of God the Holy Spirit....

Jesus said, *"Most assuredly, I say to you, he who believes in Me, the works that I do he will do also; and greater works than these he will do, because I go to My Father"* (John 14:12, NKJV).

Though it may seem the glory of God and all the evil of Hell are running on course neck and neck with one another, in the midst of evil, something glorious is about to be!

Fear is particularly highlighted to me, when I look in the spirit I do see the enemy wielding this weapon so effectively against you. In the Name of Jesus Christ I take authority! Won't you declare and decree with me?

DECLARATION: I declare over you: "Fear, be bound and be gone in Jesus' Name! Source of pain, go! Body be healed! Soul be whole! No addictions will rule! Spirit of abuse be broken! I declare you are keenly aware of the glorious awakening that has come!

Demonstrations of Love

Praying the Word of God rather than your feelings, circumstances and situations, assures you of the answer God desires.

Something is up! Though you can't quite wrap words around the stirring in your heart, you know this truth: you are sliding into the fullness of time of the demonstrations and the manifestations of God's power; yes, but more specifically, of His love!

The Scriptures make reference to God's power hundreds of times, but speak of His love *thousands* of times. Love is the force Satan despises, for love ignites all that happens. Love, God's love in you, inspires and compels you to call upon your Creator in the Name of His Son, and by the Holy Spirit, God's will is done! You don't have to fear or worry, because Jesus Christ made a way for you to take every care and concern to the Father, who loves you. What you commit to your Abba, Papa, He keeps, and then supernaturally surrounds your heart and mind with His perfect peace!

"Now this is the confidence that we have in Him, that if we ask anything according to His will, He hears us. And if we know that He hears us, whatever we ask, we know that we have the petitions that we have asked of Him" (1 John 5:14–15, NKJV).

Praying the Word of God rather than your feelings, circumstances and situations, assures you of the answer God desires. God's Word is a creative, miraculous substance, that when applied, begins to form and to create! God desires to manifest Himself in the most personal of ways to His Creation. Fill yourself full of His Word until it becomes the sound of His heart flowing from your lips.

👑 **DECLARATION: I declare that you will have a renewed love for your God! Thank Him for His love that is outstretched toward you through your Savior. Let the love of God rule in your heart. It dominates your flesh so that you pray according to God's Word.**

Order the Day

O ur God is a God of order. *"In the begin-ning God prepared, formed, fashioned, and created the heavens and the earth"* (Genesis 1:1, AMP). He planned and designed everything He created with intricate precision and detail.

Time doesn't rule you; you rule time

He divided night and day, dark and light, the land and seas—appointing them their boundaries as He pleased. The sun, moon, stars and planets He set on their courses in the heavenlies, and to this day all are upheld by the word of His power. *Everything* is subject to His command, for it is all the glorious work of His hand. You, too, are His workmanship, crafted so fearfully and wonderfully for the good works He prepared long, long ago. God gave man dominion and authority both naturally and spiritually to keep His divine order. So with your words you are to declare and decree what God would say about the way things should be.

God is an eternal Spirit. He is eternity. You are His because He created you and made a way through Jesus Christ for fellowship with your Father to be restored. You are not waiting to step into eternity someday; eternity abides in you *now!* God is not in time, He is in eternity, and eternity is in you. Therefore, time doesn't rule you; you rule time. Sometimes there seems to me to be such agitation and pressure in the spirit. This is not the way God designed things to be. You who have been given dominion to subdue the earth, and authority to trample on serpents and scorpions and over all the power of the enemy, declare Heaven's order on Earth, and command things to align to God's way and not the enemy's nor man's. Speak order to the day when there is such a disturbance in the atmosphere; it is your responsibility to keep the air clear. Order the day and don't let it dictate the way for you. Declare and decree what God has said will be!

👑 **DECLARATION: I declare over you that you will have dominion over the works of your Father's hand, and in His authority granted to you, take command. By the power of the eternal One who dwells in you, declare and decree Heaven's order and way in all things concerning you.**

God's Way

The power is always present with you, but until you say what God would say, the Holy Spirit just hovers.

God's words are final authority. Matters are not open to dispute. All things must align to the way God says they are to be. All you must do is say what God says, believing that it is an absolute truth and knowing that anything that opposes God is headed for defeat. God knows but one way to lead and that is into victory!

When God looked out in the very beginning He saw that it was all dark. If He had said, "It's dark!" It would still be dark. He saw the darkness and He knew He wanted light so He said, "Light be." The only reason light could come was because the Holy Spirit incubated over this place that was but a dark void. Even though the Holy Spirit had all the power, for He is the demonstrator, He waited on a word of God. You have to fill yourself with the Word of God and speak the Word that gives the Holy Spirit something to manifest. The power is always present with you, but until you say what God would say, the Holy Spirit just hovers.

Yes, you are powerful because God the Holy Spirit has come and taken up permanent residence within you, and in the Name of Jesus Christ, nothing shall be impossible for you! But you can sit there and think that and wonder why nothing powerful is happening. You have to say what God would say. You have to do it God's way. Do it just like God did it. The Father spoke the Word, and then the Holy Spirit brought forth light.

Always remember that all things are God's way or no way. It can be no other way. Never settle for anything less than your covenant.

DECLARATION: I declare over you that you will do things God's way. Only speak what He would say. Do what He did, for the power of the Holy Spirit manifests and demonstrates to confirm His Word.

No Weapon

"No weapon formed against you shall prosper, and every tongue which rises against you in judgment you shall condemn. This is the heritage of the servants of the Lord, and their righteousness is from Me, says the Lord."

Don't receive any words that disagree with the Word of God concerning you.

—Isaiah 54:17, NKJV

Weapons come in many forms; the most common being words. Know that there are no words strong or powerful enough to prosper against you if you condemn them and refuse to receive them.

How do you condemn words spoken against you? What do you do with words that judge and bring condemnation upon you? Anything that rises up against you, you simply say, "No!"

Thoughts and lies come from the enemy as assignments to weaken and derail you. You must be the gatekeeper of your mind and resist anything that is contrary to God's Word. No words can place judgment on you unless you allow them to. Don't receive any words that disagree with the Word of God concerning you.

👑 **DECLARATION: I declare over you that you will condemn every word spoken in judgment against you. Thoughts and lies of the enemy you don't receive or agree with. Your Father's Word is the truth. Resist any weapon formed against you with the sword of the Spirit, which is the Word of God.**

Righteous Ones

"…The desire of the righteous shall be granted."
—Proverbs 10:24b

If you are born-again, you are in right-standing with God. A righteous one are you!

You are righteous because of your belief in Jesus Christ and your relationship with the Father. The blood of His Son has given you a place to stand.

Proverbs 10:24 says, *"The fear of the wicked, it shall come upon him: but the desire of the righteous shall be granted."*

According to Second Timothy 1:7, you were not given a spirit of fear. You know you are not the wicked. You are sanctified and set apart; a righteous one. Everything the wicked would do comes upon them. No matter if it be one person, a nation or the wicked leader of a nation. What they do and whatever they fear circles around and comes back to them. Don't ever forget that. Politics can make things very cloudy, but things come back and find that one, that leader, who perpetuated wickedness.

"…But the desire of the righteous shall be granted." Just as a parent's ears are open to the sound of his or her child, God's ears are open to you and what you ask of Him. He is your Father and He loves you! He fulfills your heart's cry, oh righteous one that you are, and He grants what you desire.

DECLARATION: I declare over you that you stand righteous before your God, because of the blood of Jesus Christ. You thank God for calling you a righteous one and for granting your heart's desire.

Awake! Arise! Oh, Church!

You are a part of something so grand of Heaven upon Earth! In this hour the Spirit of God visits you with wonderful impartations to establish and secure one and all. By His grace you soar in the Spirit to see and

Stand firm and see the deliverance of the Lord!

know and hear His charge: "Awake! Arise! Oh, Church! With His everlasting Word He comforts you saying, "Do not be discouraged! Do not fear! Take up your position, Church. Stand firm and see the deliverance of the Lord!" (See 2 Chronicles 20:15; 17 and 20.)

Your position in the heavenlies and your purpose on Earth are ever-so clear now. The Holy Spirit reaffirms that you are anointed and appointed for this time! Increase comes to you spiritually and naturally, too, for all the things He has put in your heart to do!

From all over the nation, pastors, leaders, churches and ministries are receiving impartations of the Spirit and are forever changed and rearranged! Your expectant anticipation and holy desire for His presence makes all the difference in what you receive from God. His presence changes you. The world will take note that you—ordinary men and women—have been with Jesus!

👑 **DECLARATION: I declare over you that God's charge to "awake and arise" is clear to you. By the Holy Spirit you hear, see and take your place in His plan. In His presence you are changed!**

Order of Protection

It is a revolutionary generation of revelation....

No one has the authority like the sons of God! What God has planned is about to be! It is about to be for you in your day! What am I hearing Heaven say? "Order of protection!"

Now take note children's pastors, youth pastors, including college too, order of protection is given to a heavenly host. They are going forth to enable you. Teach these young ones not to fear. Show them their honor. Show them their power and their courage in His Name. Teach them no matter how small they may be. An order of protection has gone out for this generation. It is a revolutionary generation of revelation, and they will bring forth manifestations and demonstrations on the earth. The children! The youth! And the college ones, too!

Hear me now! Order of protection from Heaven! Teach them! Teach them so they will know and have faith to receive what Heaven does decree. Orders, orders from Heaven!

DECLARATION: I declare over you that protection from Heaven comes upon the young ones for this hour. Pray for parents, leaders and pastors to teach, train, guard and prepare them with the help of the angelic host assigned to this generation.

Revival in the Land

In many places throughout our great land, the Spirit of God has been poured out. Prayers were prayed and God brought revival to a people. Then the time came and the hearts grew cold and revival was no more.

Tell the ones who pray to pick them up and pray over these revival seeds, and revival will come again.

I believe I heard the Spirit say, *"Seeds. Prayers can be like seeds. They have been suspended in time from the prayers of long ago; they are now the cloud of witnesses that looks down. The seeds are there. Tell the ones who pray to pick them up and pray over these revival seeds, and revival will come again."*

He went on to say, *"Let the people come from all around to worship Jesus. Pick up the seeds. People have tried before, yet I was unable to bring forth revival. But now the time has come! My people's hearts beat as one. Now all they want is Me. Now revival can be!"*

So I write this message to you, what I believe I heard my Lord say, because now is the time and this is the day. *"Tell the pray-ers to pick up the words in the spirit and the cry for revival in the land."* In Jesus' Name these things are purposed and these things shall be, and with the Word of the Lord, we agree.

👑 **DECLARATION: I declare over you that you will pick up His heartbeat and give voice to His command. Revival in the land shall be! Cry out in prayer and water the seeds of those who have gone before, because *now* is the time.**

Expect God-Encounters

God the Holy Spirit is the resurrection glory power that pulled Jesus Christ right out of the grave!

"However, when He, the Spirit of truth, has come, He will guide you into all truth; for He will not speak on His own authority, but whatever He hears He will speak; and He will tell you things to come."

—John 16:13, NKJV

Our Lord said that God the Holy Spirit is the Spirit of truth. The Holy Spirit possesses what belongs to the Father. He will give to you what belongs to the Son. He will declare, decree and show to you things that are to come!

God the Holy Spirit is the author of the Bible. He is the manifestor of every one of God's promises to you. He is the manifestor of all the works of your redemption—all the works of Jesus Christ! God the Holy Spirit is the power of the godhead; the resurrection glory power that pulled Jesus Christ right out of the grave!

When you come to know the Person of the Holy Spirit in this way, you will begin to see what you have believed about the demonstration of His power *in* and *through* your life. You can expect God-encounters every day, as His manifested glory pours out of you just like liquid pouring out of a sieve.

Jesus is coming back for a glorious Church—and His manifested glory is in *you!* If you believe it, you will see it and be it.

DECLARATION: I declare over you that resurrection power resides in you. It's the power to raise, to save and to set free. Expect this power to be demonstrated through you. What you believe is what you will see and be!

Apostolic Pastors

There is a strength coming forth in the sphere of government. I expound to you particularly of church government, for it concerns you and the time you've come into. Many pastors are both apostolic and prophetic. Apostolic pastors don't gather up, they train up.

Apostolic pastors don't gather up, they train up.

This is the time when the church returns unto as it began—apostolic. Why? Because apostles govern. They are government. This is a time for the winning of the harvest, which is true. You must go as quickly as you can to do this thing. Souls must be won. You have got to get them in quickly now. But understand this thing: apostles stand as government in the spirit, and then they overflow into their influence in the cities, and in a state, and in a nation.

Those who carry these graces and stand in these places, you are not apostolic because you started a work, you are apostolic because God places you there and you govern in the spirit and you govern in the city.

I encourage you, Apostle. You who would grow weary in your well doing: we have need of you. Stand in your place in church government, and in the government of your cities, states and nations. Apostles see those leaders among us and they train them up. They send them out! Send them out quickly, quickly, quickly!

👑 **DECLARATION: I declare over you that you will pray for apostolic ones to stand in their place and in their grace. Let them be strengthened with might in their inner man and affect the churches throughout the land.**

The Plan for Man

... This place was a realm where dates and times of events are kept.

I was taken up into a place through a door, into a realm, and to what looked like a room. Then the walls lifted away and there were stars in space to behold. The place did expand. At the entrance I saw a creature with many eyes; he was full of knowing. Suddenly, an altar I did see, carved of stone, and it surprised me. On it were coals that seemed not to burn away. Fire and smoke rose up and seemed to speak, but I could not understand. Beings were moving around and about very slowly and deliberately with great purpose. There was a separation between them and me like sheer draperies. I could see them, yet I couldn't really see. Something was in their hands, and very carefully they would put what they held into this slot and that—almost like at a post office. Then another one would take that thing and move it up to another slot—very slowly, very carefully they handled these things.

It was very quiet; not a sound except for the sound of a horn being carried on the winds. I stood and said, "What is this place?" Suddenly, I knew this place was a realm where dates and times of events are kept. "I don't understand," I said. Suddenly there was a book, and on its page was a writing unfamiliar to me, so I could not decipher what I saw. But suddenly, it changed into what I could understand, into my language. On the cover of the book was written: *The Plan for Man.* The cover opened, and I saw the words: *Destiny of Man.* I asked the Holy Spirit, "What is this place?" He confirmed, and said, "It is the realm that I call the prophets into."

I declare and decree to you, some pastors ordained and called of God are anointed and called as apostle and prophet, too. They are gifted and enabled in those offices. I have shared with you a mystery, a secret place that God has granted to be made known. He allowed this not to just a few, not just among the prophets, but to you. Why? So that you may pray for those who carry this gifting of apostle and prophet to be comfortable to enter into that realm to see dates, times and events. Pray that once they see, they will be given utterance to speak out in their congregations and in their nations. This is a declaration and this is a decree. Take it, handle it very seriously.

DECLARATION: I declare over you that you will pray for those who are both apostles and prophets to be at ease to enter into realms where they can see, hear, know and speak by God.

Prayer for Apostolic Pastors

Please receive this declaration over you, and carry it as a prayer assignment as the Lord leads you.

...Thank You for Your visitation, and for setting in order the way of things.

DECLARATION: I declare over you that God will share with you secret things that are like mysteries. He gives a knowing and an understanding...suddenly. He may have given you a command to pray and so you shall. You will obey. You shall do as He has asked. The Holy Spirit will help you. The Holy Spirit will give you unction to pray, words to say and even order your day to give you time to pray.

Thank God for His visitation, and for setting in order the way of things for a plan inside a man. Ask God for congregations to assemble who have been called up alongside to accomplish a work. Thank your Father for establishing apostolic pastors in the land; for giving them a vision and plan to train up and not just to gather up. In Jesus' Name. Amen and amen.

Heaven's Wisdom

Wisdom is simply knowing what to do, when to do it and how to do it....

In this time you have come into, God now moves across infinity and begins the greatest outpouring of the Spirit upon humanity. He demonstrates and confirms the Word, the written heart of God for you. In this time you will have to follow God the Holy Spirit in the earth as you have never followed Him before. It is always that way in a great move of God that is worldwide. You will have to know His voice. In order to know the voice of God the Holy Spirit, you have to know the Person that He is.

The Holy Spirit is your teacher and revelator of the Word of God. The Holy Spirit reveals Jesus to you. He reveals the Creator Almighty God as your Father—your Abba—your Papa. The Spirit of God is the Spirit of truth. He is the Spirit of wisdom. Wisdom is simply knowing *what* to do, *when* to do it and *how* to do it, and you must have Heaven's wisdom in this day.

Now the Holy Spirit stirs in each and every one a knowing that something wonderful is about to be; and that something wonderful is the return of the King of kings and Lord of lords—Jesus Christ! The Spirit of God would prepare the people of God for such a return, and He would prepare the people of Earth that something is happening, for in the hearts of the people of the nations, a dissatisfaction grows.

The Spirit of God always goes ahead. He prepares you for change. Keep listening to Him. He will prepare you for change economically now. Quiet now and listen. He will tell you what to do concerning what is to come, for that is the way with God the Holy Spirit.

👑 **DECLARATION: I declare over you that the Heavenly Father will stir your heart with the happenings coming forth. Hear His sound. Know His voice. Hearken unto Him and prepare naturally and spiritually for what He shows you.**

Divine Overflow

Our God has an inexhaustible supply of whatever you need. Jesus said, *"I came that they may have and enjoy life, and have it in abundance (to the full, till it overflows)"* (John 10:10, AMP)

Jesus desires to give you an overflowing surplus of His miraculous provision!

Jesus desires to give you an overflowing surplus of His miraculous provision! He came to make you more than you are and to give you more than what you have. Noah Webster defines overflow as: *a deluge, to run over, to overwhelm, to swell and run over the brim or banks, abundant, copious.* In other words, *"more than enough!"*

Abundance speaks of inexhaustible supply. With God as your source, and planting as your lifestyle, an abundant harvest is inevitable. Operating out of the divine overflow is the Father's will for His children. This divine overflow is what I carry, and I impart this same blessing and increase to you!

DECLARATION: I declare over you that you will receive the divine overflow imparted to you. Increase comes to you spiritually, physically and financially to bless you and make you a blessing to others.

Communion of the Holy Spirit

"...And the communion of the Holy Ghost be with you all."
—2 Cor. 2:14

In Second Corinthians 2:14, Paul writes, *"...and the communion of the Holy Ghost be with you all."* The word "communion" expands in the Greek language to mean, *"May the intimate fellowship of the Third Person of the Trinity, he who is the Person God the Holy Spirit, be with you. May the ongoing companionship and partnership of the Third Person of the Trinity be with you. May you fellowship with one another now and for all infinity. May you know Him and walk with Him, talk with Him, study with Him and pray with Him."*

Wow! How wonderful of Him to grant you this intimacy through the blood of His beloved Son. Because of the time you have come into of the outpouring of the Spirit of God, you need to have a very close fellowship with the Holy Spirit. Be comfortable with Him and ready to move in His gifts, His manifestations and His demonstrations anywhere at any time.

You will never trust anyone you don't know; not even God. Who is your best friend? How did he or she become your best friend? You spent time together. You trust such a one with your life, with a loved one, with your money. That is how it must be with the Holy Spirit. That's where you are now in this time. So you know what plane to fly on, which one to get off of, what buildings not to be in, what markets to get out of…you must know the voice of the Spirit. I encourage you in your fellowship with God the Holy Spirit in these last days. He longs to make Himself known to you!

DECLARATION: I declare over you that you will partake in the intimate fellowship of God the Holy Spirit, and trust Him to lead, guide and personally direct you in all the affairs of life.

Effective Faith

"Whatever you ask for in prayer, believe, trust and be confident that it is granted to you, and you will get it."

—Mark 11:24, AMP

...Faith must have a picture held in the heart, which sees God bringing to pass what you believe.

"Now faith is the assurance (the confirmation, the title deed) of the things we hoped for, being the proof of things we do not see, and the conviction of their reality (faith perceiving as real fact what is not revealed to the senses)."

—Hebrews 11:1, AMP

To be effective, faith must have a picture held in the heart, which sees God bringing to pass what you believe. The substance of things hoped for gives image to your faith. This confident expectation places a demand upon God's power and manifests what you see and believe.

You are not trying to get God to do something for you. Through the avenue of faith, you receive what He has already done. Faith is of the heart, and its effectiveness will be greatly increased as you develop the picture of His finished work on the inside of you.

I join my faith with yours in expectation of God's visitation upon your life, your family, your business, your body and your finances. Take time today to fellowship your relationship with the God of Heaven. He will emboss on your heart what He wants you to see. Believe this! Surely He will bring it to pass!

👑 **DECLARATION: I declare over you that you will be embossed by His vision on the canvas of your heart. See what He sees. Your faith is effective because you believe He is bringing to pass what you see.**

A Supernatural Shift

The Head of the Church—Jesus Christ—is aligning His Body for the time and season you have come into.

Something is shifting, dear one! People and events are moving into position like pieces on a great chessboard, and *you* are a part of it! The Head of the Church—Jesus Christ—is aligning His Body for the time and season you have come into.

The shift begins first in your own heart. The desires of your Father well up on the inside, and a holy dissatisfaction stirs you to pray. Then, by His Spirit, things that are not of Him are moved out of the way. Things are changing on your behalf very supernaturally now. Be not surprised if locations shift, vocations change and circumstances rearrange. Divine connections made long ago come back around full-circle, for you are the Body of Christ, designed to work according to His divine order.

By the orchestration of the Holy Spirit a supernatural shift is upon you! Though this divine equipping is supernatural, it seems like the most natural thing to move and function in this place. It is by the design of the Almighty that you have been prepared and positioned for this time. *"For we are God's own handiwork, His workmanship, recreated in Christ Jesus, born anew, that we may do those good works which God predestined, planned beforehand for us, taking paths which He prepared ahead of time, that we should walk in them..."* (Ephesians 2:10, AMP).

From the graces I carry and impart, I release unto you the understanding and direction you require for this time. Leaders in particular, I encourage you to stand in your place and in your grace. Lead with all boldness and teach others how to follow the Holy Spirit as you have been trained so accurately to do. Such a time you have come into, and you are right on time!

DECLARATION: I declare over you that you are divinely prepared and positioned by the Holy Spirit for the last days. Embrace the grace to move and change and have things in life rearranged.

All Authority

The Father has purposed for you to walk in *all authority* in the Name of Jesus Christ. He has provided for you *all power* by God the Holy Spirit. Through the Word and the Spirit you have been given *all things* that pertain unto life and godliness! *"Behold, I give you the authority to trample on serpents and scorpions, and over all the power of the enemy, and nothing shall by any means hurt you"* (Luke 10:19–20, NKJV).

> *Whatever name you can name, in Christ, you are above it!*

Your place is one of great authority. In the spirit you are seated with Jesus in heavenly places in Christ (see Ephesians 2:6), where you occupy a realm *far above* principality, power, might and dominion, and every name that is named (see Ephesians 1:21). Whatever name you can name, *in Christ,* you are above it! Dominion over the enemy is your rightful place: destined for you by God the Father, delivered to you by Jesus Christ, and secured for you by the power of the Holy Spirit!

It is my prayer for you to operate in the place of power and authority granted to you by God Most High. I have great confidence in your ability to move in the power of the Holy Spirit entrusted to you by your Father, to the glory of His beloved Son!

👑 DECLARATION: I declare over you in the Name of Jesus Christ that you will take authority over principalities, powers and over all the power of the enemy. No *thing* that is named can hinder, thwart, delay, stop or destroy you. In that royal Name, release the Spirit of wisdom and revelation where your authority is concerned, and declare that you are a vessel filled and overflowing with God's nature, ability, love and power in demonstration.

The Family Name

"For this reason I bow my knees to the Father of our Lord Jesus Christ, from whom the whole family in heaven and earth is named..."
—Ephesians 3:14–15, NKJV

God Almighty, Creator of the universe and Father of our Lord, is *your* Father! God is a good Father, and He is in the business of protecting His family. As a son or daughter of the Most High, heirs with God and joint heirs with Christ, you have received an inheritance—*the power and the Name!* This is the authority the Father has divinely granted you because you are in the family.

The Father directs you by His Word and by His Spirit so that you might walk in perfect protection. It is your part to listen and follow His promptings, however slight. This listening begins in the place of prayer and fellowship with the Father, Son and Holy Spirit. In this place of intimacy with Him, His voice becomes so clear that it is not hard to hear, to see and to know which way to go, what to do and what not to do. All He needs is your time and your heart.

DECLARATION: I declare over you that you receive a revelation of the Father's love for you! You are in His family, and He has given you the Name of Jesus to implement authority. The Holy Spirit draws you into places of deep and intimate fellowship with God. He speaks to you, shows you things to come and covers you with perfect protection under His Almighty shadow.

No Other Name

There is no name like the Name of Jesus! Acts 4:12 proclaims: *"Nor is there salvation in any other, for there is no other name under heaven given among men by which we must be saved."* The Name of your Lord Jesus Christ is being revived within you. Life resides within His wonderful Name!

By the power of His Spirit you are separated and sent; commissioned to tell and demonstrate the heart of Heaven on Earth.

The Name of Jesus is above every name that has been named. (See Philippians 2:9). The One sent to take away the sins of the whole world declared in Matthew 28:18–19, *"All authority has been given to Me in heaven and earth. Go therefore and make disciples of all the nations...."* By the power of His Spirit you are separated and sent; commissioned to tell and demonstrate the heart of Heaven on Earth. If you are born again, the spirit of prophecy—which is the testimony of Jesus Christ—is upon you! (See Revelation 19:10).

The Word of God is incorruptible seed. The seed of Christ went into the earth and produced you and me. By God's design, every seed produces after its own kind. You now have the ability and the power within you to reproduce born-again souls! You have the guarantee for someone else to experience an eternity with the Creator, if you will just tell them of the Name and give them a chance to choose Jesus.

DECLARATION: I declare over you that in the authority of Jesus' Name and by the power of His Spirit, you will demonstrate the heart of Heaven on Earth. Seeds are planted and souls are won to your Father's honor and the glory of the Son.

His Appointed Time

...Readiness of heart and seasons of preparation are essential for a surge in destiny!

There are places in the spirit regarding your destiny that wait for you, but are accessed only in God's divine sequence and timing. These places are "time locked" so-to-speak. They are opened by the Spirit and in the spirit.

All of your self-effort and energy will not open or access something that is not available to you yet because the plan waits for *His appointed time*. When you come into the fullness of time for your assigned plan and purpose in God, it happens seemingly effortlessly, though *not* automatically! The plan unfolds unto you because there is an unconscious cry of your heart longing to be filled with all the fullness of God. The unveiling, revealing and unfolding transcends the reasoning of your soul.

You must be aware that these places in God are guarded and sometimes challenged by demons. *"For a great door and effectual is opened unto me, and there are many adversaries"* (1 Corinthians 16:9). For this reason, readiness of heart and seasons of preparation are essential for a surge in destiny! If there is not a readiness in heart and mind, then the surge in purpose and destiny would be too much, and failure would be the result. God's divine timing is the key to you fulfilling your destiny!

Know this today: You are not alone! You are connected to a supply of the Spirit of God, a supply of grace and of provision for the purposes God has destined specifically for you. I release these provisions and divine connections unto you for the plans and purposes He is leading you to pursue.

DECLARATION: I declare over you that the Holy Spirit is orchestrating timing, events and the plans He has purposed for you. All provision, connections and graces He imparts. In His appointed time He unlocks your destiny and fulfills every cry of your heart.

Deep Calls Unto Deep

The Father loves you and has destined your life for great purpose. It is always my heart to encourage your faith through words spoken in due season by the Spirit of God. I believe by the power of the Holy Spirit that the Word of God will never return void; God's Word will always accomplish what it was sent to do, and that is to produce fruit in the life of the hearer and doer.

"For the Spirit searches all things, yes, the deep things of God."—1 Cor. 2:10–11, NKJV

What do you hear the Holy Spirit speaking to your heart? What is He saying to you in your times of fellowship with Him? He who formed you knows you so well. He understands how to communicate most accurately and personally with you. Whether His Word comes to correct, protect or direct, He *always* has your good in mind. However He is dealing with you, I want to encourage you to trust Him. He who knows the future better than you know the past, knows how to shepherd you, His precious sheep. He tells you in His Word: *"Lean on, trust in, and be confident in the Lord with all your heart and mind and do not rely on your own insights or understanding. In all your ways know, recognize, and acknowledge Him, and He will direct and make straight and plain your paths"* (Proverbs 3:5–6, AMP).

God knows just where you need to be, when you need to be there and how to get you there. The times you have come into require such a keen awareness and precise following of the Holy Spirit.

"For the Spirit searches all things, yes, the deep things of God" (1 Corinthians 2:10–11, NKJV). Deep is calling unto deep. Will you answer? Son, daughter of the Most High God: *The world is waiting for you!*

👑 **DECLARATION: I declare over you that you will hear the cry of the Spirit. It will reach the depths of your heart. You answer your Father, and you consecrate and dedicate your life anew. You will do everything He asks of you.**

It's Your Time

The fruit of your fellowship with the Father makes you a catalyst for change!

Great grace is coming to the people of God, and *you* are a part of it! The fruit of your fellowship with the Father makes you a catalyst for change!

The Father is searching for hearts set on Him; hearts that will yield to and obey the Spirit's slightest impression. You have been in training for the time you have come into with a wonderful teacher: God the Holy Spirit! Right where you are right now, as a mom, a store clerk, a doctor, a student: know that you are a son or daughter of Almighty God. When you step out in faith and give voice to His Word, all of Heaven backs you up!

You lay hands on the sick and they recover.

You speak the Name above every other name and demons flee.

You see and know and it makes a way for someone to be free.

It's time, and it's your time!

What a day of destiny you have come into, and what a grand opportunity lies before you. Father God had faith in Jesus—His plan for the earth. He has faith in *you*, a son or daughter of God, too. On Christ, the Son of the living God, He builds His Church, and the gates of Hell shall not prevail against it!

👑 **DECLARATION: I declare over you that you are like Jesus, a child of God. Step out in faith and it brings change. Just like Jesus, don't leave anyone the same.**

The Way of Wisdom

It's a time of great transition for the Church and for the world. The Father has always known what is and what will be, *and, He has always had a way for His beloved Creation.*

"When you walk, your steps will not be hindered, and when you run, you will not stumble."
—Proverbs 4:11–12

You can take great comfort in God's ways, trusting that they are higher and better than anything you could contrive. Proverbs 14:12, says, *"There is a way that seems right to man, but its end is the way of death."* Yes, man has a way, and the world has a way. First John 2:17 assures that, *"...the world is passing away, and the lust of it; but he who does the will of God abides forever."* The only way for believers to operate in this world we are in, but not of, is to walk God's way. His way is love, and it is far above the world's way. His way is a way of wisdom. In fact, Proverbs 4:11–12 admonishes: *"I have taught you in the way of wisdom; I have led you in right paths. When you walk, your steps will not be hindered, and when you run, you will not stumble."*

When decisions must be made concerning your life, I encourage you most earnestly to seek God's wisdom for you. He will show and tell you what to do, how to do it and when. He knows the end from the beginning, and He cares for you as a shepherd does His sheep. He leads you—not just in the challenging times—but through every day of your life. Trust in your hearing of Him and learn to surrender your own will to follow His. Make it your quest and great aim to follow the Holy Spirit, who leads you into all truth and shows you things to come. Even when things don't seem to make sense to your mind, rest in the truth that *wisdom's way is a way of pleasantness, and all her paths are peace* (Proverbs 3:17).

👑 **DECLARATION: I declare over you that you will walk in love today. You will walk in wisdom from Heaven, and in supernatural peace, because you are submitted to Him and His ways.**

A Way Through

Every morning mercy is waiting for you to wake up!

In all of your hard choices, God the Holy Spirit is always there making the way for you. Where it seems there is no way in that moment...*suddenly*...God.

Psalm 145:8–9, speaking of our blessed Lord, says, *"The Lord is gracious and full of compassion, slow to anger and great in mercy. The Lord is good to all, and His tender mercies are over all His works."*

God's heart toward you overflows with compassion and mercies that are ever-new. His mercies are new every morning. Every morning mercy is waiting for you to wake up! In the mercies of God are the deliverances you need and the healings you must have in your body and in your soul. Know that He always makes a way through, and waiting every day for you is mercy. Wow, what a God!

DECLARATION: I declare over you that you will receive God's mercy, for it makes all things like new. You are mindful to extend this divine mercy to yourself and others, too; for mercy makes a way where it seems there is none.

God's Heart of Compassion

Compassion means: love, full of eager yearning. How marvelous! God is full of eager yearning over you! *God yearns for you!* It is a wonderful thing to let God be the lover of your soul. God knows you so well. He loves you so much and is eager over you.

God is full of eager yearning over you!

When God's compassion is poured out, people are glad not sad. Compassion comes in and everything changes. It happens in a moment of time. Deliverance comes, healing manifests suddenly to you. Disease, sickness, bones and nerve endings come into order. Lupus and MS no longer can be, because the Spirit of the Lord visits you. The suddenlies of God come upon you and it is a grand thing to see. Receive His compassion, and worship Him now for all He has done and continues to do for you.

DECLARATION: I declare over you that God's compassion consumes your heart, floods your soul and makes your body whole. Thank God for who He is and what He's done, and for the compassion He pours out so abundantly.

Miracles in the Atmosphere of Worship

Praise, worship and waiting on the Lord will create an atmosphere for the Holy Spirit to move in your midst.

The hour has come for God the Holy Spirit to demonstrate His power on the earth as no generation has seen! In John chapter 2, you see a glimpse of Jesus' very first miracle of turning water into wine at the wedding feast in Galilee: *"This beginning of signs Jesus did in Cana of Galilee, and manifested His glory; and His disciples believed in Him"* (John 2:11, NKJV). This sign Jesus did was a display of His glory on Earth, so that His disciples might believe that He was who He said He was: the Son of God. Everyone present tasted of the supernatural, and it was *the best!* It is just like God to save the best for last!

I believe God's glory—His presence on the earth—is the greatest manifestation of His power you will ever see. When we on Earth make contact with this power from on High, instant healings, mighty miracles, and divine deliverances will be the result, Why? *That people might believe in Him.*

You must desire the manifested presence of God in your daily life, in your home, in your marriage, in the marketplace and in your gatherings. How can you usher in the glory of God? It begins with your expectancy—your faith.

Acts 13 says that as the Antioch Church *ministered to the Lord and fasted, the Holy Ghost spoke.* Praise, worship and waiting on the Lord will create an atmosphere for the Holy Spirit to move in your midst. It is also scriptural to pray for the rain; an outpouring of God's Spirit upon the earth. (See Hosea 6:3; Joel 2:23; and James 5:17–18). I believe as you hunger for the Holy Spirit and learn to yield and cooperate with Him, He will manifest His glory in divine displays of power!

DECLARATION: I declare over you that you will take time to minister to God today and to worship Him. With your praise you prepare a place for Him to pour out His presence and power.

Only Believe

The Father loves you! I invite you to meditate on His great love, His goodness and His tender mercies revealed in today's scripture. I believe as you praise Him for all He has already done through His beloved Son, the tangible healing power of God will strengthen your spirit and quicken your body!

If you can believe, all things are possible to him who believes."
—Mark 9:23, NKJV

> **"Bless the Lord, O my soul; and all that is within me, bless His holy name!**
>
> **"Bless the Lord, O my soul, and forget not all His benefits:**
>
> **"Who forgives all your iniquities, who heals all your diseases,**
>
> **"Who redeems your life from destruction, who crowns you with lovingkindness and tender mercies,**
>
> **"Who satisfies your mouth with good things, so that your youth is renewed like the eagle's."**
>
> **—Psalm 103:1–5, NKJV**

God's words are spirit and life, and I believe they are affecting your spirit and renewing your mind and body even now as you partake of the Scriptures. Divine healing belongs to each and every one of God's children, for He's a good Father! All He asks is that we believe. Jesus assured Jairus concerning the life of his daughter, *"Do not be afraid, only believe, and she will be made well"* (Luke 8:50). To the woman with the issue of blood, He said, *"Daughter, be of good comfort; thy faith hath made thee whole…"* (Luke 8:48). And to the man with an epileptic son, to his disciples and to you and me, Jesus declares, *"If you can believe, all things are possible to him who believes"* (Mark 9:23).

I believe and stand with you for a complete turnaround of circumstances that have held you down or back physically in your body, financially in your prosperity and spiritually in your walk of faith. Your belief in the One—God's Holy Son—who saved you, healed you, delivered you, prospered you and loves you, makes a way for you now. Do not be afraid…*only believe!*

DECLARATION: I declare over you that the realm of faith—of possibility—is real to you. Circumstances change and go, for all things are possible because you believe.

Mercy Triumphs Over Judgment

"...Because he hath poured out his soul unto death...and he bare the sin of many, and made intercession for the transgressors."
—Isaiah 53:12

What wonderful provision has been made for you through your Savior, Jesus Christ! Forgiveness of sins, healing of disease, deliverance from death and destruction, the blessing of prosperity, and victory over every enemy...these benefits are all-inclusive of the work of salvation. This mighty work is the triumph of mercy over judgment! Jesus stood in your place and *"... Himself bore our sins in His own body on the tree, that we, having died to sins, might live for righteousness—by whose stripes you were healed"* (1 Peter 2:24).

It pleased the Father to bruise His own Son in your behalf.

> **"Yet it pleased the Lord to bruise him; he hath put him to grief: when thou shalt make his soul an offering for sin, he shall see his seed, he shall prolong his days, and the pleasure of the Lord shall prosper in his hand.**
>
> **"He shall see of the travail of his soul, and shall be satisfied: by his knowledge shall my righteous servant justify many; for he shall bear their iniquities.**
>
> **"Therefore will I divide him a portion with the great, and he shall divide the spoil with the strong; because he hath poured out his soul unto death: and he was numbered with the transgressors; and he bare the sin of many, and made intercession for the transgressors."**
>
> **—Isaiah 53:10–12**

Wow, what a God! What a marvelous plan of salvation He has unveiled for you. Now you stand righteous in the blood of the Son, forgiven and free, because you believed and received His indescribable gift. Meditate on what He has done for you today. Tell Him how grateful you are for what He has done for you, and share this miracle of life-giving grace with someone else. Give them the opportunity to taste and see that He is good!

DECLARATION: I declare over you that you will declare the goodness of your Heavenly Father! Thank Him for the blood of His Son, His gracious gift of the Holy Spirit, for saving you, delivering you, restoring your soul, for healing your body and making you whole.

Giving is of the Heart

It is a wondrous time in the earth! I love the Father's plan—Jesus! For Jesus is the only way for every man to come to the knowledge of the truth and into an intimate fellowship with the Father.

God always looks upon the heart; the unseen part.

When you love Jesus with all your heart, out of that love for Him you lead your life according to the Holy Scriptures. You fashion your life after your blessed Savior and give freely as you have received. Giving is a great deal more than sending a monetary donation. God always looks upon the heart; the unseen part. God sees *you* in every act of love you bestow, and He is the One who rewards. What a good Father!

With your gaze fixed on Jesus, set your affection on things above rather than on the earth. It is then that you are able to live each day consumed with a passion for the Christ—a passion to know Him and to make Him known!

DECLARATION: I declare over you that you will give cheerfully as the Holy Spirit leads you, and not out of necessity. You give because you love God and desire to be obedient to His ways. You give of your finances, you give of your time, you give of your talents and you give of your heart. Know that your Father will keep you abundantly supplied.

Work as Unto the Lord

"Whatever you do, do it heartily, as to the Lord and not to men." —Colossians 3:23, NKJV

Dear one, you are so valuable and precious to the Father! The supply you carry is of great significance. Just your presence changes the very atmosphere everywhere you go. God placed in you such specific giftings and talents, hand-picked and tailor-made for you with a custom fit. Isn't He marvelous?

So when you are given a task to fulfill, regardless of who has asked it of you, know that you are to perform that task as if God Almighty Himself made the request. For Colossians 3:23, NKJV tells us, *"And whatever you do, do it heartily, as to the Lord and not to men."*

We are all to work as unto the Lord. Whether you are volunteering in your church, helping at a civic function, performing a task for your employer or serving your family, remember to do it with *all* your heart for the glory of your Lord and King. When you keep a scriptural perspective in your serving, you become an instrument the Holy Spirit can flow through to minister to others, to glorify the Son, and to bless you. Your faithfulness is a fruit of the Spirit that yields rich rewards!

DECLARATION: I declare over you that you will work as unto the Lord in all that you do. Your heart is to serve and not to be seen. Great blessing comes to you when you serve the Lord scripturally.

Empowered by the Spirit

I believe that you are about to enter into the places you have longed for in God. He welcomes you there by His Spirit in prayer. Trust God with your life and those you love. He will never disappoint. He is faithful, and a God of great mercy and compassion.

Everything in creation responds to the voice of the Creator.

Be assured this day that your prayers make a difference in the outcome of things. Your voice is empowered by the Spirit of God as you speak His Word concerning you, your family, your job and your nation. Remember how God your Creator spoke: What He called forth, was! Everything in creation responds to the voice of the Creator. As a son or daughter of the Most High God, you speak by direction of the Holy Spirit, and all things must obey. God's Word is the final authority; all things are as He says.

You are of the I AM! Believe and receive that your steps are ordered by God, and stand your ground by faith, for it is holy ground if you are consecrated and set apart to God. If you have decided to follow Jesus as the Head of the Church, then as His Body, you are to draw your identity, your strength, your joy and your purpose from Him. I desire with all my heart for you to experience the fullness of life that God has provided for you.

Stay close to Him in the abiding place of His power. Keep your heart toward Heaven, and be filled with the knowledge of Him and His divine presence in you!

👑 **DECLARATION: I declare over you that the Holy Spirit empowers you to pray, to trust, to love, to believe and to obey. I declare that you will draw from His presence this day, and are filled full with the knowledge of God's will.**

Stay in Position

... Prayer cancels the plan of Satan and establishes the plan of God!

The Holy Spirit encourages you to stay in position for His provision through God's Word and prayer. You must remember that prayer cancels the plan of Satan and establishes the plan of God!

Stay focused on your destiny in Christ. Don't let up! Stay in there and continue to speak forth what you believe. *"For the vision is yet for an appointed time and it hastens to the end fulfillment; it will not deceive or disappoint. Though it tarry, wait earnestly for it, because it will surely come; it will not be behindhand on its appointed day"* (Habakkuk 2:3, AMP).

Know that you are not late, because God is never late. His timing is perfect, and you are right on time!

DECLARATION: I declare over you that you will not grow weary in the waiting, for God's plans are right on time. Prayer positions you for the plans and provision God is preparing for you.

Heaven Opened

I love prayer. Even as a child I liked to pray. People sometimes ask me, "How did you get to know the Holy Spirit?" I didn't know much about Him until much later in life. Most of my life I knew "Father" and "Son." It wasn't until I was 34 that I saw a Bible, and that was

For those who bow their knee in prayer, heaven opens.

under the influence of the Baptism of the Holy Spirit. The very first time I saw the Word of God, it was brand new to me. I got to know the Holy Ghost by spending time with Him, particularly in prayer.

I like what happened to Peter in the Book of Acts, when he began to pray. In Acts 10:9–11 NKJV, we read that, *"…Peter went up on the housetop to pray, about the sixth hour. Then he became very hungry and wanted to eat; but while they made ready, he fell into a trance and saw heaven opened…."*

Peter bent his knee to pray and heaven opened! Then, in verse 13, *"… there came a voice."* Watch the early Church. They were always praying, and then the Holy Spirit spoke.

You have got to hear; you've got to know. If you will pray, heaven will open for you and you will see and know. That just seems to be the way of it. The early Christians prayed and they saw. They prayed and they heard. You are no different! As you bow your knee in prayer, heaven opens!

👑 **DECLARATION: I declare over you that prayer is the key to opening the heavens. You bow your knee in prayer today and by the Holy Spirit you begin to see and know what He desires to show you.**

The Fire and the Glory

Make a decision in your heart to turn aside from what is familiar.

God has all manner of ways to manifest His presence—what we call the glory. He comes in a cloud, fire, a heaviness or weightiness, even in silence as a holy hush. In the Old Testament, Moses' first encounter with the glory is recorded in Exodus 3:2: *"And the angel of the Lord appeared unto him in a flame of fire out of the midst of a bush: and he looked, and, behold, the bush burned with fire, and the bush was not consumed."*

The fire and the glory. God will visit you, but He won't consume or destroy you. In verse 3, Moses said, *"I will now turn aside, and see this great sight, why the bush is not burnt."*

Notice that Moses *said* something. That means he made a decision about what he witnessed. He said, *"I will…."* That's decision. That is what it is going to take.

"When the Lord saw that he turned aside to see, God called unto him…" (v. 4). When God knew that He had Moses' attention, and that his heart was willing, *then* He called him. If you read on further, you see that God equipped Moses for what He called him to do. Moses received understanding of what to do, how to do it and when to do it.

Never believe that you don't have need of God and the things He would want to add to you. You may be a man or woman of God, but there is always room for more giftings. You can't have *more* of God; if you are born again, you've already got Him. However, there is a deeper understanding that you can have, which enables you to walk in everything God has for you.

Make a decision in your heart to turn aside from what is familiar. Allow God to have liberty in your life to remove, add, change and rearrange what is needful for you and for Him.

DECLARATION: I declare over you that you will give your attention to the Father and make a decision to know Him more intimately. I declare that He will add to you what He desires to give, remove what must go, change and rearrange what is needed. I declare He will visit you with His fire and glory!

God Visits You

R ight now, today, God comes into your situation and intervenes for you. Believe this. Don't challenge it—believe! Receive this and you will see this. Don't wait to see. Turn everything now into a thanksgiving for the provision that you may not feel or see, but that shall become, for it already is! Everything that is, came from the place of the unseen. So though you don't see or feel in this moment, I am witness and give testimony: what is impossible...*suddenly* becomes so.

Everything that is, came from the place of the unseen.

What was impossible before, what you thought couldn't be, now shall be. How? God visits you. He comes and gives provision. Where you had none, now you suddenly have. Whatever character that would be needful, forms for you. Things move out of the way now. What must happen? What must be reversed? What has been the report to you? What is your body, your mind, your situation, your relationship, your finances, your schooling, your scholarship, your business, dictating to you? Something of God happens for you that changes everything. Believe that. Receive this moment with God, and you shall see what is needful for you.

DECLARATION: I declare over you that you will believe and receive what wasn't before. Open a door of thanksgiving for the provision that already is, for your faith receives it and makes it so.

The Only Begotten Son

…Everything that flows and manifests through the vine, comes out into you, for you are one with the Father and the Son.

There is a grace to speak of Jesus Christ, the only begotten Son. By the direction of the Holy Spirit, I asked Him for this grace and things have never, ever been the same. He filled my mouth with an articulation of Jesus Christ. Out of the heavenlies, out of the unseen, words were given for the expression of the King Himself. Jesus took on such a place and position, and the expression of the Name above every name came forth in a new way.

Nothing must be allowed to separate you from Jesus your Savior; not religiosity, tradition or doctrine. When you say you are born again, you must see the Creator as having fathered you by the blood of His Son. There has been a supernatural, eternal conceiving, and by the blood of Jesus and the love of the Father, you have been brought forth. God is your Father, and all that is in the Christ—the only begotten Son—flows in you. He is the vine and you are the branch and everything that flows and manifests through the vine, comes out into you, for you are one with the Father and the Son.

Go to the Scriptures concerning this truth so that you will have the mind of Christ in you, and take your rightful position in the Father's heart. Out of the crucifixion and the resurrection of the Christ, you became a son or daughter of the Most High. This is who you are!

👑 **DECLARATION: I declare over you that you are one with the Father and allow nothing to separate you from your Savior, for you can do nothing apart from Him. (See John 15:5).**

The Person of God the Holy Spirit

"Nevertheless I tell you the truth; It is expedient for you that I go away: for if I go not away, the Comforter will not come unto you; but if I depart, I will send him unto you."

—John 16:7

By the Father's love for you, the symphony of the knowings of the mysteries and the secrets of the Trinity come forth.

What a marvelous plan the Father orchestrated in sending the Holy Spirit! *The Amplified Bible* names Him Comforter, Counselor, Helper, Advocate, Intercessor, Strengthener and Standby. He is all those things to you. Most importantly, He is a Person!

By the Father's love for you, the symphony of the knowings of the mysteries and the secrets of the Trinity come forth. The Holy Spirit draws you unto Himself. He shows you your Lord and your God, and speaks to you of Them. He takes you into meditations of God the Father and God the Son and the very Word that He inspired.

As you fellowship with the Holy Spirit He teaches you to follow Him, to wait upon Him, to listen and to look upon what He gives you to see. Then, He gives you the interpretation of those things that He has opened unto you. This is the Third Person of the Trinity, the wonderful Person of God the Holy Spirit. Know Him for who He is!

👑 **DECLARATION: I declare that you recognize the blessed Holy Spirit as the Third Person of the Trinity. He comforts, counsels and helps you. He advocates for you and intercedes on your behalf. The Holy Spirit stands by your side and strengthens you. He is God. You come to know Him better and to love Him more, and it is wonderful!**

Kingdom Life

When you come into your place of fellowship and belonging, you step into Kingdom life, and your heart knows you have found your "safe place" for your growth in the Christ.

It is the wonderful Holy Spirit who leads you into your God-ordained destiny. As you learn to move with Him, you often discover there is a cost to the decisions you make to follow that destiny. One decision, that may seem insignificant at the time, can ultimately have far-reaching effects in your life and the lives of others. I believe there comes a time in your life when you set about to find where you belong, and whether you realize it or not, all the while it is the Holy Spirit who is leading you into God's plan through those hunches and intuitions you experience each and every day.

One of the most important directions the Holy Spirit will lead you in is to your pastor. *Of great significance to your destiny is finding the place where you will be protected, provided for, taught and even corrected.* When you come into your place of fellowship and belonging, you step into Kingdom life, and your heart knows you have found your "safe place" for your growth in the Christ.

Be encouraged that the Father has a pastor and a congregation reserved just for you! Trust the promptings of the Holy Spirit in you, for He is the Spirit of truth, and He will only lead you in paths of righteousness. If you have found your place of provision and protection, make that commitment to stay and pray for that work and for your pastor. *You* are of great significance, and you have a place and purpose in God's Kingdom!

DECLARATION: I declare over you that God has called you to a specific place, a specific pastor and a specific congregation. He leads you by His Spirit into His best for your life. People of destiny are drawn to places of destiny, and you are one of destiny. You recognize and discern and are being drawn by the Holy Spirit to your safe place of divine provision and protection for growth in the Christ.

Heart of the Pastor

"And He Himself gave some to be apostles, some prophets, some evangelists, and some pastors and teachers, for the equipping of the saints for the work of ministry, for the edifying of the body of Christ...."

A pastor cannot pastor as he was born to do unless you are in your place.

—Ephesians 4:11–12, NKJV

There is something so supernatural about the heart of the pastor. I believe the Holy Spirit draws you to a particular pastor—not to a praise and worship team or to a great facility—but to a leader, a shepherd. People are most often like their pastors, so when I see the heart of the pastor, I see the heart of the people he oversees.

When God divinely connects you to a particular pastor, he can easily impart the plan and vision of God from the pastor's heart into yours, because just you being in the place the Holy Spirit has set you is a "God thing." A pastor cannot pastor as he was born to do unless you are in your place. You carry the giftings and anointings that come up alongside your pastor, and you draw out what God has deposited inside of him for you.

The plan of God and the vision of God are imparted to the heart of the pastor, and the pastor imparts to the people. Let the Holy Spirit lead you to the place and to the pastor He has called you to. The strength of that leadership, and the Word and vision he imparts to you, will carry you through the responsibilities of life.

👑 **DECLARATION: I declare over you that God the Holy Spirit is leading you to a specific pastor, one who teaches you and imparts God's vision and plan into your heart.**

Praying for Your Pastor

Prayer for your leader accesses and activates the giftings you carry....

Know that the keeping of your pastor in prayer is a specific assignment. The Father entrusts you to cover your leaders in the place of prayer, and it is a great honor to make request on behalf of another. Prayer for your leader accesses and activates the giftings you carry; it opens the plan of God in your pastor's heart and imparts his vision to you.

You will find that for most things God wants to do in the earth, He needs for someone to say so. He needs for His sons and daughters to declare and decree what is on His heart. God is very specific. When you pray for your pastor, God will work through him on behalf of the congregation, and the Holy Spirit will impart your pastor's heart to you. There are things God wants you to say over the vision and the plan that He puts inside of a pastor, so you have a part in that when you pray.

When you commit your heart and your prayer life to the plan and vision of the pastor's heart, know that you give of your supply, and it's a holy thing. Through praying for your pastor, the plan of God inside a man unfolds for the people of the congregations personally and reaches beyond into the cities of nations. You have a part of drawing the plan of God out of your leader's heart and into your own.

When you have received the vision and the plan of your pastor, it can become so big inside of you. You begin to see what God sees. What grows in your heart concerning the families in your congregation and the people in your city and in your region slides into its place for each and every person affected, all because you prayed.

DECLARATION: I declare over you that you will commit this day to pray for your pastor—the leader God has led you to. Your prayers make a way for God's plans to unfold in your city, region, and nation, and in your own heart.

Fellowship Your Relationship

*J*esus Christ—your beloved Lord, the Head of the Church and your Savior—*led captivity captive and gave gifts unto men*. (See Ephesians 4:8–13). He went to the highest heights and the deepest depths to secure for you the gift of pastor. My pastor always taught me that it wasn't enough just to have accepted Jesus as Savior, but that a person must also *fellowship the relationship* with the Father, Son and Holy Spirit. The Word of God was so imparted and inscribed on my heart through my pastor that when hard times came, I was always very sure of God. The fellowship that I had with the Godhead, coupled with the Word of God that I meditated upon through the leadership of my pastor, anchored and steadied me in the face of seemingly impossible situations.

When you have spent time with your Father…you know that He is faithful and true to the very Word He wrote to you.

Know that no matter what circumstances present themselves, when you have spent time with your Father you are able to stay in there until what your Lord has promised you manifests, because you know Him. You've sat at His feet, sat down at the table, had morning coffee and walks with Him. You know that He is faithful and true to the very Word He wrote to you.

Take this moment to fellowship your relationship with Him today. He loves you! He created you for this purpose—to fellowship with Him.

DECLARATION: I declare over you that you will fellowship with your Heavenly Father today. Give Him your time and your heart. Don't allow busyness to get in the way. His Word steadies, secures and stabilizes you. You are anchored in Him no matter what comes your way.

Hearing the Holy Spirit

The Holy Spirit will never step out of the character of the Godhead in His conversations with you.

When you have spent time developing a relationship with God the Holy Spirit, you will have tremendous confidence in your hearing of Him when He speaks to you.

"Will the Holy Spirit speak to my ears?"

No, the Holy Spirit will speak to your heart—your spirit. You will discern who is talking and will know whether something is your idea or His by your knowledge of the Word and through your fellowship of the Godhead. The Holy Spirit will never step out of the character of the Godhead in His conversations with you. All you know the Father, the Son and the Spirit to be, will always be reflective in His communication. He will never depart from the righteousness of the written Word. Everything He says reflects the Word, for He is the author of it.

The Holy Spirit made sure something was put in writing for you and me: He said the Word of God is like a sword. Hebrews 4:12 describes the working of the Word: *"For the word of God is quick, and powerful, and sharper than any two-edged sword, piercing even to the dividing asunder of soul and spirit, and of the joints and marrow, and is a discerner of the thoughts and intents of the heart."*

The Holy Spirit works with the Word that is inscribed upon your heart and divides between your soul and spirit. He suddenly opens your understanding and makes the Word very clear to you. When you have an impression of what you are supposed to do about a situation, your knowledge of the Word and the illumination of the Holy Spirit divide between that soulish part of you where your intellect, will and feelings abide. Your meditations on the Word of God will make it easier for the Holy Spirit to guide you into all truth and into what is right for you to do. When you know Him, you will discern that He is talking and not you, and you will know exactly what to do.

DECLARATION: I declare over you that you will hear the voice of the Holy Spirit and that you know His voice! He opens up to you understanding of the Word He inspired and separates soul from spirit. You will see and know exactly what to do and which way to go, all because of your fellowship with Him.

Ear Toward Heaven

You have the greatest authority of anyone in all the world because of the Name of Jesus Christ on your lips.

You are a generation of seeing and knowing, and of the demonstrations and manifestations of God the Holy Spirit. The power of the Trinity is upon you! You have the greatest authority of anyone in all the world because of the Name of Jesus Christ on your lips.

Because of the generation that you are, you're going to see and know a whole lot more about the end of things. You who give yourself to the Holy Spirit and separate from the stuff and noise of life, He's going to start talking to you. He's going to start showing you what you need to see about what is about to be. The Spirit of God comes in and visits with you in such a way that you will begin to see Him take hold of natural vision and give you understanding of what is in your heart. You will know beyond your natural experiences and intellect.

Keep an ear toward Heaven in this time. Sit down with the Holy Spirit and listen to what He has to say about the time and your place in it. He's going to start talking to you about love and the attitudes of your heart. He'll speak to you of your authority and walking in what He has purchased for you. He will give you understanding about what you need to do for you, and it will help you and those around you, too.

DECLARATION: I declare over you that you are listening and looking for instructions from the Holy Spirit. You have ears to hear and eyes to see what He tells you and shows you.

Watch Your Words

Words are like containers; they carry the power to create!

What you say and do is so important, because everything circles around and will find you. The good things that you have said and the good things that you have done will find you. Likewise, the bad things that you have said and done will circle around also. What do you do about the bad things? Confess them to God. Repent and then that harvest will be uprooted and will never produce the fruit that you don't want in your life.

Because of the time you have come into, everything is compacted, so things will manifest more quickly. Everything you say and do circles around to find you quickly; faster than ever before. What you have believed, you are going to see a lot sooner than you have ever seen before, so you must watch your words ever-so closely now.

A revelation of the power you possess in your words will change your life! Words are like containers; they carry the power to create! You must not oppose yourself with your words, but work with them to plant and build up rather than to dig up and tear down. I believe as you meditate on this truth you will become more mindful of what you allow yourself to think upon and speak forth. Then what circles around to you will only be a harvest of blessing from words well-tended.

DECLARATION: I declare over you that you will repent and uproot any harvest of words that did not speak life. Revelation of the power of your words has come; so you tend the garden of your life and plant and harvest only what is good.

Authority Over Fear

The Holy Spirit would ask of you, "Why do you worry so?" Why all this anxiety that I see? Oh, don't you know how well I care for the flowers of the field and the birds of the air? How much more I care about you and all that concerns you!"

When fear strikes, faith dissipates.

Dear one, I know how the responsibilities of life stack up and press in upon you. Sometimes in the many decisions to be made it seems wisdom is not even there. Then fear reaches in and grabs you. When fear strikes, faith dissipates. Fear melts your faith away, but God didn't give you this fear as Second Timothy 1:7 affirms, *"For God hath not given us the spirit of fear; but of power, and of love, and of a sound mind."*

Fear is not of God, neither is it from God; therefore, I take authority over fear of circumstances. I take authority over this spirit that so tracks your life. I bind fear and command it to go. I release peace unto you—an all-encompassing peace to surround and keep you.

Watch God work in all the areas of your life as you give Him your care, worry and anxiety. Stop yielding to fear, and the chronic thing that keeps happening to you will no longer be allowed. Spirit of infirmity lift in Jesus' Name! I release healing and health in its place.

👑 **DECLARATION: I declare over you that you have authority over the spirit of fear. What you don't allow and refuse to yield to have to go. The peace of God rules in your heart and mind, and fear has no place in you.**

He Gives His Beloved Sleep

The Holy Spirit will come to you in your quietest moment....

Oh, dear one, do not be afraid of anything that comes upon the earth. For you are the glorious Church and your light will only grow brighter now. The Holy Spirit will come to you in your quietest moment, when you are settled down. For most of you that will be at your point of sleep. He will speak to you about an event. He will always go ahead and let you know what is about to be.

Do you not know the things that you have averted; the things that have not happened, because of your faith? Because you believed and prayed in the blessed Name of the only begotten Son. The Holy Spirit would say to you today, "Be sure not to look too hard on what happened and on what you see and feel, and thank Me for what did not happen, because you trusted Me."

As I pull back the curtain, the drapery from your eyes, I reveal to you what didn't happen; what events did not occur. It will be the same up until the end. God will instruct you. The Holy Spirit will speak to you and tell you exactly what to do, what to pray and what not to do. He goes ahead and secures you.

So tonight, when you are still and quiet, be at peace and rest in the knowing that He gives His beloved sleep (Psalm 127:2). He holds the times, seasons and events in His hand, and He tells you of things to come.

👑 **DECLARATION: I declare over you that you will understand the Father's love for you. You now sleep in the presence of the holiness of His Spirit. Thank Him for mending your heart and for healing your body. Thank Him for setting your mind so free. Thank the Almighty God for saving you so completely.**

Fellowship With Your Faith

In times of crisis it can be difficult to grab hold of scriptures, but when you have been fellowshipping the relationship with the Father, Son and Holy Spirit, when all else fails, you have your relationship.

Without fellowship, your confession of the Word is just works.

You have done well to memorize and confess the Word, but too often the confession of the Word is without the relationship and fellowship of the Person of the Lord Jesus Christ. When you know the character of your Father, of your Lord and of the Person of the Holy Spirit, then you draw a tremendous assurance out of that relationship. Without fellowship, your confession of the Word is just works. Let there be fellowship with your Lord, and you will find it easier to sustain by faith what you believe of the God of the Word. The Word and God are one; they can't be separated or you're left with religion.

The Father created you for fellowship. Take time today to fellowship with your faith in the Father, Son and Holy Spirit, and enjoy Their presence!

DECLARATION: I declare over you that you will know the Father intimately. You will appreciate Him and who He is today. You will thank Him for Jesus, His Son—your Savior. Thank Him for the Holy Spirit who teaches you so well of Him. He is so real to you and not just words or religiosity.

Write the Vision

"Write the vision and make it plain on tablets, that he may run who reads it."
—Habakkuk 2:2

I would like to share with you about *vision*. In particular, the vision the Father has given *you* for your life personally. My desire is to stir you to be about what is in your heart. What has the Holy Spirit spoken to you? What has He revealed about His plans for your life? Write it down. For that and that only is what you must do. *"Unless the Lord builds the house, they labor in vain who build it"* (Psalm 127:1).

There are many *good* things you can do, but are they *God* things? How can you know the difference? God tells you to *be still and know.* More often than not it is in not in the doing, but in the resting and expectant waiting that you will know with great certainty what the Father has purposed, planned and prepared for you. As you delight yourself in Him, He will give you the very desires of your heart! (See Psalm 37:4).

I want to encourage you that *with God* all things are possible. Whatever you do must be done *in* Him, *through* Him and *for* His glory. Jesus said, *"Abide in Me, and I in you. As the branch cannot bear fruit of itself, unless it abides in the vine, neither can you, unless you abide in Me"* (John 15:4).

Dear one, what God has purposed for you *will* come to pass. Take time today to write down what the Holy Spirit has given to you. Keep it before your eyes and in your heart. Be faithful to do what you know, and what has not yet been opened unto you will be illuminated in His timing. Don't oppose yourself with your words. Agree with and speak God's Word concerning your life. What you have seen and heard through His Word, in prayer, in dreams and visions, in prophecies and in your heart, *will* come to fruition!

👑 **DECLARATION: I declare over you that you are stepping into the fullness of all God has destined for you. There is nothing too hard for Him and He lives in you. Write down what He has shown. Do what is known, and in God's timing He will illuminate and open unto you all you need to see.**

A New Sword

I come in the Name of my Commander -in-Chief of the armies of Heaven and of Earth. The Angel of the Lord accompanies me because I carry a charge to you. In this charge as the army of God that you are in the earth, the Holy Spirit would bring such enlightenment and increase and revelation to you over the Word of God deposited inside of you.

Placed in your hand is the increase, the enlightenment, the revelation of the Word you must now have.

The sword of the Spirit is the Word of God, and what you have will be increased even now. I am assigned to deliver to each and every one a new sword. Placed in your hand is the increase, the enlightenment, the revelation of the Word you must now have.

Angelic ones distribute what the Father has for you. You will see by Spirit and by Word how the charge is true for you. You will receive such increase in the knowings of Jesus Christ in you and the glory that raised Him from the dead, and you will walk in this same resurrection power! It has always been present in you, but you have not had the revelation of such a thing. You will be different now because you came into the revelation of what has been spoken and written but not understood... until *now*.

👑 **DECLARATION: I declare over you that you will receive this charge and the sword of the Lord. Increase and enlightenment of the Word of God is opened to you, and you walk in this revelation as never before.**

Secrets and Mysteries Opened

Nothing, nothing shall be kept from you! You will now have understandings that you never had before.

It is time for secrets and mysteries that have been held for this time to be opened unto you. So I come in the Name of my Commander, Jesus Christ, and with the accompaniment of the Angel of the Lord and the angels under Him.

For there are dominions and principalities in the angelic host, and Satan has perverted, but my Father's hosts are here to deliver what I bring. So reach out by faith and even extend your hand to Heaven as though to reach up and grab hold of a sword in the air, and the angels will distribute and give to you the greater, the enlightenment and revelation of the Word that is inside of you.

Everything will get done to the glory of the Son. In the Name of Jesus Christ as my Father has willed it to be, you now receive the sword that is granted unto you from the angel on assignment. *Greater than it has been* is now in your hand. You will wield this sword—the sword of the Spirit, the Word of God—that you have had thus far, but the enlightenment and revelation now zooms into you through the tip of the sword to the handle in your hand. Nothing, nothing shall be kept from you! You will now have understandings that you never had before.

Now with the other hand, receive a shield of faith that is greater than you have had before. This shield is greater than you. It is taller than you to quench the fiery darts of the evil one. My understanding from the Lord is that you have necessity of this shield. So in the other hand receive a greater shield that is distributed to you. The ability to receive, to go and to do I release unto you. For you are charged! Carry on in Jesus' Name!

👑 **DECLARATION: I declare over you that the greater has been given into your hand, the sword of the Spirit and the shield of faith, with understanding greater than it has been. Secrets and mysteries that have been sealed are now opened and revealed.**

Place of Victory

A ngels guard the portals over the U.S.A., and other nations too, when I look and see the vista, the view. When you gather around the Name of the Son and the instruments come together and make a sound of worship to your Lord, more and more you will hear the sound of the drums like a call to war.

You—the Body of Christ—implement the work that was so gloriously done by the only begotten Son.

Victory! Victory! You move and have your being from the place of victory. You implement in this time in Earth. The battle has already been fought and won. Now you—the Body of Christ—implement the work that was so gloriously done by the only begotten Son.

 DECLARATION: I declare over you that the Father opens revelation unto you to see and know what you didn't before. In His power and might you move and implement the victory won by His Son.

God Rides Sounds

You are on approach for a landing in this new move of God, and it comes with tremendous new sounds coming together.

Dear one, keep your heart open to the supernatural...the miraculous of the Spirit of God! Thank Him for this moment that He has set apart for you to listen and hear from the Holy Spirit. God breathes out, and in a split second, your ear becomes full with a sound from Heaven.

You must learn to interpret the sounds that are coming down. Some are musical, and you will recognize new sounds and new songs that are yet to be written. You are on approach for a landing in this new move of God, and it comes with tremendous new sounds coming together. Yes, mighty sounds are coming down to the glory of the King and to the honor of the eternal Father. Heaven is full of sounds, and there are just times when sounds seem to come down and musicians pick them up and flow. That's the anointing. That's the Holy Spirit affirming: "Heaven likes this sound."

These sounds come down through a portal that's been opened, and they move all around the world. From far away where it's night for some and morning for others, the sounds do make their way to the ones whose ears are turned toward Heaven to hear. Very authoritative are these sounds; they are positioning when they come forth from Heaven. They position you for the greater. He consumes the air and rides the sounds that make their way down to you!

DECLARATION: I declare over you that your ear is open to the sounds coming down. They bring understanding and help position you to move with the Holy Spirit most accurately.

Abundance to You

When I look and I see, not very far off it seems to me, *abundance to you, oh Body of Christ!* People of the congregations in the cities of nations, abundance to you and wisdom too, to know what to do with the greatness that will come to you.

In My Name you shall proceed regardless of what you hear or see.

"Oh son and daughter, know that it's true, everything about you is My love, and so it must be in the great things that come to you. Be quick to share. Be quick to give. Don't horde. Don't say, 'I've waited so long for this,' or 'Oh my, now I have so much.' Turn and look and see who is in need. Such abundance I see for you!"

"Body of Christ worldwide, congregations in the cities of nations, in My Name you shall proceed regardless of what you hear or see. Be sure to share Me. Tell them of Me. Give them a chance to choose. The world will shake. Seas will roar. Mountains will break."

Dear God, your glory comes down and moves all around. We'll not be afraid, because we trust You. We trust in what You say. We trust You and what You've written. We trust You both night and day. No matter what we hear. We trust in Your Word and in Your Spirit. We are safe and secure in what You have said and promised to us. Dear God, we'll say what You say. We'll do what You would do every day.

DECLARATION: I declare over you that you will receive the abundance coming to you and you are wise in all the distribution of it. You'll not fear regardless of what you see or hear. Trust arises in your heart, for the Father secures His sons and daughters.

Redemptive Position

Stand firm, fixed and resolute in your place in prayer and in your authority....

You have the responsibility and accountability to exert the authority that Jesus Christ paid for with His blood! Today I want to encourage you to still and settle yourself to hear from Heaven in this most exciting and important time in history.

The Father, Son and Holy Spirit are always working together on your behalf. The Father leads you to the Word, the Word takes you back to the Holy Spirit, and the Spirit reminds you of your redemptive position in Jesus.

Stand firm, fixed and resolute in your place in prayer and in your authority, and be expecting God's glory to manifest in whatever way He chooses in and through your life.

 DECLARATION: I declare over you that you will stand fixed and firm in the place Jesus secured for you, and you will pray from your position of authority.

All of Him, None of Me

My Father reaches on down into each and every heart bent on doing His will. He comes to "take the me out of me" in each and every one of you. In the place of me, He puts *Him…all of Him.* You want everything in your life to be about Him. You want your being a spouse, a parent, a child, a sibling and a friend all to be through Him and not through you. You want God in everything you say and do, and that everything be done through the Name of Jesus.

Let the presence of you be gone this year, and let the presence of the beloved Son, your Lord and Savior, come.

Let the presence of you be gone this year, and let the presence of the beloved Son, your Lord and Savior, come. Let His presence invade every space you encounter. No more of you, just all of Him.

Such manifestations and demonstrations will come because you have believed, you have declared, you have walked and paced and prayed. Face down I hear you crying out, *"God! Are not these things supposed to be? These things inside that You have shown me?"*

Dear one, these things that He has shown, they become. They now will be to the glory of the Father and to His Son, and by His Spirit, the work gets done.

DECLARATION: I declare over you that you will ask the Father to reach down and take "the you" out of you. In the place of you, ask the Father to put Himself. Desire Him to come through in everything you say and do, and ask Him to take you out of the way.

What's the Report?

Receive the report of the Lord and nothing less in every arena of your life!

When our daughter was in a terrible accident, God spoke, "Life and wholeness." But when we looked at the situation, there wasn't any. She died at the accident site. They revived her, but because of the lack of oxygen, she was all curled up in the fetal position. Twenty-three years old, graduated from St. Mary's of Notre Dame cum laude, lacrosse co-captain and student government—and now, hit by a truck on her way to work.

Her injuries were so massive; she was in coma, her body broken in so many places, the aorta to her heart was torn. She underwent surgery for her spleen, but then the surgeons said something wasn't right; her chest was expanding, and they needed to do an angiogram for her heart. Her brain was full of blood and air. Everything was saying the very opposite of what God said.

What's the report that you have been given over your life? Over your marriage? Your children? Your business? Your schooling? Over your dream? You have to choose what you will believe and say...*in spite of!* Our daughter couldn't choose. Three days out they said, "Dr. Varallo, you just need to let her go. She's in a permanent vegetative state."

"Life and wholeness. Life and wholeness. Life and wholeness for her. Remember, remember, remember. By His stripes she's been healed. By His stripes you have blood covenant," the Holy Spirit would whisper.

Days turned into weeks. Our daughter kept living on full life support. What are you living on? What is your sustenance today? What is the report to your soul, to your mind, to your emotions, to your screaming body? I have been commissioned by the Most High to tell you this day: *"Hear the report of the Lord! Receive the report of the Lord and nothing less in every arena of your life!"*

A day came when she woke up. She talked. She learned to walk again because God said, "Life and wholeness," and we believed Him. A day will come for you because you dared to believe the impossible. When everything says, "No, you can't"; God says, "Yes, you will!" I impart to you the possibilities of God—it's where I live, and it's yours to possess if you want it.

DECLARATION: I declare over you that you will receive the impartation of the possibilities of God! His report is health, healing and wholeness for you. I declare that the God for whom all things are possible displays His mighty power by stretching forth His hand to heal you!

Jesus is Your Infinity

It is a phenomenal thing to understand that it isn't how "good" people are that gets them to Heaven, and it isn't how "bad" people are that sends them to Hell. So many people have that confused!

He is not just your way out one time, but all the time.

The Scriptures tell us, *"For by grace are ye saved through faith; and that not of yourselves: it is the gift of God"* (Ephesians 2:8). By grace through faith you have eternal life!

In Second Corinthians 13:14, the Apostle Paul writes: *"The grace of the Lord Jesus Christ, and the love of God, and the communion of the Holy Ghost, be with you all. Amen."*

Paul emphasizes the grace of your Lord, and His love! It was love that gave you Jesus—He is your way out. He is not just your way out one time, but all the time. Jesus is your infinity! Every moment is infinity. Your way out is available every moment. Every moment you are enabled by the Spirit of God to choose to do the right thing; only *you must choose* to do it.

He goes on to express your need for *"the communion of the Holy Ghost."* Communion speaks of intimacy. There is no replacement for the intimacy of the Holy Spirit. Jesus Christ said to be e*ndued, filled to the full and overflowing with Him.*

When you're full of Him He becomes so big to you. You are the hardest on yourself, aren't you? See yourself from Heaven's point of view. See yourself in Him, because that is where you are in position and in relationship. Receive the assurance of His love for you today.

👑 **DECLARATION: I declare over you that Jesus is forever your way *out* and your way *into* His eternal love and grace. He is your infinity!**

Arise, Awake, Unto the Glory!

"Eagerly pursue and seek to acquire love; make it your aim, your great quest...."
—1 Cor. 14:1

A cry sounds from the heavenlies to all who have ears to hear: "ARISE, AWAKE, UNTO THE GLORY!" God, Creator Almighty, desires to restore you into the ways of His Spirit in every facet of your life. He has made the way for you to live from such a high place—in position, in authority and in the more excellent way of love.

Writing in First Corinthians, the Apostle Paul admonishes, *"Eagerly pursue and seek to acquire love; make it your aim, your great quest..."* (1 Corinthians 14:1a, AMP). Above *all* else, you are to follow after love. What you are believing concerning your life will not happen for you if love is not your way; for faith works by love. You may say, "How Mary Fran? You just don't know what so-and-so did to me." Dear one, be forgiving. No one is perfect. You are not saying that a person is morally right or wrong when you forgive him or her. Regardless of what was done or said or what wasn't done or said that you thought ought to have been, you forgive, simply because that is what God said to do. Something so glorious of God comes upon you when you let go of your natural inclinations and follow God's way.

Be kind. Kindness is a forgotten practice today. Kindness is a magnet that will attract God and people. What wonderful manifestations will come because a kind word is spoken. Kindness is a fruit of the Spirit who now lives in you! Glorious fruit will grow where a seed of kindness is planted. I believe greater manifestations of His glory are pressing in right now for you if you will put first things first and love one another as He has loved you. This love has been shed abroad in your heart by the Holy Spirit, and by His grace you can do what He has commanded.

👑 **DECLARATION: I declare over you that you will choose to forgive, to be kind and to walk in love. God's love in you is supernatural and not natural. You arise and awake and His glory causes the spectacular demonstrations of God to happen in and through you!**

The Fourth Dimension

The natural realm is the third dimension, but there is a realm in the spirit called the fourth dimension. This place is reflective of and identical to the natural realm it seems to me, only *there,* what you are believing is already done. You will see this place with the eyes of faith. God gives you eyes that you might see both in the spirit and in the natural realm. He gives you vision to *see a thing* that it might *become a thing* on this side.

He gives you vision to see a thing that it might become a thing on this side.

So though God may show you something that He desires for your life, your family, your business, or your ministry, that thing will not automatically come to pass. You have to get a picture of it out in front of you and keep it before your eyes. You will see with your natural eyes, but because you are a believer, faith shall arise in your heart and you will call that vision forth with holy words.

What do you want to change? What are you believing for? What does it look like? What does your miracle look like? If you can see that place in the spirit realm where everything is done, then by your faith you can bring it on over into the natural realm where it will become.

DECLARATION: I declare over you that with your eyes of faith you will see your miracle. You have an expectation of its manifestation, and by faith you pull it on through from the spirit realm where it is done and into the natural where it can become.

Man Looks; God Sees

Every place you put your foot, you establish God.

In Genesis 13, God set about to begin a whole new nation through the faith of one man. It took some declaring and separating on God's part, and that may be the way of it for you. Genesis 13:14 says, *"And the Lord said unto Abram, after that Lot was separated from him, 'Lift up now thine eyes, and look from the place where thou art northward, and southward, and eastward, and westward: For all the land which thou seest, to thee will I give it, and to thy seed for ever. And I will make thy seed as the dust of the earth: so that if a man can number the dust of the earth, then shall thy seed also be numbered.'"*

Abraham, which means *father of nations*, was still called Abram at that time, but God showed him what his descendants would be like. He declared to Abram, "I will give you *all* that you can *see*." What do you see? What do you see in the spirit? What do you see in the natural? Abram was to see in the natural, but the declaration God gave concerning all that he saw is a very supernatural thing that took faith on Abram's part.

Watch the terminology of the Holy Spirit when you pray; listen to how He phrases things to you. God first told Abram *"Look."* Then He showed him vast stretches of beautiful, fertile land that spanned in every direction. Then God said, *"See."* Seeing is different from looking. Seeing takes God, for God gives vision, which is seeing supernaturally. In verse 17, God instructed Abram, *"Arise, walk through the land in the length of it and in the breadth of it; for I will give it unto thee."*

You may need to walk the property of wherever it is you are trying to buy or sell. Every place you put your foot, you establish God. Because God is in you and upon you, He is every place you are. The authority, power, declaration, redemption and possession of Him accompany you. Look and see what He has shown you, and by faith, possess what He has given.

DECLARATION: I declare over you that God's vision for you is grand and glorious. You *look* with your natural eyes, but you *see* through eyes of faith. Wherever you go, you take God with you.

Free From Fear

"For you have not received the spirit of bondage again to fear; but you have received the Spirit of adoption, whereby we cry, Abba, Father."

—Romans 8:15, NKJV

Everything Jesus Christ came to do brought liberty and freedom to you.

Bondage is a place of captivity. God has delivered you from fear and the bondage it brings, and you are not to return to it. When you are held captive you are not free to make your own choices. Everything Jesus Christ came to do brought liberty and freedom to you. He preached deliverance to the captives, set at liberty those who were bruised, loosed the bound and healed the oppressed. He came to give you life and life more abundantly.

Fear is the opposite of faith, and it will paralyze you from doing what you know to do. Unless the devil can get you to fear, he can't do anything to you. Your Father—Abba, Papa—loves you, and His perfect love casts out all fear. Use your authority and speak to fear. Command it to go in Jesus' Name! Don't allow fear to be found anywhere in your life.

DECLARATION: I declare over you that you will receive God's perfect love in every part of your life, and declare that you are free from fear and the bondage it brings in Jesus' Name!

Guard Your Gates

"Keep and guard your heart with all vigilance...above all that you guard...."
—*Proverbs 4:23, AMP*

In the natural, you close and lock the front door to your home because you don't want anyone to come in and steal anything. In the spirit, the heart would be representative of the front door. You are to be the gatekeeper of your own heart. Proverbs 4:23, *The Amplified Bible*, says, *"Keep and guard your heart with all vigilance and above all that you guard, for out of it flow the springs of life."*

Above everything else that you guard, you are to watchfully and attentively guard and protect your heart—for it is where life flows. God not only told you what to guard, but how to guard it. Verse 23 goes on to say, *"Put away from you false and dishonest speech...Let your eyes look right on with fixed purpose, ...Consider well the path of your feet...remove your foot from evil"* (verses 24–27).

You guard your heart by *speaking* truth, *looking* at good and godly things, *listening* to what is just and right and *walking* with your heavenly Father by the leading of the Holy Spirit. Your eyes, ears and lips are gates to your own heart.

Gates are openings, and so they are the weakest part of a structure. That is why in the natural and in the spirit gates must be carefully guarded. God gives you this assignment and the authority to guard your gates well. Don't let anything through that would try to steal from you.

** DECLARATION: I declare over you that you are the gatekeeper of your life. You will guard the gate of your heart with all vigilance. You will let nothing and no one in to steal what God has given you.**

Bitter or Better

Be encouraged today to keep your heart tender and pliable in God's hand. It's easy to become calloused through the hard things of life, because you feel like you have to be so strong. But if you'll keep His Word in the midst of your heart, God will protect that part that is the life of you.

The disappointments and the difficulties of life come to all of us; the difference is what you do with them.

The sword of the Spirit, which is the Word of God, will help you discern between soul and spirit. That soulish part of you—your mind, will and emotions—will be buoyed up and strengthened, and will act almost like a buffer to insulate your heart and keep it soft. A hard heart is a heart in rebellion against God, which is sin. Hebrews 3:8, NKJV, says, *"Do not harden your hearts as in the rebellion, in the day of trial in the wilderness."*

The disappointments and the difficulties of life come to all of us; the difference is what you do with them. Will you allow them to make you bitter? Or will you trust in His Word and become better? *"But may the God of all grace, who called us to His eternal glory by Christ Jesus, after you have suffered a while, perfect, establish, strengthen, and settle you"* (1 Peter 5:10, NKJV).

DECLARATION: I declare over you that you will keep your heart soft and pliable in God's hand by keeping yourself full of the Word of His grace.

Assignments in Prayer

...Everything God would do in and through you requires prayer.

Your graces, giftings and anointings make a way for you. What God by His Spirit has imparted to you is divine equipment to establish and position you for purpose. How glorious it is to discover and develop what was placed inside of you!

It seems to me everything God would do in and through you requires prayer. You have to have the heart of your Father and that will only come through time spent in His presence, fellowshipping with Him, with His Son and with the precious Holy Spirit. He will speak to your heart and give to you assignments in prayer. He will lead you ever-so specifically, and you will follow Him.

I like to think of each one of us like skipping rocks in God's hand. We meet with Him in the heavenlies in the dimensions and in the many facets of Him. Then we hear Him say, "Go here in prayer today. Take care of this. Cover that. Ask this of Me."

To skip a rock across a creek, that rock has to be a certain size, a certain shape and has to be held a certain way. Be like a skipping rock in prayer, and watch where God the Holy Spirit will take you!

DECLARATION: I declare over you that you are equipped by God the Holy Spirit to pray out His plans. He leads you, guides you and directs you into places of revelation and understanding. You will pick up your assignments and be faithful to follow Him.

Don't Weary Your Faith

It is the Father's heart that you have an understanding of the time and a discernment of unfolding events. He is always positioning and securing you individually and corporately. There is a difference in the prophecies that have been given to the world and those that have been spoken to the Church. Sometimes people cross them over, and it's not to be that way.

Ask the Father in the Name of His Son for seeing and knowing concerning the events that are to come....

There are things both written and spoken unto the sons and daughters of the Most High that you are to hold before the Father and give Him remembrance of. Then there are things that are said to the world. There are events—occurrences—that you can change, and others that you can affect. Then there are those events you can only prepare for. You have to have the wisdom of God to know the difference, or you are going to weary your faith. If you pick the wrong event to change, but it's something you can only prepare for, you tire your faith.

Ask the Father in the Name of His Son for seeing and knowing concerning the events that are to come, and by the Holy Spirit, you will know the difference.

DECLARATION: I declare over you that by the Holy Spirit, your eyes are open to see events that are to be. You will pray most accurately to change, stop or to prepare.

Meet With Him

God the Holy Spirit is orchestrating things for you even in this moment....

Thank the Father for making this place in time for you to meet with Him today. As you meditate on His Holy written Word to you, let the Holy Spirit reveal Jesus Christ to you as never before.

May a new boldness come upon you and courage beyond what you've had, because of your comprehension of His love for you. God is for you not against you! He is always there making a way where it seems there is none. God the Holy Spirit is orchestrating things for you even in this moment as you give Him your heart right from the start of the day.

Be strengthened in this time with Him. For the Word declares that those who wait upon the Lord shall renew their strength. (See Isaiah 40:31).

You have spent this blessed moment with Him, and He is grateful.

DECLARATION: I declare over you that it is a joy to spend time with the Father! Thank Him for granting you this moment in time. He fills your heart with courage, boldness and love. You wait upon Him and are strengthened today.

God the Holy Spirit

G od the Holy Spirit leads all people to Jesus Christ. He takes up permanent residence with those who have believed, empowering them, counseling them and leading them daily. He is the great demonstrator of the compassion of the Godhead. Upon each and every one of us He is the Spirit of glory, power and grace.

He is the breath that was breathed into man....

Before creation He was there. He is the breath that was breathed into man; the anointing that blanketed the prophet, priest and king before the Messiah came in the flesh. The Holy Spirit overshadowed the virgin and imparted the seed of God into her, for Jesus Christ was born of the Spirit. He was the One who let Jesus know when it was time to close the carpenter's shop and take the walk to the Jordan to meet up with His cousin, John, to be baptized in fulfillment of the Scriptures. Then, when our Lord came up out of the water praying, the Holy Spirit rested and remained upon Jesus in power! The Holy Spirit led Jesus into a place of testing that He might see in His manhood and in His humanity that indeed He had the strength of the Spirit and the word of His Father to fulfill His course...His destiny!

The same Holy Spirit drew you to your Lord and abides in you today. He is the power upon you and the anointing when you stretch out your hand to heal in your Lord's Name. Know Him and the Person that He is, for He is all these things and more *in you!*

👑 **DECLARATION: I declare over you that you will follow the Holy Spirit in everything you say and do. Thank Him for who He is and for all He does. Be grateful for the gift of the Holy Spirit!**

A Heavenly Language

Suddenly! The Holy Spirit blew again, this time into the spirits of men, and where once the languages were confounded, He brought a sound of unity.

Three days after Jesus commended His spirit unto the Father on the Cross, the Holy Spirit rushed down from the heavenlies into the bowels of the earth and set the King of kings free! Death could not keep your Lord in its grip, for there was no sin found in Him. The price had been paid for all of humanity by the precious blood of God's only begotten Son. What a victory had been won!

Then, as He promised, Jesus went to the Father, and the blessed Holy Spirit came into the earth to take up universal command and permanent residence with the Body of Christ. One day, in Jerusalem, at the celebration of the Feast of Pentecost, Jesus' followers gathered in agreement—all together in one place—in the Upper Room.

Suddenly! The Holy Spirit blew again, this time into the spirits of men, and where once the languages were confounded, He brought a sound of unity. A heavenly language the Holy Spirit did give to one and all, and they were set ablaze with a passion to display the Christ from that moment forward. Speaking words they had never uttered before, they spilled out into the streets of Jerusalem. To their surprise, those gathered outside around and about could understand the words, the sounds, the wonders of God that were being declared.

Now today when you receive this gift you speak and you pray; you cry out when you don't know what to say, and the Holy Spirit becomes a heavenly language on your lips. Just as at the start, *suddenly,* all is well.

DECLARATION: I declare over you the glorious Baptism of the Holy Spirit is a gift you won't want to live without. Yield yourself to pray each and every day. This heavenly language and fire you have received makes you a witness of your Jesus so others can believe.

Shake the Place

Such power from on High moves on the earth as believers lift their voices in prayer to the Father in the Name of the Son! You may not need the place to shake or everyone present to be filled with the Holy Spirit; however, there may be circumstances, situations and even attitudes in your life and in others that need to be shaken.

"And when they had prayed, the place was shaken where they were assembled together; and they were all filled with the Holy Ghost, and they spake the word of God with boldness."
—Acts 4:31

When you pray, you are giving God legal access to move in your life. He is unlimited in the ways He can manifest Himself. If it takes making things shake, then so be it! All things must come into divine alignment with the will and plan of God.

What in your life or in the life of someone you love needs to move? What needs to bend and break? What situation or circumstance needs to shake? You have the power and authority on the inside of you to speak the Word of God with boldness. Declare and decree the Word, pray as the Holy Spirit leads, and watch God work on your behalf!

👑 **DECLARATION: I declare over you that as you lift your voice to pray, by the power of God, He moves things out of the way! Everything that is not of Him, I command it to bend, break and shake in Jesus' Name!**

Prayer Makes a Way

Prayer… opens wide a door and moves obstacles out of the way so that a path is made for the things of God to easily come on through.

The intimacy of your relationship with the Holy Spirit will be reflected in your prayer life. Prayer is what brings you into a place of fellowship with the Godhead. In times of prayer the Holy Spirit will lead you, teach you and show you the Father's heart.

It is always the Father's heart to go before you and make a way to secure you. Prayer always makes a way. It opens wide a door and moves obstacles out of the way so that a path is made for the things of God to easily come on through.

You don't pray to the Holy Spirit; nor do you pray to Jesus. Jesus taught us to go to the Father in His Name. By the leading of the Spirit He takes you into places in the spirit and places of fellowship with your Father. He is ever-present with you to counsel, comfort, reveal truth and direct you on, even in the most difficult times. Never underestimate the power of your prayer in your own life, in the lives of those you love and in the lives of those you don't even know.

DECLARATION: I declare over you that you will be obedient and faithful to pray, and in the Name of Jesus, every obstacle moves out of the way.

Royal Resistance Force

There is always a people within a people. I believe I heard the Holy Spirit say, "Tell them they are a resistance force." This is an offensive position. Resistance is a power that moves forward to bring change or to destroy. You, son or daughter of God, are a Royal Resistance Force!

The destiny of humanity is at stake, and the only ones in all the planet who can make the difference are the royal sons of God....

In a natural army we have Special Forces, who are highly trained and skilled for unconventional missions. You are a Holy-Ghost people empowered by the anointing, just as Jesus was. You are the ones who make the difference for the Body of Christ and for the world because you believe that the Holy Spirit will supply you the power necessary to pray, to resist, to change and keep things at bay.

Something terrible has been unleashed in the earth, and the only force that can stop it and change it is you. All the diplomacy, all the money of the wealthiest nation, all the armies and all the munitions cannot stop this thing—only the Word of God and the Spirit of God—which you and I carry. Hell is coming for every man, woman and child, and the only thing that can make a difference is a tremendous force—a resistance force—within the earth. Arise as the army of God and begin your march on behalf of your family, your loved ones, your neighborhood, your community, your city, your government, your state, your nation and nations beyond.

You will love where you are not loved; you will be merciful where mercy is not extended to you. You will forgive where people won't let you forget. You will love with such compassion, yet all the while you shall be hated and persecuted. Yet in your love and compassion shall the miraculous abound as you speak the Word of the Lord and reach out your hand to touch those in need. Remember who you are, oh royal and very loyal sons of God.

DECLARATION: I declare over you that you are a royal son or daughter of God! Power from on High dwells in you to be a force of resistance against the plans of the enemy. I declare that in prayer you will bring change or stop events that will affect humanity for all eternity.

Submit to God

"Therefore submit to God. Resist the devil and he will flee from you." —James 4:7, NKJV

Something wonderful happens with the Holy Spirit upon a believer whose life is passionately submitted unto the Christ. Do you know the Holy Spirit will help you submit yourself?

Everyone likes to quote our opening scripture, James 4:7, and talk about how when we resist the devil he will flee from us. This is certainly true; however, we have a tendency to leave off the first part of that verse, which is that we must first *submit* to God! There is no resisting with any accomplishment until you submit yourself to God. You submit your will, plans and life unto His will, plans and purposes. When you do that, you are empowered by the Holy Spirit to resist the devil who will run as in terror from you.

When you sit down, God sits down. When you stand up, when you pass through a room, when you go down the hall at school or work or even in the mall, the presence of God is so upon you. To the measure of your life that is submitted unto God, is the measure that His presence will stir people you come in contact with one way or the other.

I believe there are more people looking for God than looking to oppose Him. People are looking for answers, and the answer comes in the Person Jesus Christ and His Holy Spirit. Align your will unto the Father's this day, and great power will be at your disposal to resist the enemy at every turn.

DECLARATION: I declare over you that you will submit your heart, will and life to the Father, and that you are filled with the power to resist the enemy. In Jesus' Name he has to flee from you.

The Peace of God

Jesus Christ came to secure your peace. What thoughts are circling around you today? My Lord says to you, "Be still thoughts that race, decisions that press, reasonings that would exalt themselves against the knowledge of the Father God."

You are the gatekeeper of your mind, and what you resist has to flee from you.

You are the gatekeeper of your mind, and what you resist has to flee from you. You are to take captive every thought and meditate on only what agrees with the Word of God concerning you and those around you.

Keeping the thought realm clear is a battle you will win with the sword of the Spirit, which is the Word of God.

> **"For the weapons of our warfare are not carnal, but mighty through God to the pulling down of strong holds;**
> **"Casting down imaginations, and every high thing that exalteth itself against the knowledge of God, and bringing into captivity every thought to the obedience of Christ."**
> **—2 Corinthians 10:4–5**

You cannot fight thoughts with thoughts. You are going to have to open your mouth and speak to those thoughts. You don't just say any words; you speak God's Word! Make your meditation be in the Word of truth, and you will easily identify thoughts that are not of God. Then resist those imaginations in Jesus' Name. Capture and cast down anything that does not align with God's Word, and filter everything through Philippians 4:8: "…*Whatsoever things are true, whatsoever things are honest, whatsoever things are just, whatsoever things are pure, whatsoever things are lovely, whatsoever things are of good report; if there be any virtue, and if there be any praise, think on these things."* The result will be *"…the God of peace will be with you"* (v. 9).

Such a difference will there be for you in clarity of thought and mind: a mind at rest, in a tranquil state. Do your part and God will do His, and an all-encompassing peace will keep you settled and still.

👑 DECLARATION: I declare over you that you will make the Word of truth your meditation today. Speak God's Word to any thoughts contrary to His will. Cast them down and take them captive. Think only on what is godly and true, for the God of peace stills, settles and quiets your mind.

Overcomers

"Many are the afflictions of the righteous: but the Lord delivereth him out of them all."
—*Psalm 34:19*

Dear one, you are righteous today because of the blood of Jesus Christ! God didn't say adversity would never come to you as a believer in the Christ. In fact, the more you follow on to know the Lord, afflictions seem to increase. But God's Word says you are an overcomer! *"Ye are of God, little children, and have overcome them: because greater is he that is in you, than he that is in the world"* (1 John 4:4). To be an overcomer you must have something to come over.

Afflictions are simply harassments in your life. When afflictions arise, your job is to do what the Word of God says: to believe and say what God says, knowing that whatever affliction presents itself, the Lord delivers you out of each and every one.

DECLARATION: I declare over you that the Lord is your deliverer! He gets you out of anything and everything that comes. There is nothing occurring in your life that the Lord cannot deliver you out of...*nothing!*

Worth Without Measure

Anytime you feel worthless, rejected or have very little esteem because you feel you have failed, the Holy Spirit will come alongside and remind you of your worth. Worth without measure is what God the Holy Spirit, through Jesus Christ, will show you. He

Even in your worst moments, God still thinks you are worth loving and dying for.

will speak to you and say, "Hey, remember Us: the Father, the Son and Me, the Holy Spirit? We think you are great!"

This is true about each and every one of us. For God so loved.... all of us in the world. He sent His only begotten Son to die for you. Even in your worst moments, God still thinks you are worth loving and dying for.

Anytime you are bombarded with thoughts of worthlessness, insignificance and rejection, understand that those thoughts, which produce the corresponding feelings, are not from God. That's a demon harassing you, maybe even a familiar spirit, who is tracking you. Give him no place in your thoughts. He wants you to take the bait and travel down that road of failure with him, but you are a victor, and in Jesus you win! Satan knows this is true, so all he can do is bring feelings to you. With lies and deception he speaks—they are his language. Recognize this and don't be surprised.

Arise in the power of the Son and resist the very temptation to follow those familiar paths. Speak only what God says of you, for His Word is true concerning you.

👑 **DECLARATION: I declare over you that your worth doesn't come from man, a job, outward appearance or performance; it comes from Jesus Christ alone. You are a purpose. You are a godly plan. You are a divine destiny placed in the earth at just the right time to fulfill God's will and to glorify the One who counted you valuable enough to love you and give His life for you.**

Breathe on Us

The Holy Spirit will resuscitate you and restore your first love—Jesus Christ.

The Holy Spirit brings visitation to you in this moment. He breathes on you, and in His holy breath, you are washed and refreshed. You are made like new! Revived are you in your love and passion for the King. Once again you are encouraged and made bold. Fear of every kind evaporates—it is blown away by the breath of God.

The Holy Spirit will breathe on you new life. He will resuscitate you and restore your first love—Jesus Christ.

Breathe on us!

DECLARATION: I declare over you that the Holy Spirit breathes on you. Receive His restoration, refreshing and reviving, and in Jesus' Name you will never be the same.

Practice His Presence

I recognized the fact that I didn't really know the Holy Spirit like I needed to when I was a young wife and mom. I will never forget what He spoke to me to help me begin my adventures with Him. He said, "Mary Fran, you are going to have to practice My presence."

Whatever it is you do, God will do it with you.

That sounded like a holy thing to me, so I tried to figure how to do such a thing as I did the laundry and went about the tasks of the day. I soon found out the Holy Spirit said exactly what He meant; He wanted to do the wash *with me.* He wanted us to fellowship and converse while I did my work. For you it may be something else; working in the yard or at the office. Whatever it is you do, God will do it with you. He is always willing to live life with you and to fellowship with you.

All He wants is for you to recognize that He's there with you, and then He will start to speak. Most likely He won't speak to you in an audible voice; the conversation will take place in your heart. Just let Him talk. I talk out loud to Him because that's the way I do things, but you do what is comfortable for you. Just be you and let Him be Him. As you practice His presence, you will come to know Him just as you are known by Him.

👑 **DECLARATION: I declare over you that you recognize the Holy Spirit's indwelling presence. He is real to you and genuine with you. Practice His presence each and every day in the simplest of ways. The Holy Spirit is living life with you.**

Heaven's Holy-Ghost Outpouring

A deluge of unprecedented power is at hand to bring life, to revive and to saturate all who are parched and thirsting for Him.

Extraordinary momentum is building, dear one. It is as when clouds gather in heaping billows before a thunderstorm, swelling higher and growing heavier with saturation. In the spirit, clouds are gathering on the horizon of time in preparation for a storm of another kind—*Heaven's Holy-Ghost outpouring upon the earth!* Coupled with this outpouring will come the thundering and lightning of God Almighty displayed in divine demonstrations of the Holy Spirit!

When the windows of heaven were opened for the very first time, rain fell and flooded the earth, destroying every living thing except for what was preserved in the life-saving ark. This time when rain falls, it will be in the spirit! Holy-Ghost rain will fill and flood *earthen vessels* enduing you with all the fullness of the Head of the Church! A deluge of unprecedented power is at hand to bring life, to revive and to saturate all who are parched and thirsting for Him.

Outpouring is coming! Excitement mounts in my heart for all that is moving into position for the performance of God in the earth through *you!* What a time you have come into! I pray most earnestly that this divine momentum will help propel you into the hope of His calling for you.

DECLARATION: I declare over you that you will cry out for the Holy-Ghost rain to fall, filling you and all the earth with His fullness. Prepare your heart to run in the rain, just like Elijah!

Pray From Your Place

O f great importance to you in the days you have come into is your authority, particularly regarding prayer. The Father expressed His infinite love for you through the sacrifice of Jesus Christ. As a believer in Christ, you now stand in God's presence as a righteous one with His Son. *In Him* you have been forgiven,

You are seated with Jesus in heavenly places right next to Almighty God!

redeemed, sanctified, justified and glorified! Jesus obediently humbled Himself to the point of death, so the Father exalted Him to a place *above every other name.* He seated Jesus at His own right hand, which signifies a place of authority. Ephesians 2:6, says He has, *"...made us sit together in the heavenly places in Christ Jesus."*

You are seated with Jesus in heavenly places right next to Almighty God! My how the things of earth take on a different perspective when you are seated in your place! Now take that heavenly perspective to prayer and *pray from your place.* So many times you come to prayer with all of your shortcomings and problems before you and stay stuck in the soulish realm where you see and feel everything. The Psalmist David understood that realm, but he encouraged himself in the Lord. *"Why are you cast down, O my soul? ... Hope in God..."* (Psalm 42:5)! I believe if you approach God from your position of authority—the place He secured for you with the blood of His own Son—*everything* will change.

I encourage you to take your seat, dear one. Use the authority that has been purchased for you, and pray from your God-given place *far above* all principality and power and might and dominion, and every name that is named!

👑 **DECLARATION: I declare over you that you will pray from your place of authority, from your seat in the heavenlies, far above all principality and power. You will keep this position and perspective, and your prayers will be more effective.**

Angelic Hosts

Angels… will not respond to your emotions or to your need, but to your decrees of the Word of God.…

God wants you to stay steady and grow stronger in Him, for the times ahead will be more of a challenge to you than the times before. It will be by Word and Spirit that you will always overcome.

Know that angels are at attention, and their presence is notable. If you will learn to work with them, they will get things done that you cannot. They wait upon your words. Your words must be your Father's. For only to God's Word will angels respond. They will not respond to your emotions or to your need, but to your decrees of the Word of God and its application in that moment when you say what God would say.

You apply what God would say and command the ministering spirits, those to whom your Father has given the charge to keep you. Psalm 91:11 declares that the angelic ones will keep you in all your ways! Know these things. Believe these things. Say these things. Release these things, and they will manifest!

👑 **DECLARATION: I declare over you that the ministering spirits, angelic ones sent from your Father, hearken unto the Word of the Lord!** *For your God supplies all your need; effectual doors are opened unto you; favor surrounds you as a shield; the Lord is your refuge and your fortress.* **Go now, ministering spirits, and bring provision, opportunities, favor and protection!**

Liberty for All

The United States of America—our blessed land of liberty—was founded on the passionate pursuit of freedom in Christ. That freedom still rings in the hearts and homes of all who confess Jesus as Lord, who follow His ways and who fulfill His will to preach the Gospel to every creature.

"Now the Lord is that Spirit: and where the Spirit of the Lord is, there is liberty."
—2 Corinthians 3:17

This Gospel is a gospel of liberty! Everything Jesus did for you is about freedom. He has anointed you to preach *deliverance to the captives...* and *to set at liberty* them that are bruised. (See Luke 4:18). What in your life is a bondage to you? Jesus *has delivered you* from the power of darkness! (See Colossians 1:13). If the Son, therefore, shall make you free, you shall be free indeed! (See John 8:36).

I encourage you to declare your freedom from every kind of sin, sickness, disease, poverty, lack, deception, calamity, habit, fear and bondage that has held you back from walking fully in the life-changing grace Jesus supplies. I speak strength to you to stand fast in the liberty by which Christ has made you free, so that you will not be entangled again with a yoke of bondage. (See Galatians 5:1).

DECLARATION: I declare over you freedom for your spirit, soul and body, and the resolve to enforce the liberty your Savior so completely provided. The Son has set you free and you are free indeed!

The Coming of the Eagle

Repentance.
Restoration.
Revival.

I was in prayer one evening when suddenly it was as though the wall was taken back, and there was an enormous eagle coming through the air. Ah! He was so big!

Behind the eagle was the outline of the United States. The wings of the eagle spanned from the West Coast to the East Coast, and across his wings was written the word: *Revival.* Then the eagle came closer, and I could see underneath and across his throat. On his heart was written the word: *Repentance.* When he came closer, I could see he carried in his beak the word: *Restoration.*

I will never forget that encounter with the Holy Spirit. That message is so a part of me now. It is what I carry in my heart: from the heart of the Father to you.

DECLARATION: I declare over you that the Noble Eagle stands over your nation. From coast to coast his wings do span. On his heart, in his mouth, and across his wings he carries the answer for your land: *Repentance; Restoration; Revival!*

Repentance

The Holy Spirit speaks of repentance in prelude to the coming revival He longs to bring—repentance not just of sin, but of rejecting His Word. Turning away from His Word is the same as rejecting His Son.

Whatever is not right, you need to bring it to the light.

Whatever is not right, you need to bring it to the light. *"Not a creature exists that is concealed from His sight, but all things are open and exposed, naked and defenseless to the eyes of Him with Whom we have to do,"* (Hebrews 4:13, AMP).

The Father sees and knows your heart. On your knees you go and say, "Father, every place in my life that I have chosen wrongly, that I have disappointed You, that I have sinned, please forgive me. I repent. Clean me with the blood of Your Son. I'll be like new, and I'll burn bright for You. I want nothing to stand between us, dear Father. It's not about me, it's about You."

"From this day forth I will choose differently. I choose to lay down all the old ways, and I turn my life—not just my face—toward you."

"God, please just be God and do in my life what only you can do. Forgive, restore, refresh, revive and renew."

DECLARATION: I declare over you that His goodness leads you to repentance. Repent of sin—things done and undone—anything that would disappoint, displease or offend. The weight of sin is a burden you were never meant to bear. Allow the Father to remove this from you today and take sin out of the way.

Restoration

"The love of God will restore unto the Body the strength and the glory that was."

The eagle came up before me again as I was in my car. So I got out pencil and paper while I sat in the driveway and wrote down what I believe I heard the Holy Spirit say. "The love of God will restore unto the Body the strength and the glory that was."

"Oh, yes!" I responded.

"Mary Frances," He said, "Look at the eagle."

So I did.

"Where is the Holy Spirit?" He asked.

And I said, "He is in us and upon us and alongside of us."

He said to me, "Mary Fran, I come as an eagle and not as a dove."

When I looked at the eagle, I began to see the Church. Its wingspread was from the West Coast to the East Coast, and it began to change form. The eagle was made up of millions of men and women and children— believers committed to their God—people who will not compromise. The fruit of repentance is restoration. It is a recovering from the effects of sin. You will carry the glory again. You lost that glory in the garden. The glory was Adam's covering. Now God wants to pour the glory out on you and clothe you with it once again.

👑 **DECLARATION: I declare over you that His infinite love restores you. He will once again clothe you in the glory that belonged to you from the start, for your sin has been cleansed and you have a new heart.**

Revival

We are going to have to have restoration before we can have revival in our hearts. The strength of a revival is carried in the commitment that people have to the Holy Spirit and to God's Holy Word.

What have you done with My Son?

God said that revival takes shape, and as it forms here in America, all the world will watch and see. He said that all will see and all will know—all will know that the Messiah had come—that He had come *and* that He is returning!

That was the vision and that was the message. The Messiah, His Son. What have you done with My Son?

👑 **DECLARATION: I declare over you for the order of things as shown through the vision of the eagle: Repentance, Restoration and Revival shall be. Let it begin in the heart of you!**

Revival in America

"...As your nation America goes, so shall go many of the nations of the world."

I am so thankful to live in the blessed United States of America. Father God loves this nation, and I believe the divinely strategic plan He has for America is just a breath away from coming to fruition.

The vision the Holy Spirit gave years ago of the majestic eagle whose wings spanned this nation from Washington state to the Florida Keys is one I will never forget. The eagle's shadow was made up of peoples of all different ages, cultures and walks of life, yet they were all linked together in unity. His eyes, piercing and so determined, were fixed on the Northeast coast. New York and Washington D.C. He did see, for He knew what would be: an incomprehensible attack, the rallying of our armed forces, and a war to follow. He showed me these things, and then I believe I heard my Lord say, *"Mary Frances, as your nation America goes, so shall go many of the nations of the world."*

God's Spirit is hovering now, just waiting for the command of our Father. He is about to soar over this land, reaching into homes and hearts, sweeping from coast to coast, bringing *repentance, restoration and revival!* For God's plan is to reap the precious harvest from *all* nations of the earth, and the Noble Eagle—God's beloved America—carries revival in her wings, across this nation and to the nations beyond, to all who will believe upon Jesus Christ. It is time to soar!

👑 **DECLARATION: I declare over America that she will be beautiful once more with the glory of the Lord. People in unity will worship the King, and multitudes of souls will be won to the glory of Jesus Christ the Son.**

The Church Arises

The Church of the Lord Jesus Christ, His Body in the earth, takes her position now as she moves into a new place. She not only arises to the sweetness of the heavenly sounds coming down, but she takes up the sword of the Spirit. When she speaks the Word, her tongue is like a mighty weapon.

Mighty is your weaponry of Word!

By the Spirit and in the spirit, step out and begin to move in your community. Only say what God would say. Mighty is your weaponry of Word! This equipment is not a physical thing; take up this substance that is life and power and faith—an unseen force filled with God Himself—and proclaim what shall be in your community and city. You are fearless!

Leadership changes in churches and in politics, too. Leaders of cities and states change. Now it begins! I hear a mighty sound of warriors in place. Dear one, know that your fight is not with flesh and blood. Identify the Prince of Darkness and the demons, and bind and loose. Have it no other way.

DECLARATION: I declare over you that such power in demonstration you do exert, for you are a mighty force in the earth. The Word is your weapon and you wield it skillfully, and the Holy Spirit moves you into places of influence in your community.

Mighty Ones

You will declare and decree the day, and you will clear the air.

From city to city and place to place, the Spirit will draw those who have ears to hear what He is saying to the Church. Powerful is your weaponry in your words as you say, "This is how it will be! I declare and I decree!" Like a mighty warrior you do move; this army of believers I do see and hear. City to city there will be particular meetings, and you will gather and decree. You will prophesy to your days when you arise in the morning to pray. You will declare and decree the day, and you will clear the air.

You will not be afraid for what you will see or what you will hear, or even what you will feel, because of the air. But you continue like a mighty one suited up as it is decreed by Paul: in your armor one and all. Something magnificent, something grand, something glorious has begun in this land!

If you were to ask right now you would hear from other nations, too. "Something has begun here! It has begun here! It has begun!" God's hand on *nations!*

The Lord God King shall appear in the air. Glorious shall you appear as He calls you up there. In His righteousness you do dwell. Nothing, absolutely nothing, can defeat you, the Church. When you feel defeated, and things don't go like you thought they would or should, you stand up and remember the words you read today and the sound they carry. Let them beckon unto you in the way of the Christ, Lord Jesus Himself. Let His sound determine your pace. Keep your march, for His sound is so precise.

👑 **DECLARATION: I declare over you that you will see and agree with what the Church will be. You hear His sound, and you walk in the glory and the victory destined for you.**

Interpreting the Sounds

G reat orchestration of the Holy Spirit accompanies us as we gather in the Name of the Son. He orchestrates, and we interpret His orchestration of things. Sometimes it seems as though a great symphony is playing from afar, and we can only interpret but a few of the sounds.

...Remember the gate is opened! The portals are clear!

Something wonderful of God is created in such an atmosphere. Oh, dear one, remember these moments with God the Holy Spirit. When you feel that you would be absolutely down and confounded, remember the gate is opened! The portals are clear! Heaven is indeed making the way and giving the manifestation of what you have believed.

Know that angels are on assignment to remind you of His way. You must not be surprised by what you hear and see. You are moving into your greatest time, and this will be your greatest hour; and, the greatest time of opposition. If Hell can stop you, it will. It will look for every way in, but the Holy Spirit went ahead as He always does, and He told you what you would do and how it all would end.

DECLARATION: I declare over you that the Father orchestrates and brings understanding to you of His ways that will be important in these last days. He opens the portals and goes ahead to prepare the way.

Declarations and Decrees

...Great power is released through words spoken in agreement with Heaven.

The pattern of God is always to release words, utterances, declarations and decrees into the earth *before* great anointings and their demonstrations come forth. For great power is released through words spoken in agreement with Heaven.

Declarations and decrees made by the Body of Christ are opening wide the way for the plans and purposes of God to come forth. There is no mystery about what the plans of God will be, for God the Holy Spirit—the Spirit of truth—will speak very plainly about these things that are about to manifest. There will be no surprises for believers in the Christ. You will know about things before they happen. You will know exactly what to pray because you are led by the Holy Spirit, and you walk in the authority of the Son.

Whatever God is speaking to you about His plans, agree in your heart and give voice in decree. Declare the end from the beginning, and you will see His will brought forth for all humanity.

DECLARATION: I declare over you that the end is victory for you and all who receive Jesus as Lord. I declare before you ever see, for declarations of faith make a way for God's plans to be.

The Vista and View

When God opens a door, a room, a place or a region of utterances, then understandings of revelations come to you. Though physically you remain in the same location, spiritually He places you on a different plane or vista. When He does this for you in prayer in particular, you will have a greater view of things. Where it has been narrow before, the view in prayer will widen for you. It will be easier for you to grasp and hold things in the spirit for yourself personally, but also both nationally and internationally.

Where it has been narrow before, the view in prayer will widen for you.

God gives that view to you. He gives you understanding with it, too. He does this not to confuse or overwhelm, but to secure and stabilize you, because that is the heart of God. The Father is a good parent, and parents always do that for the family: they make sure their sons and daughters are very secure about anything that is getting ready to happen.

DECLARATION: I declare over you that the Father opens up new doors to you of revelation and understanding in prayer. Your vista is greater. You see further and more than you did before. You are settled and secure in the knowing of things you see and hear, and you prepare for them in the place of prayer.

Kings in the Marketplace

I believe there is coming for the kings a momentum from the Holy Spirit.

In the Old Testament, it was the kings who had the monies to bring forth what God had given the priests to do. The priests stood before the Father on behalf of the people, because in the ancient days not everyone had the Holy Spirit—only the kings, the priests and the prophets. The priests would get the word from the Lord, whether it was to build or go to battle, and take the plans to kings who had the resources to do what God had sent down to be done.

It seems to me the devil has come in, particularly in the United States where so much of the work of the gospel is supported, and he's gotten a hold of the world financial system and has squeezed almost all of the life out of it. That pressure affects our kings.

Those who stand as kings in the marketplace, those who are working in corporations, on farms, in restaurants, as lawyers, doctors and more, the Holy Spirit is talking to you. He is bringing clarity to you about your finances and your investments. Take time to pause and listen for the direction that comes to you in this moment. Don't be afraid to stop, and don't be afraid to pick up and move when everyone else is sitting still.

I believe there is coming for the kings a momentum from the Holy Spirit. He is holding some things up to you and saying, "Look! See! Understand this that I am showing to you!" Wait on Him and don't look at things through your natural understanding. Wisdom from Heaven He brings to you. Give the Holy Spirit time to affect your intellect, and then move with Him in His leadings that will position you to prosper very supernaturally even in the hardest of times.

♛ DECLARATION: I declare over you that you will pray for those in the marketplace and take time today to hear from Heaven to receive instruction and direction concerning the economy and finances. You have God's wisdom; you have His understanding; and you have clarity of exactly what to do in Jesus' Name.

Financial System Challenged

Concerning world financial markets, everything now is in a shift. There are mysteries opening that you need to be aware of so that you know what to do with your monies. The financial system even for the United States will be mightily challenged.

There are mysteries opening that you need to be aware of so that you know what to do with your monies.

How will this affect the Church? She is to be the lender and not the borrower. Something very dramatic is holding things back and waiting on you to recognize what is coming so that financially you are secure to the point you will not only have your needs met, but you will be able to help someone else who needs help. So great will be what you have. It may seem like little, but somehow it will be multiplied.

You need to know these things. They are secret things, sealed by God, only to be shared between God and His sons and daughters.

DECLARATION: I declare over you that the mysteries concerning the financial system will be revealed. You have supernatural insights into the positioning of the Church to be the lender and not the borrower. Open your eyes and see how these things will be and what will be your part.

Spirit-Led Giving

... The power to bring the return unto you is present when you are led of the Holy Spirit in your giving.

Don't ever be afraid to give. Be led of the Holy Spirit in all of your giving. If you are led of your soul, there is no power in your giving. There may be some good, fuzzy feeling, but the power to bring the return unto you is present when you are led of the Holy Spirit in your giving.

There are certain things you ought to be doing in your giving and that is giving tithes and offerings. If you are not tithing, I would ask you, "Why not?"

"Well, I don't think it's New Testament," I have heard people say.

Really? But you think miracles are New Testament and you want one! You have to find out how God wants things done, and then do things His way. When you love someone enough, you want to know his or her ways.

God is not trying to take anything *from* you; He's trying to get something *to* you. He doesn't ask you to do above and beyond without making the way for you. You just need to cooperate with Him.

Concerning giving in the Old Testament, God said in Malachi that He would circle around and rebuke the destroyer. In the New Testament, *you* rebuke him in the Name of Jesus! You bind, you loose and Heaven backs you up. That's just the way of it with God, and it makes sense to be obedient to the supernatural laws of a very supernatural God, who is your Father.

God is trying to cause the Body of Christ to become the lender and not the borrower, so you must cooperate with Him even in your finances. Be led of Him in all of your giving, and be obedient in your tithes and offerings.

👑 **DECLARATION: I declare over you that you will not withhold what is right. You tithe and give offerings out of your obedience and love for Him. There is power to produce a return on everything you sow because you are led by the Spirit in your giving and not by need, feelings or emotions. You are a cheerful, prompt giver. The Father is supernaturally making you the lender and not the borrower, and you rebuke the devourer from all of your substance in Jesus' Name.**

Spirit-Led Promptings

When the Spirit of God comes upon you to do something for Him, the passion to perform it consumes you.

"But how do I know when a prompting is from God?"

The mark of God's prompting is a leading in your heart.

Know that anytime God asks something of you, He never pushes you. The mark of God's prompting is a leading in your heart. If you are being pushed to do something, just stop. Stop everything right where you are, because pushing is not God.

The Holy Spirit leads. If you are feeling pushed to accomplish something, pushed to change, pushed to do this, pushed to give that money, pushed to sign that contract, pushed to that investment—you had better hold it. God never pushes. The devil pushes, and man pushes.

You are in charge at the hand of God, and you hold it right there and wait upon the Holy Spirit. Pause and wait, and the Spirit of God will make it very obvious to you what you are to do.

👑 **DECLARATION: I declare over you that you are led by the Spirit of God in all your dealings. The Holy Spirit never pushes; He only leads you from the inside and not outward signs or circumstances. Anything that pushes is not God. You have the discernment to know the difference, and to stop when you are being pushed to do anything by anyone. You follow the promptings of the Holy Spirit in all the affairs of life, and He always leads you into success.**

Visions and Dreams

"Then was the secret revealed unto Daniel in a night vision…"
—Daniel 2:19

In this time of the end and end-time events, there are things you must know. In Daniel's day he needed to know secrets, mysteries, matters, dreams and their meanings as revealed by God, for his very life depended upon it.

The god of this world—Satan—gives forth information creating facts for humanity. If you are working with facts, you are working with the lesser. The Spirit of God gives you a gathering of revelations, which create truth, and the truth is greater than the fact. Revelation comes out of timelessness and facts are subject to time. Facts can be changed—altered—by the truth.

Just as Daniel received the answer he required in a dream, you can expect visions and dreams. You have to receive them, and the Spirit of God will interpret them for you. Ask Him for visions and dreams that you would know His heart and what to do. Then when He wakes you up at peculiar times, be faithful to write down what you believe you have heard and seen. God will fine-tune things for you. You just believe Him and prepare your heart to receive from Him in the night season.

 DECLARATION: I declare over you that you will have dreams and visions of the night that are from God your Father. They will give you understanding so you know what to do, and the Holy Spirit will give you the interpretation, too.

Wisdom to the Wise

"Daniel answered and said, Blessed be the name of God for ever and ever: for wisdom and might are his:

God gives His wisdom to those who have understanding.

"And he changeth the times and the seasons: he removeth kings, and setteth up kings: he giveth wisdom unto the wise, and knowledge to them that know understanding."

—Daniel 2:20–21

The Word says God *gives wisdom to the wise* and *knowledge to those who have understanding.* He didn't give the knowledge to those who don't have understanding. He gave the knowledge of the times and seasons and the change in leadership to the wise, because they endeared themselves to having godly understanding.

Endear yourself to understanding what comes out of the revelatory realm—a place of seeing and knowing—and not just out of information. The maneuvering of times, seasons and kings are of God, and you can't move with God if you are working out of head knowledge. God gives His wisdom to those who have understanding.

When you pray according to Ephesians 1:17, that you would have the Spirit of wisdom and revelation in the knowledge of Him, you come into a place of the knowings of God the Son, and nothing will overwhelm you. Though the moment requires everything of you, it won't defeat you. It can feel like defeat, look like defeat, and sound like defeat, but it isn't. God says, "I am here with you, and I have nothing less than victory to give. It is as I say, and I say, 'Victory!'"

👑 **DECLARATION: I declare over you that you believe you receive the Spirit of wisdom, and the Almighty is giving unto you divine knowledge to understand the times and seasons.**

Don't Just Draw the Line

Clear the air and change the very atmosphere.

The Lord Jesus Christ is a warrior. You are of the generation that implements His victory all the way back to where the host of demonic beings came from. You are the one who draws the bloodline and says to Satan, "You can come this far and no further; now I'm going to push you back to where you came from." You don't just tell him to stop at the line, you clear the air and change the atmosphere, because if you don't, he can bring disturbance and distraction that eventually breaks you down.

You don't want to allow those spirits any room around you or your family. In particular with addiction, you can draw the line, but the demons of addiction are still there dancing, and they will try to cross that line. If you have ever been addicted to anything, it is just about next to impossible to walk free when those demons are still around you. They may not be able to break you, but they are still there taunting.

So don't just draw the line, push the darkness back. Clear the air and change the very atmosphere. You are the difference in the earth because Christ is in you. Where you are, He is in manifestation.

DECLARATION: I declare over you that you have a revelation of the difference you make because Christ is in you. Where you are, He is! You draw the line and keep things clear in the spiritual atmosphere. There is no room for any work of the enemy near you or your family.

Draw From God's Kingdom

As a believer in the Christ and subject of the King, you must draw from the Kingdom of God and not from the world system.

God in a place! How precious it is to witness God the Holy Spirit move in His gifts of healing and prophecy on behalf of the people everywhere He sends me. I believe it is the Father's will to impart His wisdom and understanding to each of us so that we will move with great precision in these times.

Jesus comforted His disciples with these words: *"Peace I leave with you; My own peace I now give and bequeath to you. Not as the world gives do I give to you. Do not let your hearts be troubled, neither let them be afraid. Stop allowing yourselves to be agitated and disturbed; and do not permit yourselves to be fearful and intimidated and cowardly and unsettled"* (John 14:27, AMP).

Let this truth sink down into your heart: You are *in this world,* but *you are not of it.* As a believer in the Christ and subject of the King, you must draw from the Kingdom of God and not from the world system. The father of the world system is Satan—the father of lies. The "system" will not get better, but you will if you give yourself to the meditation of the Word and the fellowship of the Holy Spirit. Meet with Him each day. He will show, illuminate and make plain the way for you as only He can do. Divine direction, supernatural protection, secret truths and mysteries will be given to those who wait on Him.

DECLARATION: I declare over you that you draw upon God's Kingdom this day, and partake of the wisdom, revelation and divine direction reserved and purposed for you!

Intimacy of the Holy Spirit

Times in the presence of God are holy times, and they will require the intimacy of the Holy Spirit

I am grateful for the ingathering the Holy Spirit brings for the sons and daughters of the Most High. It is your intimacy with Him that allows you to hear His sound, which draws you into His presence. In such a place the Father's heart is made known to you. He garners up a time—a Kairos—where time and destiny meet to form on your behalf.

Times in the presence of God are holy times, and they will require the intimacy of the Holy Spirit for you to hear well in these last days. The power of the Holy Spirit is like electricity. This power has always existed, but man has not always known about it, until a time came in man's knowledge that he knew and learned how to harness such a power.

So it is for you and the Holy Spirit; the Holy Spirit has always been, for He is God. Now you know beyond what you have known before. Now you learn how to move with and follow Him in His operations and demonstrations. You don't harness Him; and He doesn't care to harness you. He wants you to choose Him and to hear Him and to follow Him as He leads you.

DECLARATION: I declare over you that you will take time to develop intimacy with the Father. Reverence His power, don't negate or short-circuit His power, but learn to follow and flow with Him in His operations and demonstrations.

Ask God for Your Families

Believe as you never have before for your families! For there is a war on to divide and destroy. Believe for more of God in each and every heart. Let families come together. Let forgiveness and love reign. Let there be peace. For there will be those who will be lost this year. Make it right with this one and that—whoever is near and dear to you. For they may be gone before the year is through. Make it right, dear one, make it right.

"…Remember the Lord, which is great and terrible, and fight for your brethren, your sons, and your daughters, your wives, and your houses."
—Nehemiah 4:14b

Sometimes you think things will always be just as they are, but suddenly…in a day, things are changed, and people go away. Ask God for your family, don't delay. Unto God's glory and the delight of His heart these things are sealed and considered done. Those that you have been praying for that would receive your Lord and be born of Him, you shall see the manifestation of that if you don't back off. Stay in there; for a fight is on between Hell and you over that one. If you will do the battle in the Name of Jesus Christ and thank God Almighty for their salvation, loose the light of the glorious Gospel and bind the god of this world in his ability to continue to blind their mind, they shall be won. In a moment it will get done, and they will be Heaven bound and not Hell bound.

DECLARATION: I declare over you that as for you and your house, you will serve the Lord. You will use your authority concerning your family and speak to those entities to stop blinding the minds of those who have not believed, and to cease opposing those who have not received the glorious Gospel of Christ. Stand and fight and say, "Satan, take your hands off! I claim them for God's Kingdom, and you cannot win."

Oceans Prophecy

The prophets stand between the times, and speak of things that were, things that are and things that are about to be.

The Holy Spirit spoke, and I believe I heard Him say, "Waters, waters, waters; oceans, oceans; seas; gulfs; rivers; creeks and streams. I spoke to them all, in particular to the oceans, and I told them they weren't to cross a particular line. I did that thing. But Adam sold My Creation out, and Satan took dominion and authority here. Now My people have been redeemed from the curse, so you are the only ones I will be able to speak to, to stand up and stop some things. Some things I will not ask you to stop. Know the difference. Know the difference."

I saw waters that are going to challenge our authority. I saw waters rise so high in the sky. They roar! There was such a roar, and they are going to challenge the line God said not to cross. There will be times when you will know the future event, and God will tell you of it, and He will say, "Get on it!" The ocean is getting ready to stand up and roar and cross the line. "You are My voice, and My authority and My power in the earth, and when I tell you to stand it down, stand it down! Then there will be times I will speak to you, and I will show and tell of a mighty roar of the oceans and the waters of earth that is about to be. You cannot change this thing, do not even try. But I prepare you for it. Know the difference."

The next event concerned the earth, and it was almost as though I could hear groans. Oh my! So I wrote on a piece of paper as fast as I could the things He was showing and telling me. "The earth groans, the core moves." The core of the earth is experiencing such pressure to move, and I could see like a bulging disc in a spine. I saw the platelets of Earth sliding and moving, and some of them looked like arenas of slate moving. There will be the suddenlies of Earth: eruptions, shakes and quakes in usual and most unusual places. He did not speak to stand it down. I tell you of it so that when you see this thing, you will know that God went ahead of the thing.

In the midst of it all is the glory of God. A reviving spirit coming upon the Body of Christ worldwide, that He might empower the Church as she has *never* been empowered before.

👑 **DECLARATION: I declare over you that the Holy Spirit is telling you and showing you things to come, always securing and assuring you. (See John 16:13).**

2004 Tsunami Prophecy

During a church service in January 2004, I gave voice to what God the Holy Spirit revealed concerning the tsunami that struck Indonesia the day after Christmas, December 26, 2004. The Holy Spirit showed "things to come" so people would pray and change it, for He said of this event, "You can be changed."

"Some events you can affect; some you can change; some you can prepare for."

This event was not stopped. It happened, and many souls were lost. This emphasizes the importance of the Church taking her place in prayer, and giving voice to God's will concerning what is revealed by His Spirit to affect change in the earth. The following is what the Holy Spirit revealed.

"There's a portal. There's a portal. There's an opening. There's a portal. I see it. Here it is. There's an opening. There's an opening. There's an opening to know. There's an opening to know. Close, so close. In just a few days. No fear, no fear, no fear. It's a…tsunami, a tsunami, a tsunami. It's important. It's important. Indonesia. Indonesia. It's about to be. Be exposed foul thing. Be exposed. You can be changed. Be made known."

👑 **DECLARATION: I declare over you that the Father always goes ahead and makes a way. Be faithful to pray when He shows and makes things known concerning events that can be changed, stopped and prepared for.**

Gatekeepers

You are the keeper of the gates of the cities of the world!

As a believer in the Christ, you are called to pray and stand in the gap concerning unbelievers, leaders, events, and all that the Holy Spirit would choose to reveal. You are the keeper of the gates of the cities of the world!

All throughout the Old Testament, God set gatekeepers in place to guard and protect the physical gates to the cities and of the temple. What God did in the Old is always a pattern, and a type and shadow of the New. In the New Testament, you are also called to be a gatekeeper, taking your place in the spirit through prayer as the Holy Spirit leads you to guard and protect the working of God's plan and the fulfillment of prophecy. When events are made known, you can pick that up in prayer as an assignment from Heaven, and pray it through to expose it, stop it, change it or prepare.

There are many types of gates: The gates of Heaven; the gates of Hell. Cities have gates; minds have gates; governments, nations, states, homes, churches and people have gates. Gates represent authority and power. Search the Scriptures, and you will read of the dealings that take place, and of the counsels and rulers who meet at the gates. You must guard and protect these openings as the Holy Spirit shows what He wants you to know.

God told Abraham in Genesis 22:17, *"...your descendants shall possess the gate of their enemies."* You are Christ's, and Abraham's seed, according to the promise! You have been granted access to the gates of people and places— to those who would oppose the plans of God. Through the Name of Jesus Christ you have authority to guard, protect and watch over the things of God and to keep the enemy out.

👑 **DECLARATION: I declare over you that you are called of God to be a gatekeeper; to watch over and guard the spiritual gates of your family, church, city, state and nation. The Holy Spirit alerts you of assignments from the enemy, and you declare, decree and pray in authority and don't allow anything in that would steal, kill or destroy.**

An Unction of the Holy One

The Spirit of God gives unto you an unction. An unction is simply a knowing inside of you. The knowings in you will come out of your fellowship with God the Father. God will be able to speak deep within your heart because you are giving Him your time.

"Ye have an unction from the Holy One, and ye know all things." —1 John 2:20

When you are at the cusp of understanding what the knowing is, His illumination comes to the knowing, and you see. I believe revelations and understandings of the knowings inside of you are becoming clearer to you now. By the end of the year, some of you will make awesome decisions—to build, move, go or stay. You have to listen beyond your intellect with spiritual ears to what the Holy Spirit would speak to you concerning your life, and trust in the unction He gives.

DECLARATION: I declare over you that the Holy Spirit is the Spirit of truth. He is the revelator of the Words of Jesus Christ. He gives unction—insights and knowings—unto you. You know where to go, you know what to do and what not to do. In all your decisions you follow the unction given by Him.

The Miracle of This Nation

This nation will not forsake her God nor the things that she should do.

Oh, this nation. The miracle of this nation. The glory of this nation. It may seem to you that this nation has given up her godly way, but I say, "This is God's nation and this is how it will be."

The glory of the Lord upon this nation through and through. This nation will not forsake her God nor the things that she should do. This nation chooses rightly because the Church—the believers within—arise and speak and say, "Wait a minute now; this is the way, and we're going to walk in it. This is the way."

On all the broadcasts near and far they say how it will be financially in this nation and internationally. But the Spirit of the Lord speaks and says, "That is not the word of the Lord to you. Don't be taken and blindsided by these words and reports that are given to you. For I say you are My people, and I have provision for you. It comes from the north, the south, the east and the west—miraculously! Supernaturally."

You are the Kingdom of God. Where the Kingdom is, the Kingdom rules and laws change! Your borders are lined with a line of glory so that things are known and things are seen that otherwise would slip through. Suddenly, there is a drawing of the glory line on the borders of you. What would deceive and slip on through will now be exposed and be shown to you. Those who know what to do, their ears will now hear and their eyes will now see. The truth of the Almighty shall be revealed to them. Then they will know better how to lead, how to protect, and how to prosper you. I look and see this outlining of your borders; miraculous things concerning you.

DECLARATION: I declare over you that you agree concerning your nation, and you declare and decree: "This is God's nation and this is how it will be! You were a miracle from the start and are still near and dear to the Father's heart."

Truth Shall Reign

Flashing before me are many cities. So I say this is how it will be. For in the streets I look and see this thing that moves like a plague. It slithers along down this street and that, and thinks it can take this one and that one, but it has been seen and is found out.

The glory of God will shine on through, and the truth of the Gospel will be known by you.

I declare and I decree: "Michael! Now! Now! The battle is on! What thinks it can so deceitfully move is now exposed amongst you. I watch as this thing would slither on its way, head toward those in authority, and want to wrap itself around and confound, and put to sleep the leaders of the land. Saying to those who are born again, "Oh, Christian," like a lullaby I hear, "Lay down and go to sleep. Christian pray-ers, one and all, lay yourself down right now. Rest and sleep. Go to sleep, do not pray…." "No!" I say, "No!" This is how it will be in the cities of the earth. The glory of God will shine on through, and the truth of the Gospel will be known by you. What would deceive you, confound you, lie to you, manipulate and control you, will be exposed, even now.

Decisions will be made; this one and that one will be removed. The glory of the Lord moves through the land. Who dare try to confound God's sons and daughters? It will not be so. Truth shall reign, not a lie and not deception. "Watch and see as I move from city to city. The watchers on the walls, the guardians at the gates, those who know the portals over your land, are well aware of My plan. They pray it on in, and they pray it on through, so that these things of Me can happen for you."

"The lullaby of Satan will be heard, but My sons and daughters shall arise, and they'll say, 'As for me and my house that's not how it is going to be. I will not put the Word of God down.'" The Word of God in your mouth and His love in your heart consume you. You move forward with His plan, and His march continues on, for the glory of the Son.

👑 **DECLARATION: I declare over you that the spirit of apathy that would cause such a slumber, be bound over you in Jesus' Name. Entities that roam the streets thinking no one sees—God sees and shows, and now you know. Deception and lies are exposed! Your eyes are open to the truth, and the glory of God shines through you: this is how it shall be for you and your land.**

The March is On

I look at the borders of Israel, and her borders are illuminated with the glory of God.

A suddenly there will be internationally. I look at the borders of Israel, and her borders are illuminated with the glory of God. She is steady in the land, she is steady in the air, and she is steady in the sea. She knows what to do, exactly how and exactly when. She waits on no one or for anyone's permission.

Her face is turned toward God Almighty it is true. She knows what time it is and exactly what she is supposed to do. The Church of Jesus Christ in Israel and throughout the nations recognize her time. For these are the born-again ones; the Spirit-filled ones; the ones who won't back down. They know, and they see, and they interpret rightly, and the march is on.

DECLARATION: I declare that God keeps Israel. She is steady in You, O Lord God. She knows her time and exactly what to do.

The Daughters of the King

I did look and see a company of women. The daughters of the King in congregations in the cities of nations I did look and see. Some are quickened as they go about the chore of the day, whatever that may be. A holy visitation comes to this one and that, and the schooling of the Spirit that has been seems to increase.

A holy visitation comes to this one and that, and the schooling of the Spirit that has been seems to increase.

Quickly now a going forth seems to take place. A positioning prepared for these daughters. They are so courageous. They are so brave. Not an easy thing always to do, to say, to be, to lead, to create, to declare, to decree. But these daughters don't look for easy. They just simply know the Father's heart. Above all else they wish to do, is please Him in what He expected of them before everything is done and through.

Dear God Almighty, the daughters of You are given voice to lead in all fields. When I look and see, they will be one of those that are interviewed in science and space, in health, in government, in media, production and direction, and in commerce, too. These ones by Your intervention shall speak. They shall say. They shall be given a platform to say and do.

Something wonderful, O, God Almighty, is happening because of You. The daughters of the King do hear and obey. My, oh my, as they turn into next year, such changes that come, not for some and not for few, but a multitude. They are readied and prepared by You.

DECLARATION: I declare over you that your Father God speaks to you, and so with this prophecy you agree. You are ready and prepared by Him to go, to say and to do.

The Price has Been Paid

What Jesus bore, you need not bear.

Healing for your physical body is received first in your spirit—your heart—by faith. For you will become outwardly what you see and believe on the inside. That is why it is so important for you to take time to plant the seed of God's Word in your heart concerning healing, for it will spring up into a harvest of health and healing in your body.

I believe it was given unto the Prophet Isaiah to look and see afar off, to see Jesus that day on His march toward the Cross, the only door to His divine destiny. God revealed to the prophet the wounds, the pain and the suffering the Savior endured, and he recorded it so you could see what he saw. (See Isaiah 52–53). Jesus willingly took every sin and sickness upon Himself that day. Isaiah 53:4–5, says, *"Surely he hath borne our griefs, and carried our sorrows: yet we did esteem him stricken, smitten of God, and afflicted. But he was wounded for our transgressions, he was bruised for our iniquities: the chastisement of our peace was upon him; and with his stripes we are healed."*

The price for sin was paid with Jesus' own blood! He made the way for each and every one to become God's sons and daughters, and to partake of the blessings of God's Kingdom. Healing is one of the blessings He secured for you! It is yours today!

When symptoms, sickness and reports contrary to the will of God try to come to you, remember what your Savior has done. See every sin and every sickness washed in the blood. Search the Scriptures and see as Isaiah saw. What Jesus bore, you need not bear. The price has been paid, dear one. Receive your blessed promise of healing today!

👑 **DECLARATION: I declare over you a new view of what Jesus has done for you. See Him as the prophet did, and see the price for your healing paid. Remember, reflect upon and receive your purchased healing today!**

U.S.A. God's Way

As weapons move across the U.S.A., those who are in the know, know. They know, they watch, and *suddenly!* Some to be exposed and some things to be taken care of very quietly.

A nation under God no matter what it sounds like or looks like, that is what this nation is.

U.S.A., U.S.A., U.S.A., U.S.A. God's way. Founded by the King of kings and Lord of lords. The seeds are planted deep in the U.S.A. A nation under God no matter what it sounds like or looks like, that is what this nation is. From north to south and east to west and at the corners, angelic ones do know, the U.S.A. is under the Creator Almighty.

It ends gloriously to the honor and the glory of the King, in this nation and nations beyond.

👑 **DECLARATION: I declare over you that God Almighty will have His way concerning the U.S.A. Believe and say, "One nation under God," and that is how it will stay.**

Word and Spirit

God always has a people within a people.

When called upon in that day, there will be those nations who say, "But we are busy." For so it was in the ancient of times, too, on behalf of Israel. "We have this to do, we have that. We must be about this over here, don't you know. We cannot join you, we have this, and we are moving over here, and we are doing over there."

But then there will be those few, strong and mighty of heart, that come together, and churches, too. For it soon shall be very clear that there is but a remnant here of Word and Spirit. But Word and Spirit you must be.

Do not compromise the way of the Holy Spirit in those things that you do. For what you thought you would build, and what you thought would make things grow, did God say that for you? Is that the way to go for you?

God always has a people within a people. Always, always from the ancient of times, and so it is today.

DECLARATION: I declare over you that you will not compromise the Word and Spirit of God. In all things you go His way and answer, "Yes," when you are called upon to pray.

Understanding Released Unto You

I look to the spring. I look to the fall. I look to next year, and the next and the next. I look and I see wonders and signs. Some will get it and some will not. Some will say, "Oh, so what." Like in Your day, my Lord, when they didn't have an understanding of what they were seeing.

An understanding of the times beyond what you have known....

But there are those, oh Lord God, in your Body, who do understand. As it was given to the men of the tribe of Issachar to have an understanding of the times for their nation, so it is for these who partake of these words. An understanding of the times beyond what you have known, on behalf of what you are to do for this nation and beyond. I release this understanding unto you today. Never the same in Jesus' Name.

DECLARATION: I declare over you that you will receive this impartation and understanding of the times. Seeing and knowing is released unto you so you know how to pray and what to do by His leading.

Liberty of the Spirit

Learn to follow Him in all you say and do, and your trust and confidence in Him will become so natural, though supernatural it will be.

The blessed Holy Spirit longs to visit with you. He knows the heart of the Father—all that your Abba, Papa carries in the depths of Himself—and the Holy Spirit is the One who communicates and conveys that to you.

By His power He drew you to the Father and the Son. He keeps on moving on your behalf, always explaining, revealing, declaring, disclosing, transmitting, manifesting and demonstrating as only He can do. There is no one like Him! He is God, and He will never-ever leave you.

Give God the Holy Spirit liberty in your life today. He will lead you into all that is good. Learn to follow Him in all you say and do, and your trust and confidence in Him will become so natural, though supernatural it will be. Where the Spirit of the Lord is there is liberty for you!

👑 **DECLARATION: I declare over you that the Holy Spirit abides in you, and wherever He is, there is liberty. You are free to follow, free to flow, free to see and free to know which way to go.**

Your Heart is Greater

The angel of the Lord brings visitation and healing in His wings. The wonders of God have begun! You cannot know these things with your mind; only with your heart. If you try to know these things with your mind, you will lose. Your heart is much greater than your mind. Your heart—your spirit—will live forever. The mind that you receive in Christ for all eternity is very different than what is housed in your earth suit now.

Believe with your heart the wonders of God!

Believe with your heart the wonders of God! I am commissioned of the Almighty to bring deliverance to you. I bring healing to you and it begins today. A visitation of God the Holy Spirit begins this moment for you as never before, and it will only increase upon you, because it is time.

DECLARATION: I declare over you that you will receive this holy visitation of Jesus, your Lord. Delivering power has its way; healing makes things right. You believe these wonders of the Holy Spirit with your heart and not with your mind—for your heart is the eternal part.

If Only You Knew

Let the Holy Spirit fill your heart with Father's delight.

In prayer one day, the Holy Spirit reminded me of an expression I heard when we adopted our first child, our daughter. She was six-months-old when we adopted her, and she had been with the same foster parents for all that time.

My husband and I were so excited! We had prepared the house for her, decorated the nursery and filled her closet with the most beautiful clothes. We had waited for this moment to bring her home with such anticipation, but when I went to pick her up, she pushed away and arched her back at me. She looked back longingly at the caseworker with whom she was most familiar, and the caseworker said, *"Oh, little girl, if only you knew."*

I believe the Spirit of God would say to you, "If only you knew! If only you knew what I have prepared for you. If only you knew the wonderful plans that await you! Such grand and glorious times are ahead for you; and provision too...if only you knew!"

We wanted so badly to be her Mom and Dad. Didn't she know? Couldn't she understand? God wants to be your Father—your Abba, Papa—your Daddy God. The Holy Spirit longs to be your demonstrator and your manifestor of the works of Jesus Christ.

All the way home in the car she was silent. Though she didn't yet speak any intelligible words at her age, she didn't even make a sound. At dinnertime she just chewed and swallowed and looked. Bedtime came, and not so much as a whimper escaped her lips. But then in the morning we awoke to the most wonderful sound: the sound of a baby laughing!

Oh, child of God, if only you knew what has been imparted to you for what is to come. Don't let your ideas and fears hold you back from Him. Let the Holy Spirit fill your heart with Father's delight.

👑 **DECLARATION: I declare over you that your understanding is opened to what the Holy Spirit has imparted to you for this time, and you will flow with Him in anticipation of all He has prepared and provided for you.**

Everything Heeds Your Words

Sometimes the situations you find yourself in have come because of your words. You must not oppose yourself with your words. You look at your circumstances or situations; you consider your body and whether or not

Some put into motion a manifestation that cuts your destiny short.

you are in good health, and then you begin to say things based on what you see and feel. It's easy to do that, and we've all done it. But you need to be saying the greater of yourself. The truth is the greater, the fact is the lesser. You don't deny the fact, but you agree with the greater because that is what is true of you.

Sometimes by your words you cut yourself off from your destiny. You alter the provision for your race. Sometimes, you even cut your race short by your words. It is as though I can see on the horizon all sorts of destinies of the sons and daughters of the Most High, and the destinies are waning because of the words of those to whom the destinies belong.

Everything was created at your Father's hand in agreement with His Son by the power of His Spirit, and you were brought forth to walk in this land and to take up command. All of creation hears and heeds your words. Your words identify you, for you are a son or daughter of the Most High. Some of you put into motion a manifestation that cuts your destiny short because of things you see, feel and hear and have decided to agree upon. You stop your destiny. Yet it's the greatest time of all times for the sons and daughters. You must watch your words, and not cut your race short.

👑 **DECLARATION: I declare over you that you will repent of agreeing with and speaking words contrary to what God says of you. You will renew your mind with the Word of truth, and refuse to say anything that would oppose God's Word, cut short your race or thwart your destiny.**

Great Courage

Each and every one of you will have to know how you believe and what you believe....

God's presence is always, always upon you. He is omnipresent—which means He is everywhere. He is in you, and you take Him with you wherever you go. You are not trying to get into His presence; His presence is already in you!

Walk with courage and boldness as never before, because of this presence you carry. Each and every one of you will have to know how you believe and what you believe, and be ready to stand for what you believe. For this time you were created; to bring forth on behalf of the beloved Son. What you haven't had, but have had need of, will now manifest unto you.

No more doubting shall there be. It's that kind of day. Great courage arises in your heart and much is made known unto you both personally and concerning family, friends, cities, communities, states, regions and nations. This is necessary to be, for these knowings will be a demonstration unto leaders too, of cities, of regions and of nations. Where you go makes a difference.

DECLARATION: I declare over you that you walk in great courage because of God's presence in you. The boldness and knowings He has granted to you are necessary for those around you and for those in authority.

No Compromise

I had a pastor who does not compromise this word of faith that we preach. Dear one, settle in your heart that you will not compromise no matter the cost.

"But what saith it? The word is nigh thee, even in thy mouth, and in thy heart: that is, the word of faith, which we preach."
—Romans 10:8

Angels are assigned to help you concerning where once you would compromise. It is dangerous to walk about in compromise, for demon forces are watching ever-so carefully that would see the end of each and every son and daughter of the Most High. Take them out early; he would if he could. Bring them to demise if he could.

Greater is the One within you, and greater yet shall be the demonstrations of His power and love through you. Do not compromise the Word that you have believed, for it will save your life.

DECLARATION: I declare over you that you will not compromise the message of faith, for it is life to you. It delivers and protects you continually.

You are the Happening

You will do the greater works!

Greater works than have ever been are at your hand. For the greater works that Jesus spoke of and said we would do, it is time now to do. *"Most assuredly, I say to you, he who believes in Me, the works that I do he will do also; and greater works than these he will do, because I go to My Father"* (John 14:12, NKJV).

Don't wait for something to be. Don't wait for something to happen. *You are the happening!* You have come into the greatest of days. Glorious one that you are—son or daughter of the eternal God—Creator Almighty and Father by your confession of His Son. You are a child of God. Eternity already abides in you; it's the person that you are. For does not God Himself inhabit you? Eternity He is and so are you.

You must think this way: be eternity minded. You were in the Son before the foundations of the world. You have, *"...been born again, not of corruptible seed but incorruptible, through the word of God which lives and abides forever"* (1 Peter 1:23, NKJV).

DECLARATION: I declare over you that a revelation of eternity in you quickens you to do what you were born to do. You are not waiting for something to happen; you will step out with the Holy Spirit and do the greater works spoken of in John 14:12, and glorify Jesus Christ.

The God of Miracles

I have believed in miracles since I was a child. God has always been the God of demonstration to me. When you are challenged and confounded with the relationships of life—circumstances, situations and crisis—you have got to know the God of miracles.

When you are challenged and confounded with the relationships of life—circumstances, situations and crisis— you have got to know the God of miracles.

Years ago, an evil day came to our household. But, because of the Word of God inside of me and the Word of Faith teaching from my pastor over many years, there was no compromise inside of me concerning His truth and the words of my Father. Everything of covenant was fixed in my heart. Everything of faith was in place. Because of the fellowship of the Holy Spirit that I had developed all those many years, what was needful was there on that evil day. The miracles and the demonstrations of God that I had seen helped too, because I trusted Him, and I knew what He could and would do.

He is the God of miracles, and He will always, always come through.

DECLARATION: I declare over you, now is the time you will develop fellowship with the Father, Son and Holy Spirit. You will not wait for crisis to hit. Your daily time with Him prepares and takes you through any situation that comes against you. You are armed and ready, for He shall be the God of miracles to you.

He is Today!

Let me tell you about the Christ that walks the streets today.

The Spirit of the Lord is faithful to do what you believe Him to do. The great manifestor of the works of Jesus Christ is faithful to do what is impossible for the greatest of minds and medicine to perform!

You've got to know what God says about what the blood of His Son did for you. It is a time when the Spirit pours Himself out upon you, and stirs you up with the giftings and anointings that were purposed and planned, so that you will go forth to a world that is scared, that has children and loved ones in ICU or on drugs, dying, oppressed, distressed, wiped out. You must tell them the God of miracles is *today*—not in days of old, not in ancient of times. He is today! The Word of God says so, and you need to choose to believe it.

Let me tell you about the Christ that walks the streets today. This Jehovah Rapha—the Lord who heals—walks the streets with you if you will be bold and courageous to step out and proclaim Him as Lord.

DECLARATION: I declare that Jesus Christ is the same yesterday, today and forever! He will always heal, always deliver, always perform what was written and spoken of Him. I declare over you that you will step out in faith on His Word and by His Spirit and proclaim and demonstrate His power through your hands.

The Fire of Yahweh

God is a Holy God! His fire comes down on one and all; like liquid fire raindrops it does fall. Liquid fire I do see, burning out impurities from you and me. Depression must go, fear and poverty, too. Sickness and disease cannot abide in you.

...Believe and receive and you shall see a fulfillment....

Holy fire of Yahweh has come; liquid fire to each and every one. Liquid fire visits you. Yahweh's fire is a holy thing. No more confounding of our minds. Yahweh's fire clears them all. No confusion can remain, nor diseases and their pain.

Fire, fire liquid fire consuming sin, consuming curse, making things right both day and night. No fretting, no worrying and cares of the past. It's a new place and yet another facet of God's great grace has come.

Holy fire brings deliverances, too. Children I see. Moms' and Dads' children return unto you before the year is through. Returning unto Christ. Some brand new before the year is through.

Now hear the word; believe and receive and you shall see a fulfillment of all the things you have believed and received this very day. For Yahweh's fire has visited you, and nothing can be the same in Jesus' Name.

👑 **DECLARATION: I declare over you that Yahweh's fire will fall on you! Holy fire will set you free! It will burn out sin and all impurity. Everything changes and is made right. Your body is well, your mind is clear; in Jesus' Name you have no fear.**

Forget the Past

It is hard to look back when you are reaching forward.

The Apostle Paul understood something about letting go of the past. In Philippians 3:13, he wrote, *"But this one thing I do, forgetting those things which are behind, and reaching forth unto those things which are before."*

Sometimes people have so many regrets about the past that they can't live life for today. Yesterday and it's happenings are gone. You cannot go back to that day and change it. You can only change today. Give all of your regrets, disappointments, frustrations and failures to God. Don't let yesterday define who God made you to be. There is an anointing that abides within you and upon you, and that anointing is God the Holy Spirit. He is trying desperately to get your attention about the time you have stepped into, because it's different than anything you have known before. He knows that if you keep looking back at the way things were—even at the good things—that you're going to get stuck. You will get stuck in your personal life and in your anointing. The Holy Spirit is leading you on.

Make a conscious decision to forget what happened yesterday; leave it all behind and go on and live life to its fullest today. It is hard to look back when you are reaching forward. God has wonderful things ahead for you, and He is very interested in your future. You are not to build altars on your past failures or even on your successes or the way things once were. I want to encourage you this day, choose to forget those things that are behind, and reach for those things God has so lovingly planned and placed before you.

DECLARATION: I declare over you that you will forget the past and press ever-forward, for the future is bright. You will stay focused and present in what God has planned and not where you have been. It is a new time, a new day, and it has got to be God's way.

Never Alone

I want you to know today that you are never, ever alone. I know sometimes it can feel as though *Where did everyone go? Doesn't anyone care? Doesn't anyone know?*

"I am with you always, even to the end of the age."
—Matthew 28:20b

There are many things we don't understand. If you ask the Holy Spirit for understanding, He will give you what is needful for you, to stabilize and secure you. For the things He doesn't show you, you will just have to wait.

If fear is troubling you in the waiting, and wondering is pressing in on every side, I speak to the confounding of your mind in Jesus' Name. Fear will not rule or overtake you! You have the mind of Christ, and you have a warrior's spirit.

A spirit of grief, too, can try to overtake when you feel weak and that you've made mistakes. You have to take hold of that, and continue to say what God would say. If you stay with a grieving inside yourself, the master of it is death, and you start drawing death to you.

I speak healing and strength to your heart. A relief now comes to you, and it is well in Jesus' Name.

DECLARATION: I declare over you that you release the grief you have held inside, for you want life and not death to abide. Healing and strength now come to you; and in Jesus' Name you are whole and free.

Arise and Be Healed

"...Jesus Christ maketh thee whole: arise...."

Health and wholeness are the Father's will for you. Spirit, soul and body, God wants you well, and has made provision for it to be so. By Jesus' stripes, healing has been appropriated for every physical affliction or emotional wound you might experience. It is the living Word of God alone, and your faith in His power, that makes you whole: sound, unbroken and entire.

God's Word is health to *all* your flesh. (See Proverbs 4:22). The Lord is your shepherd; He restores your soul. (See Psalm 23:1, 3). He heals the brokenhearted, and binds up their wounds. (See Psalm 147:3). He bore our sins in His own body on the tree, that we having died to sins, might live for righteousness—by whose stripes we were healed. (See 1 Peter 2:24).

By the power in Jesus' Name I release restoration, healing and wholeness unto you. I release the life of God to your body, broken relationships and wounded soul. I take authority over a spirit of infirmity—*be exposed and be gone!* I command the spirit of divorce trying to rip marriages apart to *go* in Jesus' Name! I clear the atmosphere for the Holy Spirit to move in and minister grace and peace where strife and sickness, discord and disease have taken up residence.

DECLARATION: I declare over you that it is Jesus Christ who makes you whole. You arise with strength in your inner man, and use your authority to rule over any power that would try to exalt itself against the knowledge of your God and His will for you.

Power that Produces Salvation

G race is a super-abundant supply of whatever is needed to put you over in life. It is the power that produces salvation in your life. Titus 1:2 says, *"For the grace of God that brings salvation has appeared to all men."* Grace is an all-inclusive word that means deliverance, safety, preservation, healing and soundness. This grace has appeared to all men!

This great grace bestowed upon you is a gift from God Almighty. It is His divine ability poured out upon humanity.

"For by grace are ye saved through faith; and that not of yourselves: it is the gift of God" (Ephesians 2:8). This great grace bestowed upon you is a gift from God Almighty. It is His divine ability poured out upon humanity. Grace has made the way that you could not have made for yourself. Because of this life-changing power, you now have access to the Father and His heavenly blessings as Hebrews 4:16, *The Amplified Bible,* demonstrates: *"Let us then fearlessly and confidently and boldly draw near to the throne of grace (the throne of God's unmerited favor to us sinners), that we may receive mercy for our failures and find grace to help in good time for every need (appropriate help and well-timed help, coming just when we need it.)"*

Such provision your Father has made for you. His great grace is poured out for you. All you have to do is receive it!

👑 **DECLARATION: I declare over you that you receive the Father's great grace and all it provides. Every favor and earthly blessing He has abundantly supplied. Thank Him for the gift of grace—divine ability that He poured out on your humanity.**

A Passion to Know

If you're not ready to pray about what is pressing in upon you, ready to burst forth into your understanding, then you're just not ready to do it.

In Mark 11:24, Jesus, your elder brother, is talking. He's trying to communicate something to you. *"Therefore I say unto you, What things soever ye desire, when ye pray, believe that ye receive them, and ye shall have them."*

What things soever you desire. A desire is a passion within you. When our daughter was in a coma, and given up to die by medical science, or at best, live in a permanent vegetative state, life and wholeness for her was a passion within us. Desire—that's what God waits for! "Who will bow their knee in such desire that I might open the heavens and reveal the day and time in which we live? Who has that kind of desire? My Son, Jesus, came; He gave all; He made provision for all! Will no one have such a passion in their heart?"

What things soever you desire. The Holy Spirit is passionate about this. There is something for you to know and to take hold of with Him in this scripture. The kings of ancient times learned to take what they didn't know and understand and lay it on the altar. They would bow their knee and hold that thing up to God and say, "Help me! Show me!" Then suddenly…the heavens opened and illumination poured forth, and they knew what they didn't know before. For those who bow the knee, the heavens open.

Heaven opens for those who have a passion to know. God says, "On My timetable of eternal things, in this place of timelessness, you can know." There are things you can know because it's simply time. If you're not ready to pray about what is pressing in upon you, ready to burst forth into your understanding, then you're just not ready to do it. The Holy Spirit needs your attention now. What do you desire? Let it stir a passion within you to know, to understand and to do!

DECLARATION: I declare over you that you cry out with a passion to the Father, for you desire to know what the Holy Spirit longs to show. Bow your knee to Him in prayer, and the heavens will open and pour forth understanding in Jesus' Name.

It is Finished!

As Jesus hung on the Cross, suspended between life and death, He uttered these words and breathed His last breath: *"It is finished!"* What a glorious victory was won as the Son accomplished *everything* the Father required of Him. Yet to those looking on, Jesus' death appeared to be nothing more than absolute defeat.

> *Faith is not what you can do; it is your belief in the Son and what He has already done.*

So often in your own life what you are facing or walking through "appears" to be your ultimate demise; and your senses—what you see, hear and feel—generally concur. *But* Jesus Christ made a way where there was no way. He *is* the way! *In Him* you live and move and have your being. (See Acts 17:28). You can do all things *through Christ.* (See Philippians 4:13). First John 5:4 says, "And this is the victory that *has overcome* the world—our faith." Your complete trust and total reliance on the Son of God *through* every circumstance is your faith in action. Faith is not what you can do; it is your belief in the Son and what He *has already done.* And the Son said, *"It is finished!"* (John 19:30).

Dear one, no amount of striving, straining or worrying is going to change your situation. Jesus was, is and will always be the way, the truth and the life *through* the tests and trials of this age. I encourage you to meditate on the Scriptures concerning your place *in Christ*, which is your spiritual position. I believe His words of life will buoy up your faith, strengthen your spirit and quell the sea of thoughts and emotions that rise up and try to distract and derail you from appropriating your triumphant standing. My prayer is for you to live *in* the victorious One, knowing that *"it is finished!"*

👑 **DECLARATION: I declare over you that you trust in the finished work of Jesus Christ, who has already overcome every battle victoriously, and that you surrender your propensity to strive and strain, for through Jesus the way has already been made.**

Pray for the Miraculous

Pray that the miraculous would come on through....

The Spirit of the Lord says to you, "Pray the miracles on in! They are waiting just out of sight for you. Both in finances for your nation and internationally, too.

"Pray, dear one! Pray that the miraculous would come on through, for you've seen only in part, but it has begun, and it is My heart."

"In medicine and in science, too, watch and see the miraculous discoveries that you hear about. Miraculous! It happens *now!*

"New stars they shall see. New planets, too. Do not fear the asteroids that they show to you."

DECLARATION: I declare over you that these prophetic seeings and knowings are becoming clear to you. In expectancy, you lift your voice and ask the Father for the miraculous to pour forth into the earth and upon all men.

The Evangelists are Coming

Evangelists shall seem to come out of nowhere in the days ahead. For it is true and it has been said, but now it's upon us.

A surge is coming to the Body of Christ worldwide. An evangelistic anointing will pour out on not some and not a few, but on a multitude, and they will run, run, run!

That evangelistic anointing will pour out on not some and not a few, but on a multitude and they will run, run, run!

They will lift the Lord Jesus high that all men would be drawn unto Him. Oh my, what a glorious sight! Angels on assignment to each and every one. Spirit of the Lord will instruct you on how to work with the heavenly host. It is the Word of God that they respond to. They wait upon your words, oh Church.

Then there will be those that God will send with His words. People will hear, and people will bow their knee. Nations and leaders will bend. Like on a great chessboard so it is and so it shall be—everything moving into place for the finality.

DECLARATION: I declare the evangelistic anointing will wash over you. It shall be in preparation for the time of the end.

You are the Prophet of Your Own Life

No one has more authority in your life than you.

You are the prophet of your own life! No one has more authority in your life than you. God has granted this liberty to you to choose Him—to choose life!

God wants you to know that He desires for you to take charge of your life. So often we leave the decisions and directions for our lives up to other people, to circumstances or to fate.

By the prompting of the Holy Spirit, I want to encourage you this day to realize the amazing person you became when you received Jesus Christ as your Savior. You became a God-child, a God-woman, a God-man. Radical, but true. You are not God, but you are like Him. A man, woman or child filled with God Himself. He came to take up residence in you when you were born again. With the help of the leadership of the Holy Spirit, there is absolutely nothing you can't do!

DECLARATION: I declare over you that the words you speak today will dictate your tomorrow. I declare that you will choose your words wisely to form and create what God says of you. Nothing and no one is responsible for your life; take responsibility and prophesy your own destiny.

Let the Sons Arise!

Revelation is pouring forth from the Holy Spirit to the people of the congregations in the cities of nations. The idea of you being a God-man and a God-woman is really true. It has been tiptoed around, and the religious spirits in us couldn't hear it, so we could not receive.

You can't think differently until you hook up with the One who thinks so magnificently.

God Almighty is in you! Why do you think there is anything you cannot do? If you think you can't do something, you won't. For your life follows your most dominant thoughts. You can't think differently until you hook up with the One who thinks so magnificently.

You are one with God. You are God's tent—His flesh. When you realize that Christ is in you, and the two have become one, you see that your body is like a glove for Him, and you are a carrier of His heart. God's heart is people.

A door is closing behind you, and a great one is opened before you. By the leadership of the Holy Spirit, just like Jesus had when He was here in the flesh in one man, God is here in the flesh in many men—His sons and daughters. This is a new sound to your ears. The new sound that comes is a voice of revelation from the Holy Spirit. Know that you are a son or daughter and not a servant.

Something has happened. You can hear God in ways you could never articulate before. With the new sound for a new place comes a new grace. It so positions you and opens up your understanding, that things become clearer to you than ever before. Eagles would soar, lions would roar…let the sons arise!

👑 **DECLARATION: I declare over you that you receive this new sound and the revelation that it brings. You are a son or daughter and not a servant. You carry the Christ wherever you go, and His power flows through you just as it did through Jesus.**

Your Gift Makes Room for You

"A man's gift makes room for him, and brings him before great men."
—*Proverbs 18:16, NKJV*

According to the Scriptures, your gift will make a place for you. You were purposed for this end-time, dear one, and there is a place for the gift that you are to fit. You don't have to be some star-spangled person to fulfill what is in your heart. You don't have to be some flashy preacher in order to receive from God. All you have to be is a son or daughter to God the Father who loves you so dearly.

He knows that before you'll be led by the Spirit outside the confines of your four walls, He has to take care of you personally. He has got to settle some things in your life so that you are freed up to tell people about Jesus.

Don't look at yourself and say, "I'm not this," or "I'm not that." You are what you believe. What do you believe? If you believe you are a son or daughter of the Most High God, then carry yourself like a son or daughter. You are going to believe what you know. How well do you know your Father and your elder brother, Jesus Christ?

The manner in which you know them and trust them and believe them will be the constant reflection of your life. I don't mean you won't have anything bad happen. Bad things come to everyone; it's what you do with the bad things that determines the outcome.

God positions you just where you need to be in this time, with all of the giftings and anointings He so purposed for you. They fit you so well and make a way for you now, and the Father is pleased.

👑 **DECLARATION: I declare over you that you receive the giftings and anointings the Father has purposed for you, and you are led by His Spirit to the place where you will fit perfectly.**

Forever Encouraging

There are many paths you can go down concerning the whys and why nots of things. But all that does is take your eyes off of the Father and the faithfulness of Him, and puts them back on yourself and your problem or situation. Your focus turns to the medical report that you or your loved one received, or the rejection you feel because you were

A good parent … makes the way for the success of his children.

divorced, or that you have never been married. These are things that Satan wants to beat you up with, yet your Father God doesn't even begin to touch such things with you. Your Father is forever encouraging you. A good parent does that. He makes the way for the success of His children. He doesn't tear you down, He builds you up.

See yourself the way God sees you. It will change your whole attitude, and you will start to talk differently. The more positive you are the more you are like your Father God.

Be encouraged today in God's view of you. Stay focused on the picture He paints on the canvas of your heart. Let go of the questions, and see and agree with the bright future He has prepared for you.

DECLARATION: I declare over you that the Father is forever encouraging you. He always sees you through no matter how it looks to you. I declare that you will change your view; see yourself through His eyes. Know that the Father is so pleased with you.

Rivers of God

This river of healings is here now for you!

There are rivers and flows of the Spirit that come forth from the throne of God. Rivers of healings run. There are rivers, too, that come out of the great plans placed inside of God's men and women. Your leaders have rivers inside of them, with great, extraordinary plans and things to occur. You must pray so that the plan of God inside the man doesn't get thwarted, stopped, stumbled over or diverted in some way.

The rivers of God wind around, move and flow, and the Holy Spirit will direct and help you draw out of the rivers as only He can do. He leads you in the way you are supposed to go, and gives you an avenue of expression for the anointings and the giftings that are inside of you.

At times a tributary forms, where the rivers converge and one flow moves into another. In the river of healings, things in bodies and in minds change and rearrange. This river of healings is here now for you! For those with cancer: I curse the very cells of cancer in Jesus' Name. The root, the source of pain, I uproot you. Depart, now! Disappear and dissipate! No more pain in Jesus' Name.

A healing balm I extend unto the family of you, where generational conditions would try to follow and weaken you. I take authority over the spirit of infirmity that would try to live amongst you and yours. I command it to depart. From the river of God there are healings now released, and restoration of people's hearts.

👑 **DECLARATION: I declare over you that you step into His healing river and receive all that you need. You are restored, refreshed and renewed by Him!**

New Family

The enemy is the one who tries to perpetuate the works of darkness, particularly through the lines of family. But don't you know the sinless, spotless blood of Jesus Christ has paid the price? You are in a new family, with a new Father—God Almighty!

The curse has been broken by Jesus Christ, your elder brother.

Satan has no legal right to continue to keep you bound. He whom the Son has set free is free indeed! Get a revelation of this truth and enforce it in your life. Be the one who breaks the cycle and no longer yields to the familiar. The curse has been broken by Jesus Christ, your elder brother.

I take authority over demonic activity that would keep you bound, controlled and manipulated by abuse and abusers. Spirit of addiction, lift! Be gone! In Jesus' Name, depart! You have no rights. You have no authority in the life of a believer in the Christ or his house. Depart from God's family!

👑 **DECLARATION: I declare over you that you will set yourself in agreement with the Spirit of truth. The curse is broken, and you are free indeed!**

Through the Door

The manifestations of God in your life will not be any greater than the fullness of God in your soul.

"**Do not earnestly remember the former things; neither consider the things of old....**"

—Isaiah 43:18, AMP

A great door of utterance and Holy Spirit ability has opened unto you, but you cannot go through to the glory of Jesus Christ carrying what you've carried in the past. You have to let some things go or you just won't fit through the door!

One thing you simply cannot carry and still expect to go on with God, is unforgiveness. You have to forgive, or you are going to be stuck. If you stay in the place where someone hurt you days, months, or even years ago, you keep yourself in a place of remembrance, and will end up repeating the same thing in every relationship going forward.

The manifestations of God in your life will not be any greater than the fullness of God in your soul. If your soul is stuck in a place of your remembrance, then you keep nursing and rehearsing that hurt. The Holy Spirit's idea is to reverse it, get it off of you and out of your way, so you can come through the door into the greater of God that awaits.

If unforgiveness has been keeping you stuck, I want to help you break the cycle today.

👑 **DECLARATION: I declare over you that you will choose to forgive. You will let go and no longer hold guilty and accountable that person, those people, that circumstance, that situation. That relationship will no longer have a part in your life. It will not control you. I pray that you set those people, that circumstance, and that situation free. I pray it off of you. You are free to go on. Mark it today, in Jesus' Name you have forgiven.**

Words are Like Seeds

Dear one, what you say is what you are going to get. This is a principle that was set forth into motion by the Creator Almighty. Every seed is going to produce after its own kind, it is law. Words are like seeds, so make sure you are planting seeds for the harvest you desire to reap in your life.

Your words pull things to you like a magnet.

The Holy Spirit can lead you even in what you speak! The more you know Him, the more you will speak like Jesus. If you think you can, you believe you can and you say you can, then you can! Nothing will be impossible for you if you believe and operate according to God's laws. You can believe and succeed!

Everything that has arisen has a solution, and the Holy Spirit will help draw the knowings you need up and out if you are speaking light and life over yourself. Your words pull things to you like a magnet. There are all kinds of laws in this dimension of the spirit, and you must be aware of them and learn how to operate in them. Creation began with words, continues with words and ends with words. What power you carry in your words! Use them wisely.

👑 **DECLARATION: I declare over you concerning words that have been spoken—words even from your own mouth, that would control and manipulate, steal your worth and your esteem—they are cursed, for they are not God's words. I pray that you forgive yourself for the words of doubt, destruction and death you have spoken over your life. You are free to move on, to have good relationships, good circumstances, and good situations to the glory of Jesus Christ.**

The Passion and Power of God

As you come into a greater knowing of the Person of the Holy Spirit through your fellowship of Him, you are better able to follow Him in His orchestration of the gifts of the Spirit.

You are a vital and valuable gift to God the Father and to the Body of Christ. I am stirred to encourage you about moving with God the Holy Spirit in His gifts. He desires to flow in demonstration upon your life so He can manifest God's love and power to and through you to the people you come in contact with every day.

Romans 8:14 says, *"For as many as are led by the Spirit of God, they are the sons of God."* Notice a son of God *follows* the Spirit of God. As you come into a greater knowing of the Person of the Holy Spirit through your fellowship of Him, you are better able to follow Him in His orchestration of the gifts of the Spirit.

It helps to understand that the nine gifts of the Spirit are not separate from the Holy Spirit, they *are* Him! In the time you have come into, there is a marked increase in the gifts of the Spirit in the Body of Christ, particularly in the revelation and power gifts, because they are so demonstrative of the passion and the power of God on behalf of the people.

It is time for the gifts of the Spirit to come forth in greater measure, and the avenue they will come through is *you* as a believer in Jesus Christ. Be encouraged that the stirrings you experience concerning the seeings and knowings of things are from God. I pray you would respond to these promptings, and become increasingly comfortable and confident moving in them, giving the Holy Spirit liberty to flow through you on behalf of family, friends, neighbors, and even strangers. Expect it!

DECLARATION: I declare over you that a greater manifestation of the Holy Spirit and His gifts operates in and through your life! You will flow in gifts of healings, working of miracles, gifts of faith, revelation gifts, the word of wisdom concerning a person's future, the word of knowledge concerning their past and the discerning of spirits, which is the ability to see angels and demons. The gifts of the Spirit operate through you at God's command, and people are helped, healed and exceedingly, abundantly blessed.

Time of Anticipation

It's harvest-time in the earth! This is the time our Father has looked toward with great anticipation since the beginning of time. James 5:7 says, *"...Behold, the husbandman waiteth for the precious fruit of the earth, and hath long patience for it, until he receive the early and latter rain."*

The outpouring of the Holy Spirit has begun falling like rain in all the nations of the world.

The precious fruit of the earth, *souls*, are being gathered into the Kingdom as never before. In these last days, I believe we will see entire cities born again in a single day, just as in the Book of Acts. What an exciting time to be alive!

The Spirit of God is deeply impressing your hearts concerning the time and the season in which you live. The outpouring of the Holy Spirit has begun falling like rain in all the nations of the world. You are in a time of great anticipation, but also a time of patience, staying steady with your Father God, and accepting only those experiences in the spirit which line up with His Holy written Word.

I am a witness to the supernatural power of God in healings, deliverances and the infilling of believers with His Holy Spirit. What an awesome sight to see God the Holy Spirit moving among His people! Every time people receive the Lord Jesus, rejoice along with the angels in Heaven, knowing this is the greatest miracle of all!

DECLARATION: I declare over you that you receive the outpouring—rain in the time of the latter rain. You anticipate His mighty power in demonstration. You follow the Holy Spirit in His wonderful workings: healings, deliverances, miracles, and above all, salvations!

The Orchestration of God the Holy Spirit

...In an atmosphere rich with His presence, the Holy Spirit speaks and reveals the Father's heart, and it changes yours.

It is a glorious thing to witness the magnificent orchestration of God the Holy Spirit! The many facets of the Almighty One are spectacularly displayed in glory, power and grace. It is wonderful! For in an atmosphere rich with His presence, the Holy Spirit speaks and reveals the Father's heart, and it changes yours.

In His presence, such a Spirit of seeing and knowing illuminates your understanding of His plan for you corporately and individually, too. Suddenly, miraculously—by the Spirit of wisdom—you have a knowing of what to do. A place of great depth and width and height you cross a threshold over into, where destinies become ever-so clear. In His glorious anointing, pain in bodies, addictions, and demons have to go. Minds are made clear and broken hearts are made whole.

Suddenly these things are, because there is a momentum and increase coming from God to do what must be accomplished. The Holy Spirit is imparting His ability to all of you for the days you have come into, for Jesus is coming quickly!

DECLARATION: I declare over you that Heaven is coming closer to Earth, and the manifestations of God the Holy Spirit are increasing upon you. You flow in them, you see in them and you know in them.

The God of the Supernatural

It is your Father's heart that you be uplifted in your spirit and soul today. God—the Creator of the universe, the One who knows the end from the beginning, the One for whom *nothing* is impossible—is working *all things* together for your good!

He is the God who will never leave you nor forsake you....

The world would have you think and believe all hope is lost. But why would Christians listen to the world? The world doesn't know God. The world doesn't know the God of miracles, the God of supernatural provision, the God who provided manna in the desert, water from a rock, who fed His prophet meat morning and night by the mouths of ravens in famine, who opened the heavens to bring forth rain. He is the God who will never leave you nor forsake you, *and He is your Father!*

I tell you with all boldness by the Spirit of grace: *"Fear not (there is nothing to fear), for I am with you; do not look around you in terror and be dismayed, for I am your God. I will strengthen and harden you to difficulties, yes, I will help you; yes, I will hold you up and retain you with My victorious right hand of rightness and justice"* (Isaiah 41:10, AMP).

👑 **DECLARATION: I declare over you that you receive Him as the God of the supernatural that He is. There is nothing He cannot do. The world will know that He is God, and there is none other beside Him.**

You Will Come Through

"Dwell in the land and feed on His faithfulness."
—Psalm 37:3b

Something so big of God is moving into position, and the enemy would love nothing more than to delay it through distracting circumstances. Try as he might, he cannot stop the plans and purposes of God from coming to pass.

I encourage you to do as Psalm 37:3b says to do: *"Dwell in the land and feed on His faithfulness."* Stir yourself up and put yourself in remembrance of what your Father has done for you, what He has done in the Old Testament and New, and of all He has promised you. He is faithful, and He will come through. In Jesus' Name, so will you!

DECLARATION: I declare over you that God's plans will prevail, and that you will stand your ground and declare and decree the Father's faithfulness to you.

The Secret Place

Your Abba, Father has created a secret place for you where His character, His presence and His virtue abide. God's invitation to you is expressed in Psalm 91:

His invitation is for you to come to Him.

"He who dwells in the secret place of the Most High shall remain stable and fixed under the shadow of the Almighty (Whose power no foe can withstand).

"I will say of the Lord, He is my Refuge and my Fortress, my God; on Him I lean and rely, and in Him I (confidently) trust!"

—Psalm 91:1–2, AMP

Your Father is beckoning you to come. He has provided your every need. All provision is found in His presence. If you have a need, please don't wait for God to come to you. His invitation is for you to come to Him. He loves you so!

👑 **DECLARATION: I declare over you that you receive His gracious invitation and you accept. You will come to Him, for He has provided all that you need in Jesus Christ, His Son.**

The Power of Repentance

Your prayers of intercession truly do make a way for the captivity of the bound to be turned!

It is on my heart to write to you about the power of repentance. I pray as you read these words today, that God the Holy Spirit will quicken you to pray most effectively concerning the destiny of those who do not know your Lord. Believe for a great deliverance of souls from the power of darkness, and for their glorious translation into the Kingdom of His dear Son. Your prayers of intercession truly do make a way for the captivity of the bound to be turned!

At the Apostle Paul's Damascus Road conversion, Jesus sent him forth to the Gentiles for this purpose: *"...to open their eyes, in order to turn them from darkness to light, and from the power of Satan to God, that they may receive forgiveness of sins and an inheritance among those who are sanctified by faith in Me"* (Acts 26:18, NKJV).

Know it is your Father's heart that all men be saved and come to the knowledge of the truth. In the Name of Jesus Christ, repent on behalf of those who have not believed in the Son of God. Your intercession on their behalf makes a way for sin to be forgiven and captivity to be turned. Today is the day of salvation!

👑 **DECLARATION: I declare over you that you pray the convicting power of the Holy Spirit would fall and rest heavily on those who are separated from the Father and have not received Jesus as Lord and Savior, evoking repentance in each heart. Command the god of this age to loose the minds of those he has blinded and kept bound. Eyes be opened! Eyes of the heart see! Souls be set free, in Jesus' Name it is done!**

Know the Season

Just as I do, I am sure you can sense a remarkable change in the pulse of things in the earth. You have been brought into a *new time* and a *new place* in the spirit. It is here and now that the giftings and anointing abiding in and upon you will be drawn by the Holy Spirit up and out into manifestation. In the season you have come into, you will have to make some choices to allow the Spirit of God to draw upon these giftings inside of you. Will you choose to go the way of God in this new season? Will you choose Jesus Christ and not yourself? Do you truly understand that it is not about you, but about *Him,* and about the multitudes who don't yet know Him?

Begin to reach out more than ever before, expending your energy and your love to make a way for those who will walk through eternity's door.

It is time to reach out now—beyond yourself—into your community, to the people all around you. Begin to reach out more than ever before, expending your energy and your love to make a way for those who will walk through eternity's door. You have but a short time, for it is the season of your Lord's return!

DECLARATION: I declare over you that you know the time and season that is upon you, and you choose Jesus Christ and not your own way. I speak the blessing of the Lord over your sphere of influence. May there be a supernatural increase over all that concerns you. You are blessed to be a blessing! I declare that the favor of the Lord opens doors of opportunity for you to walk through to share of the Savior's love, of His power to save, and of His soon return!

A Supernatural Supply

You must recognize the season God the Holy Spirit has brought you into, and be willing to change with it.

Something new has begun! Just as things begin to change in the natural when it's time for the seasons to change, there are changes in the spirit, too. Though the date marking the passage from one season to the next doesn't necessarily mean the leaves have all fallen off the trees, or that buds have burst forth after the long, dormant winter; you can see and even sense that certain events are connected with different seasons. You must recognize the season God the Holy Spirit has brought you into, and be willing to change with it.

Many of you have gotten comfortable doing what you've been doing, which has been good and has been God. But the Holy Spirit is giving you new marching orders! He says, "I'll give you supernatural comfort when it seems what I'm requiring of you is uncomfortable in the natural. There is grace equipping you for the race ahead of you!"

You are never without a supernatural supply from God Almighty! He is with you and in you, seeing you through in all that you pray, say and put your hand to.

DECLARATION: I declare over you the grace you need to change. What seems uncomfortable and new, suddenly becomes easy with a supernatural supply of His grace.

Seeing and Saying

God uses a learning gate that is so vital to us both in the spirit and in the natural, and that is the eye gate, the gate of seeing. Since the beginning in Genesis, and all the way through His Word, God does a great deal to get our attention to show us things so we can see and believe they shall come to pass. The Holy Spirit will paint a picture on the canvas of your mind, and you will see exactly what He sees, so you can pray and ask that of Him.

The Holy Spirit will paint a picture on the canvas of your mind, and you will see exactly what He sees, so you can pray and ask that of Him.

In the Book of Ephesians, Paul prayed that we would have *"the Spirit of wisdom and revelation in the knowledge of God."* Wisdom and revelation are the seeings and knowings of God. When He shows you something you see it, and then you know it. You can see something and have a passion for it, but it is the Word of God spoken concerning it that brings forth faith upon it. Faith is going to cause what you see to come to pass, because faith is released in your words.

Be encouraged this day that the vision you have seen, the one that burns within you, this thing you see and you say, by God's grace and for His glory, it all comes to pass.

👑 **DECLARATION: I declare over you the Spirit of seeing and knowing is operating in you, and you speak and release words of faith over what you see. You thank the Father for bringing to pass the glorious vision He has painted on the canvas of your mind.**

Moves of the Spirit

History reveals much about the outpourings of God, and shows us we are ripe for revival and harvest!

God is a God of order. When He purposes to pour out His Spirit upon the earth, it is always in step with events in the natural realm. History reveals much about the outpourings of God, and shows us we are ripe for revival and harvest! Notice anytime there is a World War declared, something huge happens spiritually for the Body of Christ in the United States that spreads to nations beyond.

At the turn of the century, the Holy Spirit was poured out as never before in the history of our nation. On New Year's Eve He visited a Bible school in Topeka, Kansas, where the students found scriptures on speaking in tongues, came together, and said, "We ought to be doing this if it is true." Suddenly it spread to Azusa Street, and from the West Coast to the East, our country was aflame with the Baptism of the Holy Spirit. For 10 years people came from all over the globe to partake of this glorious gift, and the outpouring spread worldwide. As the movement began to wane, World War I broke out in 1914, with full U.S. engagement three years hence.

On the heels of World War II, the healing revival swept the U.S. Thousands were healed, and tens of thousands were born again, bringing restoration and life to the Church and nation. Then in 1967, The Six-Day War broke out in Israel, while simultaneously the Charismatic Renewal was underway. God fell on all denominations in the U.S. We were engaged in The Gulf War, Operation Desert Shield and Desert Storm in the early '90s, followed immediately by a visitation of the Spirit. The Holy Spirit touched a man in South Africa named Rodney Howard Brown, and sent him to the U.S. to awaken the Church. He stirred up our joy that we might be quickened again by God's presence. Finally, our country declared a War on Terror in 2001, following the attacks on the soil of our beloved America. Now, the last outpouring of the Holy Spirit presses in and is ready to burst forth upon us. Always God goes before to make ready a people who will lead. He makes a way! Make no mistake about it, the times and seasons are in your Father's hand, and the final outpouring of His Spirit is at hand.

👑 **DECLARATION: I declare that God will pour Himself out on your nation once again—one last time before the end!**

Deep Truth Revealed

God will show you things before they are, and it is deep truth. There are those things you can change; there are those things you can affect; and there are those things you can only prepare for. As it was with Noah, he couldn't stop the flood, but he could prepare for it.

"He revealeth the deep and secret things: He knoweth what is in the darkness, and the light dwelleth with Him." —Dan. 2:22

In Zechariah 6, five angels came into the earth. One commanded, and the other four were for the four directions of the planet: north, south, east and west. The four rode out and then came back to the fifth horseman, and said, "This is what we have seen; this is how it goes for man."

When I looked I did see armies wanting to move. I knew and had understanding of Special Forces, for just months before the Holy Spirit revealed about a drop that would come in North Africa. Special Forces went into Somalia and had to back off. Then they went in near Syria and had to back off. Just recently they went in and got the man they wanted.

There are secrets and mysteries sealed that are to be unsealed and opened up over cities, leaders and nations. *"He revealeth the deep and secret things: he knoweth what is in the darkness, and the light dwelleth with him"* (Daniel 2:22).

Sometimes you come to a place in prayer that is so big. It is something that will affect more than just you, your city, state or even your nation; it's something worldwide, and you've got to get in there and pray. It was this way for me when in a church service I started to pray for something concerning an attack. I saw weapons and I said, "There's movement; there are automatic weapons." It has something to do with Alabama, but it's not in Alabama." But I couldn't get there in prayer. Later, we would hear on the news that one of the leaders of the terrorist group that attacked a mall in Africa was from Alabama, and that was the connection. A year before the attack, God was showing us and asking us to pray. He will ask you to dig and mine things out in prayer so you can effect change, protect and preserve life, and bring His plans to pass.

DECLARATION: I declare over you that you follow the Holy Spirit into places of prayer. By His grace you will speak to things that are revealed. In prayer you will make a way for God's will and plan to come to pass for man.

Your Words Create

For some things you have to get words out there so things can start to form....

While ministering in Canada, I suddenly turned, and said, "This is what I see: It's your Prime Minister and our President. They are meeting behind closed doors." No one knew of this meeting. It was before the recent air raids in Iraq. But the Holy Spirit knew, and He said, "Loose the wisdom! Give them wisdom! Keep it secret! Give them wisdom as they collaborate to do this thing." So I simply said what I heard Him say.

Three days later I was home, and it was announced that the Prime Minister of Canada and our President had met behind closed doors, quietly, to discuss this thing. Only the Pastors and the people of that congregation heard me say these things.

For some things you have to get words out there so things can start to form, because words create. Your words create! What you say is so, now! Understand this truth, and give voice to what the Holy Spirit knows and shows. What you see and say can make the difference and bring change.

DECLARATION: I declare over you that what the Holy Spirit shows you in prayer, you will say and declare, so He has access to move and form what is spoken.

First-Name Basis

The Spirit of God sees and knows all things. Unless the light of revelation comes, you won't know Him like He wants you to know Him. *"That I may know Him, and the power of His resurrection, and the fellowship of his sufferings, being made conformable unto his death"* (Philippians 3:10).

> *Unless the light of revelation comes, you won't know Him like He wants you to know Him.*

In times of prayer and fellowship with the Holy Spirit, He reveals more of Himself each time you allow Him to. He reveals His nature, His graces and His desire to draw nearer to you. As I was in prayer, the day came when the Holy Spirit drew near unto me. "Mary Frances," He said, "When I speak to you, do I call you, *The* Mary Frances?" I said, "Why no, Holy One!" "Then why do you address me as *The* Holy Spirit each time we fellowship? I am Holy Spirit." I said, "Oh my, Holy One. Why have you never told me this before?"

From that day on, when I fellowship with Holy Spirit, He becomes nearer and dearer to me every day, as we are now on a first-name basis. Revelation comes, and the light of His Holy presence will also flood your soul as you listen and hear Him call your name. Holy Spirit wants to be on a first-name basis with you, too.

👑 **DECLARATION: I declare over you that you have ears to hear Holy Spirit call you by name. As He draws near to you, you in turn will draw nearer to Him than ever before. For He longs to fellowship and talk to you everyday, pouring His nature and graces upon you, for He has many things to reveal unto you.**

Blessings in Obedience

Now is not the time to draw back, but to press out of your humanity into His divinity!

In Deuteronomy Chapter 28, the Lord speaks of the blessings of obedience and the curse of disobedience. As you obey the Lord your God, you have many blessings promised to you. *"The Lord will bless everything you do and will fill your storehouses with grain. The Lord your God will bless you in the land He is giving you. The Lord will send rain at the proper time from his rich treasury in the heavens to bless all the work you do"* (Deuteronomy 28:8; 12a, NLT).

I encourage you to remain focused on your end-time destiny. Things are lining up with the plan of God. With God all things are possible! As you stay true to what God has placed within you to do, you will experience supernatural living. Proclaim what the Holy Spirit has spoken to your heart. Release your faith and receive it as yours, for it belongs to you! There is much for you to do, and it is by your fellowship with Him that you will be encouraged to believe all that He has so lovingly promised you.

If God has placed desires in your heart, they will certainly bring increase and blessings into your life as they are accomplished. It is God's plan for you to operate out of His divine overflow. He freely gives you all you need to fulfill what He has put in your heart to do. Now is not the time to draw back, dear one, rather it is time to press out of your humanity and into His divinity! God the Holy Spirit dwells within you with resurrection power to cause the impossible to be possible for you! Expect change. Expect things to be rearranged. Continue to prophesy your destiny by the Word and Spirit of God. Get ready for the demonstrations of God in your life and family. He has equipped you for the work of the ministry of Jesus Christ!

DECLARATION: I declare over you that you will choose to be obedient to God in everything you think, say and do. Press into God as you never have before and Holy-Ghost power will be released. Things change! They are rearranged—supernaturally—in Jesus' Name!

Born Again for Success

The presence of Almighty God invades a place. He is the Spirit of glory, power and grace. The Holy breath of God comes in, and in His presence wisdom is given. Questions are answered. Lives are delivered. Healings are manifested. Pain in hearts, souls and bodies is removed.

In every arena of your life, let His glory be.

There are wonderful times in His presence to be had. In every arena of your life, let His glory be. You are the Kingdom of God that has come into the earth through Christ Himself. The Spirit of the Lord has taken up permanent residence in you. Jesus said that *all authority* and *all dominion* had been given to Him, and then He turned and said, "*You go* in My Name!" Use your authority. Use your dominion, or Satan will.

Always remember, you were born again for success. Of all the people who will find their way, it will be you, because you are a son or daughter of the Most High, and the light has come and the glory of the Lord is upon *you!*

DECLARATION: I declare over you that in the Father's glory everything is changed; souls and bodies are rearranged, lives are delivered and hearts are made like new. It is all because of Jesus! You demonstrate this glory as a son or daughter, and all men will be drawn unto Him.

Disappear and Dissipate

No one walks in any more power than what he believes.

God wants you so sure in your place of authority, that when you speak, even the winds will obey you. Jesus said we will do what He did, and He did a lot of talking to the elements. You have the authority to command things to dissipate and not be.

When storms are brewing and threatening the life and property of you and your family, you tell them, "Disappear and dissipate!" Don't just tell them not to hit or come near you, because that storm is swirling around trying to find a place, so you've got to tell it to cease.

How is it possible to talk to the wind? Because we have a miracle-working God, and He gave us authority through His only begotten Son. No one walks in any more power than what he believes. Demons know if you truly believe, and they will push it.

What do you really believe? What do you truly expect? That is exactly what you are going to get. You are going to walk in whatever you decide to believe of the Word of God. Fellowship with the Holy Spirit until you are so sure of His character and of how to move with Him in every situation.

👑 **DECLARATION: I declare over you that you will know your Father and His limitless power. He has given you authority over all the power of the enemy, and that includes storms. You speak to inclement weather and command it to disappear and dissipate in Jesus' Name, and it must obey.**

Going Over to the Other Side

Discouragements and delays have a way of testing what you truly believe. You have come through the floods and through the fires only because of Jesus Christ and the leading of the Holy Spirit. Even in the most difficult of times, God is with you, speaking to you to assure you and to tell you how to get to the other side of every difficulty.

The Holy Spirit will encourage you, comfort you, counsel you and give you the wisdom and truth you need in the middle of the storms of life.

Jesus told His disciples in Mark 4:35, as they got in the boat at the end of the day, *"Let us go over to the other side."* Of course a storm rose up, and everyone thought they were going to perish. But Jesus was fast asleep with His head on a pillow! The disciples, alarmed at their circumstances and riddled with fear, woke Jesus up. The Lord rebuked the storm, the winds and the waves ceased, and they proceeded to the other side as Jesus had declared from the beginning of the journey.

I want you to know today, that no matter what it looks like, you are going over to the other side. That may not negate the storm or the hard things you may walk through, for this planet is cursed. Though you are redeemed from the curse you are not immune to it. When the curse gets on you, speak to it. The Word of God has told you that legally you are free from the curse; therefore, it has no right to you or your household.

The Holy Spirit will encourage you, comfort you, counsel you and give you the wisdom and truth you need in the middle of the storms of life. Jesus made the way, and the Holy Spirit will show you the way and lead you through. You are going over to the other side!

👑 **DECLARATION: I declare over you that you speak to the curse when it entangles you, and tries to keep you from fulfilling your destiny. You are going to make it through and over to the other side in Jesus' Name.**

No Division

In all of His utterance, the Father, the Son and the Spirit agree.

"That there should be no schism in the body; but that the members should have the same care one for another."

—1 Corinthians 12:25

I have learned something about the voice of the Spirit of God. He never ever brings division. The Holy Spirit does not do that. Division and schism can come from man's decision over his interpretation of what the Spirit of God has said. The Word of God will divide rightly for you concerning the voice of the Spirit, both spoken and written.

The Holy Spirit says there is no division in His voice. In all of His utterance, the Father, the Son and the Spirit agree. They are in unity, and that is how it should be for you and me.

DECLARATION: I declare over you that you will not allow strife and division between yourself and any member of the Body of Christ. Just like the Trinity, agree in a spirit of unity.

Rooms and Realms

There are many rooms in the spirit that you are welcome into. I believe when there is a visitation of the Holy Spirit, He opens realms to you. A room in the spirit can be like a realm in the spirit. Realms are where you gain understandings, where revelation comes unto you, and you are welcomed into these places.

Realms are where you gain understandings, where revelation comes unto you....

The two words, room and door, are apparently very important to the Father, for they are so often used in Scripture. Very significant events take place in rooms: the Passover meal was held in a room. The Day of Pentecost occurred in the Upper Room. To enter a room you come through a door in the natural realm, and it is this way in the spirit realm. Concerning these places in the spirit, the Holy One showed me the Prophet Elijah—a type of the Christ, and his successor, Elisha—a type of the Church. God had directed Elijah to anoint Elisha in his "room"—in the place of the prophet. The Holy Spirit was already planning, positioning, securing and making ready for what was to come, just as He has done for you with His own Son for this time you are in.

Time was created for you. It's a place—a realm. Paul said in Second Corinthians 4:18, *"That which you cannot see is greater than what you can see."* Know that there is more than what you see in the natural. There are places, doors, rooms and realms in the spirit for you to access. The Holy Spirit takes you into places with Him, and opens up revelation to position you, to give you understanding of the time, to secure you and prepare you for your going forth at this time of the end.

DECLARATION: I declare over you that the Holy Spirit is opening up rooms and realms of the spirit to you and giving you wisdom and revelation so you can see. He positions you, secures you and prepares you for this glorious time.

The Latter Time

... The Spirit of God is taking you into greater understanding and revelation of the Christ.

The early Church in the Book of Acts went everywhere and spoke the Name. The revelation they walked in was a former revelation, and that is what you have been carrying thus far. But you are stepping over into the latter time, which is the greater.

As you step on over into this latter time—the latter rain—this latter position of the Church, revelation is coming to you that is greater concerning the Name of Jesus Christ. You will respond differently, you will speak differently, you will do differently and expect differently, because something of the Spirit of God is taking you into greater understanding and revelation of the Christ.

Greater shall it be now for you, for you have crossed over and stepped into the latter time, and the greater is about to begin!

** DECLARATION: I declare the Scriptures say the latter shall be greater than the former. Expect the greater to flow now for you; greater wisdom and revelation of the Christ. Greater in every area of your life.**

Ask Me for the Grace

Some time ago, the Holy Spirit began to wake me up in the middle of the night, and I could hear myself preaching Jesus. I had never really gotten to do that, but I could hear myself doing it down in my spirit. I'd get up out of bed, trying not to wake my husband, and tiptoe to the bathroom mirror to see myself preach about my Lord. But when I got there, my reflection just stared back at me, and nothing would happen. This went on night after night, week after week.

I have watched the atmosphere change as God the Holy Spirit comes upon the words spoken of the only begotten Son.

I wanted so badly to be able to say what I could hear myself saying in my spirit. Then one day the Holy Spirit said to me, "Ask me for the grace to speak of Jesus the Christ."

And then it began. I think it is my happiest place—the expression of the Christ—to be able to speak of Him in all that He is. I have watched the atmosphere change as God the Holy Spirit comes upon the words spoken of the only begotten Son. Suddenly, everything takes on a different hue. Everything begins to change because you speak the Name.

Ask Him for the grace, and the grace shall be given! A great grace arises in the hearts of the sons and daughters to preach the Christ! On the bus, on the train, on an airplane, in the marketplace, on the street corner. You'll challenge the very system itself with His Name. You'll speak the Name and the atmosphere is charged, for your voice causes the molecules to shatter. Your voice is the voice of the Creator's son or daughter. This is the time that you've dreamed of. This is the time you've waited for.

Will you speak it? Will you proclaim the Christ and all that He is? Will you continue? Or will you hesitate? Oh, no more, dear one, shall it be that way. You're going forward another way. It's going to be very different now for you. Nothing is going to be the same. He brings you into a place, and stirs you to the very core of the fiber of your spirit. He proclaims and declares to you that things are like new. He takes hold of your destiny and your provision, too.

DECLARATION: I declare over you that you have the grace to speak of the Christ. You will proclaim His Name and the works that He does. You'll not be ashamed, but bold and sure to show and tell of your Savior.

Speak of Jesus

Be the light that you were born to be. You are a force!

A time has come like never before to speak of Jesus at every opportunity. Work His Name into your conversations wherever you can. Make it a point to find out if people know Him. Most people say, "I'm a Baptist," or "I'm Methodist. I'm a Catholic, a Presbyterian or a Lutheran."

That's religion and denomination; that has nothing to do with relationship. When someone responds that way, Jesus Christ is not his or her Savior and Lord. Help them to know Him. Be the light that you were born to be. You are a force!

Love will compel you to the lost. God's love in you will send you beyond the walls of the church, outside the confines of the mind, of religion, of ministry, of opinions about yourself and others, past the doctrines of men and the opposition of the enemy, to the very heart of those He died to save. Tell what you see and know of Him, and demonstrate His power wherever He sends you.

DECLARATION: I declare over you that you will speak of Jesus with everyone you meet. The Holy Spirit will help you to see and know if they believe, and give you words to help them receive.

Drawn Into Destiny

G od waits for you to come and walk with Him—to sit with Him every day—right where you live. He has things to share with you, and things for you to do that He longs to tell you.

Satan reminds you of the past, while all of Heaven is trying to draw you to your destiny.

When the word of the Lord comes to you, things begin to turn for you, but if things from the past are allowed to live on, then little by little, you will be overcome by what used to be. Satan reminds you of the past, while all of Heaven is trying to draw you to your destiny.

Please, no longer look at what was not. Look into the eyes of the Christ, and be led on into what the Father has had for you before the universe began.

I take authority over things that have controlled and used you. I take authority over such, and I cut the cords of connection to people, past relationships and experiences that are holding you back from your destiny. Be free, in Jesus' Name.

DECLARATION: I declare over you that you look into the eyes of your Lord and not to remembrances of the past. Ungodly cords and connections are now broken, and you are free to move forward into your destiny.

Get Up Over It

In all of your dealings in life you have to get up over the situations in position and authority and address them from your seat in the heavenlies.

When I tell someone to "get over it," I mean it. What I want is for a person to get up in vista and view over whatever is bothering him or her. Get over and above that thing which so provokes. Don't stay low, because then that thing has got the upper hand, and it controls and has dominion.

Even God Himself does not control your life. You say, "Lord Jesus, You just be in control of all my life." But He says, "No, you make decisions for your life out of My Word and out of My Spirit's leading."

In all of your dealings in life, you have to get up over the situations in position and authority and address them from your seat in the heavenlies. From that place you will be clear to hear from God the Holy Spirit. Desire Him to take hold of the very Word He authored and pierce your heart with it. I want your hearts to be pierced and to arise to a new level in God that you haven't known. To experience Him in such a way in the presence around and within you, that you are keenly aware of what you have never known before.

Suddenly you are astute. Everything is acute to you. Everything is razor sharp. When you walk into a place, you are very much aware of more than what you can see, because suddenly you understand that what you can't see, is greater. You call to the unseen to become the seen. You do that; you were born for that. No one else on Earth can do it but you!

👑 **DECLARATION: I declare over you a revelation that the unseen is greater than what you see. You will rise above situations and circumstances to declare and decree what will be. You will speak from your place of authority in the heavenlies.**

Prayer Changes the Atmosphere

Concerning the lives of others, there are things you can do to help them to choose rightly. You must understand that a person has the liberty and the freedom to choose what he or she will. Your prayers take things out of the way so that a person can better choose. However, you cannot control anyone. When you see someone walk away and do what he or she never should have done, even though you prayed, you cannot take the responsibility for his or her choice.

"For we wrestle not against flesh and blood, but against principalities, against powers, against the rulers of the darkness of this world, against spiritual wickedness in high places."
—*Ephesians 6:12*

Prayer changes the spiritual environment or atmosphere momentarily around people, so that they can better understand and choose, but *they* still have to make the choice. You can't live someone else's life for them, or force them to choose the right way, but you can pray and bind things. You have to move with the Holy Spirit and follow His leadings in prayer. You are a mighty force. You first have to believe this for your own life, or you aren't going to make a difference and stand up and fight for someone else's life.

Hell knows people, and familiar spirits know how to push all the right buttons to get people off track. But you know Jesus Christ, and you know the Word of God. You're going to have to really know Him like the sword of the Spirit that He is, and wield the Word skillfully in the place of prayer in these last days.

DECLARATION: I declare over you that you will clear the air in prayer, and change the atmosphere around hearts and minds so people can better choose the Christ and the ways of God for their life. You pray the Word and follow the Spirit in the place of prayer, and He always leads you into victory.

A Way has Been Made

… The Holy Spirit has already been where He is leading you now!

Change is upon you! Great change in the Church, and for the world. The Father's heart is always to go before you and prepare the way in times of transition, to anchor and steady you from within when everything outwardly is shifting. *Know that the Holy Spirit has already been where He is leading you now!* He knows your future better than you know your past!

What is the Holy Spirit leading you to do? Where is He directing you to go? Have you been stuck in a place not moving forward and unable to step into the new; not free to be who God has created you to be, or to do what He has created you to do? He makes a way for you now by the Spirit of grace. *His ability* moves you into a new place! Yes, change brings with it the new and different for you; the unfamiliar and uncomfortable, too. But when you yield to God the Holy Spirit as He prepares and positions you for your place, upon you will rest an abundant supply of His mighty grace!

 DECLARATION: I declare over you that the Holy Spirit is leading you forward through and into places He has already been. You are released and free to move with Him into the new. An abundant supply of His great grace rests upon you this day and makes a way where there was none before.

Don't Give Up

I don't ever want you to think that because things are not going smoothly, that you have missed God. There are times in life where you have to face opposition, particularly in the time *Don't let difficulties deceive you!* you have come into. For the things that are going on in your life right now, I want you to understand that just because it is hard and you are not seeing what you want to see right away, don't give up on what is in you to do.

If you allow your circumstances, time constraints, lack of friends, lack of support, or lack of finances to convince you that you are supposed to abandon what you have carried in your heart, then you are laying down the destiny that God purposed you for in the earth. Don't let difficulties deceive you!

Many people look at the difficulties and assume that is God telling them they are not supposed to do thus and so. Don't do that to yourself, or to God. Some of you weren't even supposed to be born—yet there you are! Some have been so challenged along the way it ought to be over for you, but you're still standing. No one should have any confidence in you—but God does.

If you keep looking at what *you are not* instead of who He says *you are,* then you will never ever do a thing. You've got to have more fight in you than that. If something isn't going the way you think it would have or should have, pause and talk to the Holy Spirit. But don't give up or think you have missed it because it doesn't happen the way you envisioned it. Sometimes the way you envision something is out of your own self and not out of God's vision. Just because the packaging looks a little different than what you thought, doesn't mean it isn't God.

No matter what it looks like in these last days, keep moving, unless God stands in front of you and says, "Stop!" Don't let circumstances, situations or lack stop you. God will make it very clear whether to take a left, a right, to keep coming or to halt. Be encouraged today that God is for you, and He is always positioning you for success!

DECLARATION: I declare over you that you will not allow contrary circumstances to dictate the Father's will for you. You will stay true to the vision He's placed in your heart, and in Jesus' Name, you will finish what you start.

God's New Firebrand

You frustrate your grace and you weary your faith by not being in your place.

Many people have been hidden by the hand of God in preparation for the time you have come into. You have wondered why you had so much inside of you, and why you have put up with so much for such a long time. It is because of the call of destiny upon you, and the dream of God inside of you. Destiny isn't something elusive that you are always trying to get to; destiny is something that you are!

Dear one, you frustrate your grace and you weary your faith by not being in your place.

Some of you have been so frustrated. Perhaps you have misunderstood your place. Some people are starters, some are builders and others are finishers. If you think you're one when you're really another, then you frustrate your grace and you certainly weary your faith. It's a time to know the Spirit's voice and not assume or presume anything.

God Almighty starts to bring forth His new firebrand. Be ready for changes. You were born for this time; the greatest time in history!

DECLARATION: I declare over you that by the unction of the Holy Spirit you will know your place and understand the giftings you carry. You are a blessing wherever you go. God keeps you busy with the joy of your heart. You will work as unto the Lord, to His glory and to your Father's honor.

Change of Seasons

Dear one, you have begun to experience a change of seasons. The Bible says, *"While the earth remaineth, seedtime and harvest, and cold and heat, and summer and winter, and day and night shall not cease"* (Genesis 8:22). I believe just as there are seasons of weather, there are seasons of time in your life. The different seasons on Earth can be compared to the seasons in your life, and each has a specific purpose. Some are seasons of preparation, some are planting seasons, and others are times of harvest.

> *"While the earth remaineth, seedtime and harvest, and cold and heat, and summer and winter, and day and night shall not cease."*
> —*Genesis 8:22*

Some seasons are short and others last longer, but I believe the seasons of your life are divinely ordered. Acts 14:17 says that God, *"gave us rain from heaven, and fruitful seasons, filling our hearts with food and gladness."* In this scripture, the word "seasons" is plural, meaning more than one. By this verse, I believe all the seasons of your life can be fruitful.

I encourage you to make every season in your life a "fruitful season." If you are in a time of preparation, do all that you can to equip yourself to fulfill your destiny. If you are in a season of sowing, sow with purpose in faith. Wherever you are on your "seasonal calendar," purpose to receive all that God has for you during this time.

DECLARATION: I declare over you by the Holy Spirit that you will have understanding of the time and season in your life. You are led by the Spirit and know when and what to plant, where to sow and how to harvest. He guides you through every season, bringing you to fruitful fulfillment in Jesus' Name.

Changed in the Glory

"But we all, with open face beholding as in a glass the glory of the Lord, are changed into the same image from glory to glory...."
—2 Cor. 3:18

God the Holy Spirit is speaking to His Church for what is about to be, and in some places, has already begun. He wants you to have an expectation and to be stirred in your heart, poised and ready to move with Him in this hour. What is coming? *The glory! The manifested presence of God!*

He wants you to experience His glory! In His glory, *anything* can happen, and does—prophecy, visions, miracles, signs and wonders—magnificent manifestations of God the Holy Spirit!

In the Old Testament, the manifested presence of God saturated Moses for 40 days, changing his countenance until his face shone so brightly with the glory he had to cover it with a veil. This time, the glory will not only shine on you, but will shine *through* you. In the New Testament, Paul writes of the glory: *"But we all, with open face beholding as in a glass the glory of the Lord, are changed into the same image from glory to glory, even as by the Spirit of the Lord"* (2 Corinthians 3:18).

You are changed into His image in the glory! When you received God the Son, Jesus Christ, as your Lord and Savior, God the Holy Spirit took up permanent residence in you. God the Holy Spirit is the Spirit of glory. You are a vessel that has been permeated by His divine presence! You now carry a knowing of Almighty God, a revelation of Jesus Christ, and the power of His Holy Spirit everywhere you go.

👑 **DECLARATION: I declare over you that the glory of God will change you to become more and more like Jesus Christ! You are ready for God's glory in manifestation and demonstration in you, upon you, to you and through you!**

Pursue God Through Prayer

I am so grateful for the fellowship we have been granted through the avenue of prayer. Prayer is simply giving voice to what is in your heart and in your Father's heart. Your supply of the spirit is vital to the plan of God for your life personally, and for God's plans that are unfolding in the earth.

It is your Father's heart to give you understanding of the time you are in.

Be encouraged to pursue God through prayer in a greater dimension. You can stir yourself up in the things of God, and be hungry and thirsty to know God through His Word and by His Holy Spirit.

Things are changing so quickly now, and as His son or daughter, He desires to speak to you of things to come. He says through the Prophet Jeremiah: *"Call unto Me and I will answer you and show you great and mighty things, fenced in and hidden, which you do not know, do not distinguish and recognize, have knowledge of and understand"* (Jeremiah 33:3, AMP).

It is your Father's heart to give you understanding of the time you are in. Stay quiet before Him, and lift your heart in worship and adoration to Jesus Christ. The One who is faithful, trustworthy, loyal, incorruptible and steady, will reveal, unveil and unfold what is hidden. He will open unto you the understanding you require for this hour.

☙ DECLARATION: I declare over you that your heart will passionately pursue God through prayer. You will call to Him, and He will answer you. By His Holy Spirit He will reveal, unveil and unfold hidden mysteries and open your eyes to see, know and comprehend in this time of the end.

Be Fully Persuaded

You must walk by faith in such a way that the unseen becomes the greater of worlds to you.

As the leaves were falling in Nashville, and their rich colors dotted the landscape, I watched in the natural realm as one season was preparing to move into another. Know, dear one, that you are moving spiritually now from one season to the next in the time of church history.

God the Holy Spirit is sweeping through congregations in the cities of nations asking every believer: "What do you *really* believe? How sure are you of the Jesus you call Lord, and of His redemptive works?" It is unaffordable not to be fully persuaded!

Galatians 4:4, tells us, *"...when the fullness of the time had come, God sent forth His Son...."* You have entered a fullness of this time, and you must be fully persuaded that all God has spoken to you through His Word and by His Spirit is so. You must walk by faith in such a way that the unseen becomes the greater of worlds to you. Be fully persuaded to call those things that be not as though they were...*because they already are!* Though you can neither see nor feel what you believe, be fully persuaded that they are so because God *said* they are so. His promises are true—how persuaded of them are you?

👑 **DECLARATION: I declare over you that you trust your Heavenly Father! What He says is true, and you are fully persuaded that what He promised, He shall do.**

You Rule and Reign

"God disarmed the principalities and powers that were ranged against us and made a bold display and public example of them, in triumphing over them...."

—Colossians 2:15, AMP

It is your right and responsibility to stand in your purchased place and give voice to God's Holy Word.

The position you have been granted as a believer in the Lord Jesus Christ is one of authority! In a grand display of His power, Almighty God stripped the enemy of his rule over you. He has been overruled by the Greater One who now dwells in you by the power of the Holy Spirit! Satan *has been* defeated! Jesus *has risen* victorious over death, Hell and the grave! By the Name of Jesus—through faith in that Name: the only name under heaven by which men might be saved—you now rule and reign with your righteous King!

It is your right and responsibility to stand in your purchased place and give voice to God's Holy Word. When you do, angels hearken to perform what you utter, demons scatter, and a way is made for the will and plans of the Father to be made manifest on Earth.

👑 DECLARATION: I declare over you that you will speak and command, declare and decree according to God's Holy Word. You give voice to the Word of God, and angels hearken, demons scatter and God's will is performed.

No Fear Here

Make time for the Holy Spirit, because if you don't, circumstances and situations will fill that time.

Dear one, let God the Holy Spirit direct you at your first awakening. Where in the Word does He want you to study with Him? What does He long to show and open to your understanding today? What verse would He take you to? Where are you inspired to turn? Learn to follow Him through the Word that He authored, and then let Him direct and speak to you from there.

Make time for the Holy Spirit, because if you don't, circumstances and situations will fill that time. The devil wants to take your time. He wants to steal your joy. He wants to take your time from the Third Person of the Trinity, weaken your faith and give you fear. Fear is an entity! It is an alien to you. Fear wants to defeat you; kill you if it can. Rob you if you let it. *You* have to declare and you have to decree the way it will be by the unction of the Holy Spirit, but you'll have to meet with Him first.

DECLARATION: In Jesus' Name, I declare over you: "No fear here! No fear in you! No fear in your life! No fear in your health! No fear in your wealth! No fear in your business! No fear anywhere or in anything concerning you!" (2 Timothy 1:7).

You are a Voice

You carry in you the power of eternity! Everywhere you go the atmosphere changes because of the life of God that abides on the inside of you. When you have made the Word of God your meditation, the words you speak impart life, health and faith—the power of possibility.

People in your life need to hear from Heaven.

You are a voice in the earth in this hour! Your friends, your family, your co-workers, all need a word from God. Your police chief, your mayor, your governor, your congressmen and your senators need a word from God. People in your life need to hear from Heaven, and you carry the sound and words of life they must have. You are a voice!

All of creation hears you. That is why when you speak, body parts will form, bleeding will cease, tumors will recede, cancer will die. It hears you. Your voice is hallmarked because you are a son or daughter of God. You are a believer, and your voice has taken on the embossment of the Christ.

Only the sons and daughters of the Most High can carry that word out into the marketplace, into the government, into the family and extended family. Only *you* can do such a thing!

👑 **DECLARATION: I declare over you that you carry within you eternity, faith, and the power of limitless possibility. Your voice will have a sound and all things will hear and respond. They must obey when you speak in the Name and the authority thereof. You will carry this sound to the people you meet, and they will hear from Heaven.**

Mighty Army Arising

Marching are you to the sound of your Lord, the Chief Commander.

I hear the sound of a mighty army arising. For a great awakening of Christ's Body throughout the whole Earth has come. Marching are you to the sound of your Lord, the Chief Commander.

Daniel 7:27, declares our end from the beginning, *"And the kingdom and dominion, and the greatness of the kingdom under the whole heaven, shall be given to the people of the saints of the most High, whose kingdom is an everlasting kingdom, and all dominions shall serve and obey him."*

My prayer for you today is for the Holy Spirit to anoint your ears for the new sounds that God is bringing down; sounds to lead and direct you in this time.

DECLARATION: I declare over you that you will awaken to the sound of your Lord, commanding His army to arise. Your ears are anointed, and your heart is receptive to heavenly sounds that are coming down.

What Do You See?

The Spirit of God is your teacher. He will teach your mouth what to say, and show you what to do if you will listen to Him, watch Him, and then follow. He will often say to me, "Mary Fran, what do you see? Declare and decree My mercy." He has taught me to declare what He shows me.

Say what you see, for the Lord is ready to perform His Word!

We have entered into the time of seeings and knowings. What do you see? Over what are you to declare and decree God's mercy?

God said to Jeremiah in 1:11, *"...Jeremiah, what do you see?"*

Jeremiah answered, *"I see a branch of an almond tree"* (v. 11).

Then the Lord said, *"You have seen well, for I am ready to perform My word"* (v. 12).

My Father asks of you, "What do you see? What you say you see, I perform! Your words will not return void to Me! Oh, what do you see?"

The seeings and knowings of things you have entered into as never before. The demonstrations of God are upon you, and nothing will ever be the same again. Say what you see, dear one, for the Lord is ready to perform His Word!

DECLARATION: I declare over you that you see with eyes of faith and declare what God says is to be. The words you speak will not return empty and void, for the substance of faith causes God to perform.

The Power of Possibility

... God brings His supernatural upon your natural!

It is God the Holy Spirit who opens your understanding of the Word that He authored. The very Word that framed the worlds, also frames your world. What power is released through the spoken Word of God! The power to produce, to create, to change and rearrange; to call things into divine order as they were designed to be by the Creator Almighty. When you give voice to the living Word of God, it brings His supernatural upon your natural! It turns your impossible into possible, and makes a way where there was none before!

When you were born again, it was God the Holy Spirit who revealed Jesus Christ to you. Jesus is the door you came through to partake of all the Father purposed and prepared for you. You have done well to confess the Word you have believed, but it is your relationship with the living Word Himself that will carry you through the hardships of life.

When you know the character of your Father, of your Lord, and of the Person of the Holy Spirit, then you draw a tremendous assurance out of that relationship. Without fellowship, your confession of the Word is just works.

Let there be fellowship with your Lord, and you will find it easier to receive by faith what you believe of the God of the Word.

DECLARATION: I declare over you a greater revelation of the power and purpose of your relationship with the God of the Word. By your fellowship with Him will He supernaturally sustain and carry you through what seems impossible for you!

A Revelation of the Christ

Such a glorious revealing, unfolding and unveiling of the Word were given to John the Revelator on the Isle of Patmos. In Revelation 19:11, the heavens opened, and John saw Jesus sitting astride a white horse. What a magnificent sight to behold his victorious King

Know Him for who He is—for He is faithful to you!

arrayed for battle! John called the righteous judge: "Faithful and True." Dear one, wherever you find yourself today, and whatever you might be facing, I would say to you: *"Know Him for who He is—for He is faithful to you!"*

What is your need? What doors have been closed and seemingly locked to you? What provision has been delayed? What symptoms persist? He is the God of the impossible, and it is His delight to care for you. His mercies are new, His provision is abundant, His supply is limitless, His timing is perfect. Call upon Him who is mighty to save, to heal, to deliver, and to bring you all the way through. His Name is Faithful and True!

May you see and know the Christ for who He truly is, and may you be so awakened by and consumed with passion for your Lord, that nothing shall by any means move you. Arise now as the son of God that you are, in the power of your King, and for His honor and glory, for the whole Earth awaits!

DECLARATION: I declare over you a revelation of the Christ in all of His glory! And unto you I declare an abundance of all that He secured for you: supernatural provision, wholeness in body, soundness of mind and limitless possibility. Arise in the authority of Your King and His Kingdom!

Believe You Receive

...There must be a receiving on your part of what you have believed.

There is so much of God for you to experience. You will have all eternity to come to know the many facets of Him. The more you know Him, you will find that you just want more of Him! One thing I have learned about the Creator Almighty is that, *"God is not a man, that he should lie; neither the son of man, that he should repent: hath he said, and shall he not do it? or hath he spoken, and shall he not make it good?"* (Numbers 23:19–20).

Whatever it is you are believing for from your Father, be it healing in your body, restoration for your soul—the mind, will and emotional part of you—for breakthrough in your finances, or direction for your life, there must be a receiving on your part of what you have believed. Jesus said in Mark 11:22–24, *"...For assuredly, I say to you, whoever says to this mountain, 'Be removed and be cast into the sea,' and does not doubt in his heart, but believes that those things he says will be done, he will have whatever he says. Therefore I say to you, whatever things you ask when you pray, believe that you receive them, and you will have them."* Until you reach forth with your hand of faith and *take* what has been so miraculously secured for you, you have not received it. For when you have received, then you can move into a place of thanksgiving for what your Father has already done.

When you truly receive what you have believed, your heart yields tremendous gratitude to your Father, to the Lord Jesus Christ, and to the precious Holy Spirit. Words of gratefulness deepen the relationship between you and the God of Heaven. He loves to hear the sound of your heart toward Him, whether written, spoken or in song, thanking Him each and every day. Receive what you have believed, and cross over into a new place of thanksgiving to Him.

DECLARATION: I declare over you that you have faith that believes *and* receives what it believes! Gratitude now fills your heart with thanksgiving, and you express your gratefulness to Him in new ways every day.

Doors Have Opened

It is a new season, dear one. In this time we have come into, such wonders of God shall be unto you and me. I declare: "In the world of the spirit in the heavenlies, holy doors open, extending great mercies. In the world of man, doors of unusual opportunities and provisions

See yourself as the eternal person that you are!

have opened for you. Out of your great Kingdom authority in the Name of Jesus Christ and by the power of the glorious Holy Spirit, you shall keep what is so miraculously given!"

Your Father God has secured every spiritual and earthly blessing you will ever require or desire. (See 2 Peter 1:3). Through your knowledge of Him, by your fellowship with Father, Son and Holy Spirit, and through the revelation of who you are, you will walk in the fullness of all God has purposed and prepared for you. Your position in Christ is one of authority and dominion on this earth. From God's Kingdom within you, you rule and subdue what is of this world. His Kingdom has come, and of His government there shall be no end. (See Isaiah 9:7).

See yourself as the eternal person that you are! For with a Kingdom perspective of your place and position, you will pray differently, you will think, talk, walk and do differently. Doors have opened, and everything changes now.

👑 **DECLARATION: I declare over you that you will take the royal place and position purchased for you by Jesus Christ, and you will walk in your Kingdom dominion and authority everywhere you go.**

The Fruit of Faithfulness

"But the fruit of the Spirit is love, joy, peace, longsuffering, kindness, goodness, faithfulness, gentleness, self-control."
—Galatians 5:22–23, NKJV

There is always a contending in the spirit for the plans of God to come to pass in your life. When your heart is so full and the desire so strong to do what the Holy Spirit has given you to do, the waiting can seem so long.

All the while God is preparing you for your specific place, and preparing a place and a people for you. Trust in His timing, and rest in the grace for each moment, for He takes such care to prepare. Faithfulness is staying true to what the Father has shown you. Staying with it no matter the cost. The faithfulness of your heart cannot be denied. For all the time—even years—that you've stayed so determined and true, where you remained and saw things through—God saw you, too.

He now activates what has been dormant on the inside. The Holy Spirit stirs up what has been there all along, because now it's time.

DECLARATION: I declare over you an activation of what has seemed dormant and gone. Now you will stir up once again the desires the Father placed in your heart, for you know the time has come for you to start.

Be Unstoppable!

When things don't go the way you thought they would or should in your life, there is a temptation to become discouraged, to give up or to quit. Don't you know that is what the enemy wants for you? But the Father has made every provision for you to overcome and to come on through. Jesus won the victory for you!

Put your head down and go on through; don't let anything deter you!

The devil will do anything he can to stop you. He'll do anything to stop the giftings and anointings that you carry. I know this to be true. I encourage you right now, wherever you may be today, whatever has happened or has yet to be, just put your head down and go on through; don't let anything deter you! As you speak the Word and follow the Spirit, you are unstoppable!

You are free to do what is in your heart to do. It is the thief who comes to steal, kill and destroy. (See John 10:10). Don't let him destroy or steal from you. What God has ordained before time itself is upon you.

DECLARATION: I declare over you that you resist discouragement that would weaken and deter you from fulfilling your destiny. You will not stop and you will not quit. You are coming through just as Jesus did. He won the victory for you!

The Place Called There

Supernatural provision was God's way in that place called "there."

There was never "a day of miracles," for miracles have always been, and are for every day. But, there are sounds now coming forth that would bring you into an awareness of the miraculous. There are leadings from the Spirit of God that you must consider. He leads you to the place called "there."

"There" is where the prophet had to hear. He had to hear to go "there." The prophet was told to go to a place in the time of famine, and that God Almighty would give the supply in most unusual and supernatural ways. A brook would flow when there was no water in the land. Ravens would come with food that they normally would eat themselves.

Supernatural provision was God's way in that place called "there." You must expect it. Supernatural things will be around and about those who go with expectancy wherever the Holy Spirit leads.

👑 **DECLARATION: I declare over you that you follow the sound of the leading of the Holy Spirit. Believe and expect a supernatural supply of provision to flow wherever He sends you.**

Your Part of the Promise

The Holy Spirit caught my attention with something in Psalm 91, in *The Amplified Bible*. *"He who dwells in the secret place of the Most High shall remain stable and fixed under the shadow of the Almighty, whose power no foe can withstand."*

All the promises of God require something from you...

Notice that "dwelling" starts with you making a choice. A decision on your part must be made to take your place in His presence. Have you ever noticed that all the promises of God require something from you? I have found that even though "God has said," you have to war for the fulfillment.

The promises of God are not automatic; you have a part in believing and receiving what the Father has so lovingly provided through the Son and conveyed to you by the power of the Holy Spirit. Have a fixed determination today not to miss out on anything that has been provided for you. Do your part to dwell in His presence, and receive the wonderful blessings the Father has promised!

DECLARATION: I declare over you that you decide to dwell, live and abide in Him at all times, and the promise of His divine protection will keep you. You will contend for all He has written and spoken, and will believe the fulfillment is yours.

Obtain the Victory

Your victory isn't in just your hearing… you must hear and do in order to obtain the victory.

Dear one, concerning the things you are believing, some manifest immediately, and others you might not see right away. However, those things are still yours because they are in your heart. I know people who get upset with God when things don't just "happen." But you must consider that your victory isn't in just your hearing—as wonderful as that is; you must hear and *do* in order to obtain the victory.

You must hear and study the Word for yourself, but if you don't do what you are hearing, either the written Word or the inspired Word of the Holy Spirit to you, then you can't get upset with God about that. *Only doers of the Word have the victory.*

Jesus Christ won, so you win! You have the victory, you have the ability in Him, but you have to do something with the victory and the ability. You have to do whatever it is the Holy Spirit is directing you to do.

👑 **DECLARATION: I declare over you that you are a doer of the Word and not a hearer only. You do what the Holy Spirit directs, and the blessings of God flow to you.**

Hear Our Sound

You, the Church, take up your spiritual weapons of warfare, for Jesus the King is soon to return. Each of you must declare and decree who you are in the Christ. You carry this passion every place you go.

We are here to do what You ask us to do.

Dear Father, hear our sound: in music, in song and in the beat of our heart. In silent prayer and cries to You whispered in the night: hear our sound. Be it loud or be it soft: hear our sound! We are here to do what You ask us to do.

Let Your fire and anointing fall on us, O Royal King. Your sons have chosen to battle conditions, situations and weather, too. We let nothing stand in the way of our worship of You, and our hearing of the decrees that come from Heaven straight from Your heart to ours.

Your presence upon us in this moment causes us to see and know Who You are and who we are—a people with wisdom beyond our years, and power beyond that of the greatest force known to man. We arise in this knowing and are on the march to fulfill Your command; hear our sound!

👑 **DECLARATION: I declare over you that a sound arises from Earth to Heaven in response to Him. It's a sound of worship, praise and thanksgiving. It's the sound of His army arising and assembling.**

Unity of the Spirit

"Endeavoring to keep the unity of the Spirit in the bond of peace. There is one body, and one Spirit, even as ye are called in one hope of your calling..."
—*Ephesians 4:3–4*

All peoples, nations, tribes and tongues shall hear of the only begotten Son before the end does come. There will be those that gather in this battle from other camps of influence and leaderships it's true. For out of different camps and denominations will come those who will hear the call and catch the fire, too.

This thing of unity that the Body of Christ has tried to do, will suddenly come upon you as the fire does fall upon this city and that city. Cities of believers will come together, and they will intercede for souls to be won. People from all denominations and non-denominations too, will gather in the Spirit of unity. Some will even gather in stadiums, and together in unison, they will worship the Christ.

It is a wonderful thing to see, and it can only be done in the unity of the Spirit and not by the flesh. Man has tried to bring different peoples and denominations—Christians one and all—together, and it hasn't worked. But now it will, because something awesome, wonderful and miraculous has begun by God Himself.

You are a force to be reckoned with! Hell will not take the souls of men. For you are on the march now, and you wear your armor well. It blinds, it so gleams and shines with the holiness of God. It blinds the demons as you pass by. Multitudes, multitudes! Decisions will be made, and the Body of Christ will ride together, because soon and very soon there shall be the return of your King!

DECLARATION: I declare over you that the unity of the Spirit is coming upon the Body of Christ. It will create a mighty force of resistance against the enemy. Believe and agree you will experience divine unity, because this is how God said it will be.

The Government of God

Here you stand in the corridor of the time of the end. It is a time for the government of God to rule and reign in and through each individual divinely bound together by love. *"Of the increase of his government and peace there shall be no end,"* (Isaiah 9:7). Christ's government is the power to rule oneself according to His Holy written Word, and to be a living demonstration and testimony of His love and grace in the earth.

Christ's government is the power to rule oneself according to His Holy written Word....

At the same time you are learning to walk in your liberty in the Christ, something else is trying to take form. A one-world church is on the rise. Satan is always perverting the things of God. When God brings a Spirit of unity to the Body of Christ, then Hell steps in with a very charismatic leader and says, "Let's all meet under one roof, for we are all of one faith. We will call it the *One-World Church*."

That is not going to work, for that is not what God is about. That is not what unity looks like. Be aware of the time, dear one, and let not any enticing words deceive you. The Word and the Spirit divide all things for you—know them well for the time you have come into.

DECLARATION: I declare over you that the sword of the Spirit, the Word of God, divides all things for you. The Spirit of truth will lead you into only what is right and of the light. A oneness there will be, but only by the Spirit of unity.

Generation of Prophecy

What was spoken of you and this day, is coming to pass....

What a magnificent time it is to be on the earth! It's a glorious time in church history, and the history of the world. It's a time when the blessed Holy Spirit pours Himself out upon you. In the ancient times, there were visions and dreams given to the prophets and they spoke out what was to be, but the fulfillment of what they saw and said was not manifested in their time. It's as if prophecy gets fused to time. Time continues through a matrix of generations, and when it comes to a particular generation, the utterance that is fused to the time for that generation, is released.

Things foretold have been kept for this time. You are the generation of prophecy. What was spoken of you and this day is coming to pass, and will continue until your beloved Lord comes and calls for you. You will hear the sound of the horn, and suddenly the righteous ones will be no more. *Suddenly!*

The prophets of old looked into and inquired of this time. Sometimes they didn't even have words to describe it, though they tried. For the glory, the power, the miracles and salvations will culminate into something so grand upon and through you! You are the generation that they saw and said, declared and decreed would be. Here you stand at the threshold of all that is ready to burst forth upon the earth. You are in the matrix of the end time, and so now the prophecies come forth. It's wonderful, and it's time!

👑 **DECLARATION: I declare over you that, just like Jesus, you are of a generation that has been foretold. The fusing of time and prophecies that has come, and the releasing of the words and their power, rests upon your generation for this final hour.**

Break the Seal

In Daniel 12:4, *The Amplified Bible*, an angel appeared to Daniel the Prophet and gave to him prophecies, visions and knowings of things he had no understanding of, but was obedient to do. Many times you will hear things you don't have all the understanding of yet, but if you are obedient in receiving the word of the Lord, the Holy Spirit will give you understanding. Only with understanding can you have belief and faith for the end-time revelations that are given.

"But you, O Daniel, shut up the words and seal the Book until the time of the end...." —*Daniel 12:4, AMP*

It was given unto Daniel to scribe, to write these things down, and to seal them up. There are certain catalysts within the matrix of time that catapult out those prophetic utterances to a particular generation. You have come to such a place in the matrix, where it is the time of revelation for an end-time generation. *"Then many shall run to and fro and search anxiously through the Book, and knowledge of God's purposes as revealed by His prophets shall be increased and become great"* (Daniel 12:4b, AMP).

The things written of in Daniel, which have been sealed for thousands of years, *now* are being made known to you! Daniel heard but did not understand. He asked, *"O my lord, what shall be the issue and final end of these things?"* (v. 8). *"And he, the angel, said, 'Go your way, Daniel, for the words are shut up and sealed till the time of the end'"* (v. 9). The Holy Spirit said to me concerning the seal spoken of in Daniel, "Break the seal!"

The secrets and mysteries that have been held—graces and information that He can bring revelation upon—have been sealed and held for now, for the time of the end. I know, because the Word tells me so. The seal over end-time revelation is broken now for you. The word of the Lord comes forth, and is revealed by His prophets. It shall be increased and become great, for a window has been opened for the prophetic voice for end-time positioning and purpose!

DECLARATION: I declare over you concerning the knowings, prophecies, visions and eternal end-time revelations that have been broken open in your generation, and I release the Spirit of wisdom and understanding to fulfill your destiny and God's purposes.

The Prophetic Voice

...Prophets are not an echo, but a voice!

The words of the prophets launch you into destiny. Their utterances come from Heaven to ignite you, position and catapult you into a place as the end-time generation that you are.

In the natural, when you consider spaceflight, there are launch windows for rockets and different crafts. A launch window is a time period where the vehicle must be launched in order to reach its intended target.

In the spirit there are windows—prophetic windows—and launching times even for the Body of Christ. At the appointed times, God brings in voices to speak. For prophets are not an echo, but a voice! You are in the time of the prophetic voice, and God positions prophets to speak and say to the Body of Christ and to leaders of nations so that things will be altered, turned, changed and prepared for.

It is the time of the voice. It is happening now. It has begun. Things are being said, and things are being done, all to the glory of the Son.

DECLARATION: I declare over you that you hear and receive the prophetic utterances sent to position and prepare you for end-time events. You believe His prophets, and you shall prosper. (See 2 Chronicles 20:20b).

Timeless One

It is a defining time in the earth. As never before, there is a coming together of things in the spirit and in the earth, and all is becoming acutely defined. What stirs in my heart in this moment is *the Kingdom*. The Kingdom of God is within you! It is all around you! I want you to be ever-mindful that abiding in you is the power that transcends time, causing the eternal part of you to be timeless. You were born again out of a place of timelessness. Who you really are—spirit being; the immortal, eternal part of you—existed in Christ *before the world began*. (See Ephesians 1:3; 2:10).

> *The way to live in the system without being dominated and controlled by it, is to speak the language of the Kingdom.*

You came into the earth with the plan, purpose and destiny of the Creator upon your life; but every step of the way in walking out His divine plan is a choice on your part. The Kingdom of God is invisible; it is not something you can see, *but the demonstrations and the manifestations of the Kingdom of God through you,* the whole world can see. This Kingdom that you are constantly moving through and are immersed in on Earth is one of revelation and dominion. You need to know and believe this, or you will be a citizen that is subject to the world's system, and it will become the greater, because it is what you will think about, talk about and believe. Though you must live in the world, the system is not to control you. *The way to live in the system without being dominated and controlled by it, is to speak the language of the Kingdom.* Your vocabulary must be Kingdom speech. You say what God would say—all day. The language of the Kingdom is faith. What you believe and say is what brought you into the Kingdom, and it is the way you must continue to operate.

Make the determination today to live Kingdom-minded, for it will change everything for you.

👑 **DECLARATION: I declare over you the power to walk in the dominion and the demonstration of the Kingdom, and to operate as a timeless one, who lives and moves from the Kingdom of God within you!**

Have Faith in Your Dream

...The things of God are to be contended for, bathed in prayer, spoken, declared, decreed and agreed with....

It is my desire to encourage you today, and to stir up in you the dream Father God put in your heart. What do you carry inside of you to do? Is there a place the Holy Spirit has branded upon your heart, or a people that you long to reach? A ministry to birth or a business to build?

Ephesians 2:10, in *The Amplified Bible*, declares, *"For we are God's own handiwork (His workmanship), recreated in Christ Jesus, born anew, that we may do those good works which God predestined (planned beforehand) for us, taking paths which He prepared ahead of time, that we should walk in them, living the good life which He prearranged and made ready for us to live."*

What God has purposed for you is *good,* and, it's already *in* you! But, as with all the things of God, it is going to take faith to bring your dream to pass. Know this: the things of God are to be contended for, bathed in prayer, spoken, declared, decreed and agreed with, and in the fullness of time, they *will* come forth.

Don't let the dream God put in your heart die. Have faith in your dream! I know for some of you, situations and circumstances have dimmed your dreams and desires. For others, so much time has passed since that dream burned bright, that you have almost forgotten it. Remember that God is not in time; He is the eternal One. He lives in you; therefore, eternity lives in you, and you are not limited by time.

Dare to dream, dear one! Believe that you will see your dream through to its fulfillment, for this is where your Father already sees you!

👑 DECLARATION: I declare over you the resolve to see the dream in your heart come to pass. Renewed strength is released now for you to pray out, speak out and walk out the dream your Father has given to you!

Seeing in Prayer

With a prophetic place in prayer, come the giftings and equipment to see. Often I speak these things out when I pray. I release this Spirit of seeing unto you this day. It is necessary now for you to see and know and to pray, because of the time you have come into.

It is the wisdom of God that He would go before events and say who you are in Jesus Christ.

The Holy Spirit will lead you in the place of prayer, opening up to you what He knows and desires to reveal. As you are faithful to pray and say what He shows you, events that can be affected and changed will rearrange in Jesus' Name. Other events are going to happen; you can only prepare for them. Discernment I release unto you, so that you will know the difference.

It is the wisdom of God that He would go before events and say who you are in Jesus Christ. He speaks to you of the force that you are—the resistance force in the earth—so that you can pray and speak, declare and decree, and bring hope and salvation to those in your family, community, your nation and in nations beyond. He stirs the Church to awaken, and to arise to her place in prayer. For the fight is in the spirit, so that is where you must do battle.

You make an eternal difference, dear one! Take your place and resist the things that would try to devour you, your house, your city and the multitudes who do not yet know your Jesus.

DECLARATION: I declare over you that you will receive the impartations of seeing released unto you. You will operate in a greater measure than you did before. You step up in prayer, in utterance, in wisdom, in revelation and in discernment to make a difference in the course of events and eternities.

Knowings in Prayer

When the Holy Spirit reveals what has been concealed, it is for you to see, to know and to pray.

In praying for leaders, as the Holy Scriptures direct you to do, you will often be taken to nations and events that are taking place. When the Holy Spirit reveals what has been concealed, it is for you to see, to know and to pray.

If the Spirit of God brings up a matter that you have already touched upon in prayer, then the matter is not settled; and therefore, it requires your attention. Follow the leading of the Holy Spirit in prayer, for He is the Spirit of truth, and He knows all things. He communicates these knowings to you, and shows you what to do. As you give voice to His promptings concerning what He makes known to you, He will give you the understanding and the words to say as you pray.

God the Holy Spirit is very specific. He speaks of people, places and events. He reveals plans, shows faces and exposes enemy maneuvers hidden under the surface. He highlights weaknesses where the enemy plans to strike and destroy. By His leading, you speak to those knowings and command them to be exposed. Strengthen, fortify and pray protection over people and places that are being threatened. The Holy Spirit is your magnificent teacher, helper and guide in the place of prayer, and He can be trusted.

Believe you receive this impartation of knowings that I carry, and you will increase in your seeing and knowing in prayer. A marked difference you will see, and notable fruit will follow. Give voice today to what the Holy Spirit reveals, and you will hinder, delay, stop, thwart and expose plans once concealed.

👑 **DECLARATION: I declare over you, by the direction of the Holy Spirit, that you step into the knowing necessary to pray for events being planned in your land. You lift your voice and make a decree concerning lives and destinies, and expose and reveal what was concealed.**

The Fellowship of His Presence

God has much to say to you and much to impart. He is always making a difference for you. It is magnificent to know God— what you do know of Him. It seems like just a thimbleful compared to what you will come

... The fellowship of Him can be every moment.

to know of Him. Every day is greater than the day before as you lend yourself to the magnificence of the fellowship of His presence.

There is a difference between relationship and fellowship. You can have relationship with someone and think about them from time-to-time, yet not have the opportunity to see them and actually spend time with them. So different is the way of God your Father with you. You have relationship with Him through Jesus Christ, but the fellowship of Him can be every moment.

You can acknowledge God all day long as you go about your day. It is your choice. The fellowship of His presence makes all the difference. It is magnificent to have an awareness of His indwelling presence, the ability to talk to Him, share ideas with Him, to hear His voice gently leading you, directing and even correcting you. You can have relationship with someone but never enjoy that relationship because it requires a tangible fellowship. You can have relationship on paper, in legal document and contract, but if you never move beyond that to enjoy a person's presence and fellowship, then something is missing.

It's the same with the presence of God. He's ever-present. Enjoy the fellowship of His presence this day. Things will change for you, and they will never ever be the same again.

👑 **DECLARATION: I declare over you that the presence of God changes your heart; it changes your mind. It affects your affections and turns them to Him.**

Healing of Tumors

...If you have a lump, a bump, a tumor or cyst in this moment of time—suddenly—your God visits you.

The Holy Spirit reminded me of how He sweeps through among the peoples and all lumps, bumps, cysts and tumors seem to go right out the door. Suddenly, they are no more.

This anointing I carry, and want to release upon you. So, if you have a lump, a bump, a tumor or cyst in this moment of time—suddenly—your God visits you. Oh please, won't you receive? Just lift your hands and let Him visit you, and suddenly what was on you, will be no more.

There shall be a difference. I trust my God. I know He's true, and I know He visited you. What was there is changing now, and soon will be no more in Jesus' Name.

DECLARATION: I declare over you in Jesus' Name that you receive the anointing released in this moment of visitation. In His Name you believe and receive. In His Name you are changed!

Take of Mine

As you gather around the Name of the Son to worship and adore Him, God the Holy Spirit takes what belongs to the Father and communicates that to you. I love *The Amplified Bible* translation of John 16:14, *"He (the Holy Spirit) will honor and glorify Me, because He will take of (receive, draw upon) what is Mine and will reveal (declare, disclose, transmit) it to you."*

"… The Holy Spirit will honor and glorify Me, because He will take of, receive, draw upon what is Mine and will reveal, declare, disclose, transmit it to you."
—*John 16:14, AMP*

It is by the power of the Holy Spirit that you receive all the Father has secured for you through the blood of His Son, and it is in His manifested presence that the anointing touches and changes you: spirit, soul and body. In Luke 4:18, Jesus declared and demonstrated that the Spirit of the Lord was upon Him, anointing Him to preach, heal, deliver and set the captives free. In the anointing, confusion of mind will suddenly find clarity of thought. Mind binding spirits have to lift as they did in the ancient of times when the Holy Spirit came upon the prophet, the priest and the king. Spirits of addiction, and foul things, too, will lift from people in the presence of God. The brokenhearted ones, who are torn so deep in pain, so suddenly will experience the hand of God mending what was torn in two. Sickness and disease quakes in His presence; it cannot remain in bodies when He comes in His glory to each and every one.

This glorious presence He transmits to you, receive of His anointing, healing, clarity, deliverance and liberty. "Take of Mine," the Father says, "I did this for you."

👑 **DECLARATION: I declare over you that you will take what the Father has given you. Receive it by faith. Everything changes and rearranges. In His manifested presence, you cannot stay the same.**

Christt the Healer

God's truth is that Jesus Christ, your Lord and Savior, is the Healer, too.

I want you to know today that the glory makes everything all right. Don't be afraid of the reports you have heard, for the Spirit of truth lives on the inside of you, and He is the greater!

God's Word was authored by the Holy Spirit, and He now brings revelation upon the Word that will quicken your ears to hear and to receive His revelations. Your heart will be soft in God's hand. He will emboss the truths of His Word upon your heart, and no man can steal them from you.

Now, by the leadership of the Holy Spirit, I declare and decree concerning your body. I curse disease in Jesus' Name, and I release healing and health to you. God does such things so quickly, it is true. I see the facts; I see the reports—how they have startled the very heart of you. The truth is greater than a fact! God's truth is that Jesus Christ, your Lord and Savior, is the Healer, too.

I speak life to you! Death go, life be! Normalcy be! I speak this to you, particularly concerning children. Jesus said not to keep the children from Him. If you have a child who needs healing, place your hand on him or her in this moment while the glory is upon you. In the presence of a miracle-working God, the Holy Spirit manifests Christ the Healer.

Today the glory came, and all is well with you in Jesus' Name.

👑 **DECLARATION: I declare over you that you will never forget this day! The Father visited you in a most profound way. Words were spoken, His glory came, and you will never be the same.**

New Place, New Grace

You have come into a season of *new begin-nings*, and unto you is opened a new grace to accompany this time. Everything is changing in accordance with the divine will and purpose of Almighty God. It is all for good, Amen!

...God never changes, and His Word is a stabilizing anchor....

Welcome the new, and embrace the grace afforded you for this leg of the race. Though seasons change, remember that God never changes, and His Word is a stabilizing anchor, able to keep and steady you as you press toward the goal for the prize of the upward call of God in Christ Jesus. (See Philippians 3:14, NKJV).

Know that anything God asks you to do, He gives you the ability to do, for that is His grace! *With Him*, nothing will be impossible for you. Hold fast to your profession and waver not, for your faith is a living substance that brings forth the evidence you have been hoping for!

👑 **DECLARATION: I declare over you that you will embrace the grace that is necessary for new places in God. In Him you remain steady, stable and secure.**

Prepared in His Presence

... The fire of God is changing you and making you ready for the time of the end....

The love of God overwhelms my heart. He is so merciful and gracious. To each of you the Holy Spirit imparts a divine enabling to proclaim the Gospel of Jesus Christ in the places and to the people He has called you to.

God's ways are perfect and wonderful. He has brought you into a glorious time in the earth, and by His Spirit He prepares you for what is to come. It would seem that the fire of God is changing you and making you ready for the time of the end—a place in time between the sixth and seventh millennium. It is as though you are all on pause, awaiting His next move.

Be encouraged that we are all in this together. We are all experiencing the pressure that is around us, propelling us upward. Abide in the secret place of His presence, and you will be safe and secured by His love. Listen to His voice and become intimately acquainted with Him and His ways.

DECLARATION: I declare over you that the fire of God will change you. His Holy presence will prepare you. You will be equipped and ready, secured and steady, to move with His Spirit in the time of the end.

All is Well

All is well, dear one; *all* is well. I encourage you to anchor your soul in the Word in the midst of the uncertainty swirling about in the world, and give voice to your faith in this hour. For *faith calls those things which be not as though they were* (Romans 4:17).

God's Word is eternal; it is the only substance that will affect change, bring hope and produce life!

As one seated in heavenly places with the King of kings and Lord of lords, you have authority to declare and decree what will be. Rise up and speak God's Word, which is His will, in the face of adversity. Declare what He has said over your family, over your life, over unstable markets, over struggling marriages and ailing bodies. God's Word is eternal; it is the only substance that will affect change, bring hope and produce life! *"The words that I speak to you are spirit, and they are life"* (John 6:63, NKJV). So fear not; only speak the Word, for all things are being set in order and brought into divine alignment for His purposes and for good.

The Father sees and knows your heart in all matters. He loves you so! Everything you do in faith pleases Him greatly, and it is His good pleasure to give you the Kingdom. May you know the fullness of Him in this most critical time, and may you rest in His immeasurable love, grace and peace, knowing that truly *all is well!*

DECLARATION: I declare over you that God is your refuge and strength in troubling times. His Word rises up in you, and you speak with authority in the face of adversity. You will stay filled with His fullness, and it anchors and keeps you steady.

The Heart of the King

"The heart of the king is in the hand of the Lord...."
—*Proverbs 21:1*

The times and seasons are in your Father's hands. He rules with righteousness over all the works of His hand. Highlighted to you in this most unusual time—the time of the end—are the governing authorities at all levels: from the leaders of nations to the heads of homes. Leaders are front and center now, and it is your right and responsibility to pray accordingly, scripturally, so that the Father's will be done.

Let not what you see and hear concerning the leaders and nations consume you with fear. Meditate on the truth of God's Word, and give voice to what He has already settled in Heaven concerning matters on Earth. Proverbs 21:1 assures you, *"The king's heart is in the hand of the Lord, like the rivers of water; He turns it wherever He wishes."* In Psalm 22:28, you are reminded: *"For the kingdom is the Lord's, and He rules over the nations."* Psalm 103:19 declares: *"The Lord has established His throne in heaven, and His kingdom rules over all."*

Take comfort in First Thessalonians 5:1–10, *"But of the times and the seasons, brethren, ye have no need that I write unto you. For yourselves know perfectly that the day of the Lord so cometh as a thief in the night. For when they shall say, Peace and safety; then sudden destruction cometh upon them, as travail upon a woman with child; and they shall not escape. But ye, brethren, are not in darkness, that that day should overtake you as a thief. Ye are all the children of light, and the children of the day: we are not of the night, nor of darkness. Therefore let us not sleep, as do others; but let us watch and be sober. For they that sleep, sleep in the night; and they that be drunken are drunken in the night. But let us, who are of the day, be sober, putting on the breastplate of faith and love; and for an helmet, the hope of salvation. For God hath not appointed us to wrath, but to obtain salvation by our Lord Jesus Christ, Who died for us, that, whether we wake or sleep, we should live together with him."*

Agree with the Word of God concerning leaders; meditate on His truth, and no matter what you see, hear and feel, trust that His will and ways will prevail!

DECLARATION: I declare that the king's heart is in the Father's hand, and He turns it as the rivers of water. You ask the Father in Jesus' Name to turn the hearts of your leaders toward Him, that they would rule rightly and even choose Him before the end does come.

For Such a Time as This

"For if you keep silent at this time, relief and deliverance shall arise for the Jews from elsewhere, but you and your father's house will perish. And who knows but that you have come to the kingdom for such a time as this and for this very occasion?"

...You have been anointed and appointed, prepared and positioned, for this day.

—Esther 4:14, AMP

The Eternal God has always been and will always be. You were created in His image, and spirit you are, just like your Father. In His orchestration of events, He placed you on Earth at the time of His choosing. With such purpose and precision He has positioned you, dear one, and it is a marvelous thing. You are on Earth at the time of the end. Giftings, equippings and understanding you must have for this time.

Know the hour you are in, for it is late. Your Lord is soon to return, and there is Kingdom business to be about. Just as Esther was placed in a royal position of influence and authority for the saving of God's people, you have been anointed and appointed, prepared and positioned, for this day. You are highly favored of the King, in right standing through Jesus' blood. You've been given His Name and Heaven's authority to back up all you command.

In this time of the end, be fearless, son or daughter, for you have been brought to the Kingdom for such a time as this! This is what you have waited for. It is what you were born for. You are right on time!

👑 **DECLARATION: I declare over you God's divine positioning is moving you into your place in this hour. I release every gifting, anointing and the favor necessary for you to perform all that He has prepared for you to do, because it is time.**

You Have Become New

"Therefore, if anyone is in Christ, he is a new creation; old things have passed away; behold, all things have become new. Now all things are of God...."
—*2 Corinthians 5:17–18, NKJV*

Whatever you have done, and wherever you are now, the past is far behind. As a born-again believer, your past does not exist. The Cross of Christ has made a way for all humanity to step into a place where old things have passed away and all things have become new...and all things are now of God.

The Father knows where you are, and what you have done; He knows your entire life. What has been washed in His blood is not only forgiven, but also forgotten. It is by faith and not by feelings that you can say, *"I have been crucified with Christ; it is no longer I who live, but Christ who lives in me; and the life which I now live in the flesh I live by faith in the Son of God, who loved me and gave Himself for me"* (Galatians 2:20–21).

If old habits, mindsets and patterns of living are hindering you from crossing over into your royal redemption, remember that forgiveness has been extended to you. Let go of what you have done or left undone. Let go of your shortcomings, pride and fears. Allow the truth of God's Word to reign, and all things will become new.

Our Savior's sacrifice secured a heavenly home for all who believe. Eternal life abides in you today! For when you are born again, all the power you need to overcome—in this life—lives in you through your faith in Jesus Christ! *"For whatsoever is born of God overcometh the world: and this is the victory that overcometh the world, even our faith"* (1 John 5:4).

👑 **DECLARATION: I declare over you that the eternal life abiding in you has canceled out your past and made all things new. Yesterday, today and forever, you overcome through the blood of God's victorious Son!**

Faithful and True

It is a blessed privilege to stand in your place as a son or daughter of the Most High God! Particularly in this time of great change in the earth, the revelation of your sonship provides you supernatural peace, comfort and assurance of His steadfast promises.

"But the Lord will arise over you, and His glory will be seen upon you."
—Isaiah 60:2, NKJV

Dear one, He who made a way, the One who *was*, who *is*, and who *is to come*, is named *Faithful* and *True*. He is everything His Names speak of Him: *He is faithful to you!* His truth is greater than your fact! Whatever the world and the god of this world try to do, your faith in the One true God overcomes! Greater is He that is in you than he that is in the world!

God's glory—His manifested presence—is growing brighter upon the righteous ones! *"For behold, the darkness shall cover the earth, and deep darkness the people; but the Lord will arise over you, and His glory will be seen upon you"* (Isaiah 60:2, NKJV).

Increasingly, as you gather corporately to worship your Lord, you experience a "glory silence;" a "holy hush," where in His presence you sit in utter silence and bask in His magnificent glory and splendor. It is wonderful! Healings are abundant. Bodies, minds and situations are changed and rearranged in His presence! I encourage you to stay mindful of the power you possess as a righteous son or daughter, walking in the knowledge of the victorious One, and transforming the world with the glory of the Son!

👑 **DECLARATION: I declare over you that His glory will be upon you, and brighter it will grow against the darkness that appears to be swallowing up the earth. You speak, "Light be," from your heavenly seat (see Ephesians 1 and 3), and deep darkness will be dispelled in the light of His glorious presence.**

Prayer of Thanksgiving

The Lord God Almighty keeps this nation and nations beyond.

My Father, thank You for this moment in time that we have been brought into with You. Holy Spirit, I know that everything You do glorifies Jesus Christ, Savior and Lord of all. Holy Spirit in this place, You are the Spirit of glory, power and grace. Thank You Holy Spirit for the magnificence of Your presence.

Mighty are Your works, Holy Spirit. Mighty, mighty are Your demonstrations and manifestations. You remind us in this moment of time—in this moment, this portal, this opening—*if the Lord God Almighty doesn't keep the nation, it is not kept.* And I thank You, Lord God Almighty, that You keep this nation and nations beyond.

So let the people rejoice. Let the people give thanks for what is. Let the people rejoice that the Lord God Almighty keeps the cities. That the Lord God Almighty keeps the nations. That the Lord God Almighty keeps the congregations. Let the people rejoice.

DECLARATION: I declare over you that you rejoice in God your Savior! You thank Him that He keeps your nation. He keeps your city. He keeps your congregation. You lift your voice in thanksgiving, praise and worship to the Lord God Almighty, for He alone receives the glory for all that He does on behalf of His beloved Creation.

The Fathers and the Sons

The fathers shall call out to the sons, and the sons shall come to their fathers of the spirit. There will be present in the lands around the world, the spirit like that of Elijah the Prophet. The glory of the Lord shall be seen upon the Church, and the fathers will lead the sons, and the sons will honor the fathers, and many will be the souls that are won because of it.

"And he shall turn the heart of the fathers to the children, and the heart of the children to their fathers, lest I come and smite the earth with a curse."
—Malachi 4:6

Then suddenly there is that last soul in before the Lord God Almighty comes in a cloud and calls unto Himself a glorious Church. There will be many souls, many harvests, even after the Church is gone, for the Spirit of the Lord shall remain, and continue His wooing of the lost unto the Son. They, too, shall agree, and cry out, and be one with the Son.

It has all been a process even unto this day, the fulfilling of biblical prophecy. The manifestations of those things spoken to people personally and corporately will move quickly now among the congregations in cities of nations worldwide. The Lord shall come, and the estrangement shall be no more. There will be a oneness, it will seem, from city to city and nation to nation. Not of same tongue or color. A suddenly of the glory right before the Lord Jesus stands in the air. But a restoring must come first.

And so it shall be: a turning from what causes you to sin, and great revival shall begin. An awakening shall come upon the lands. Multitudes, millions, billions of people, will rush into the Kingdom of God. Quickly, very quickly: cities that shall come in a day. What has been spoken shall be fulfilled as it has been until now. God has not failed in His purpose and plan. He will continue throughout the tribes of man. And then the day will come, dear God, to the glory of Your Son.

👑 **DECLARATION: I declare over you that you will be secured and positioned through revelation and prophecy that brings understanding of the times and events soon to be. You will have great expectancy and align your heart to His manifestations that would draw together the fathers and the sons.**

God Wants Your Care

Cast your care on the Lord…

Oh, how your Father cares for you! First Peter 5:7, in *The Amplified Bible*, tells us, *"Casting the whole of your care (all your anxieties, all your worries, all your concerns, once and for all) on Him, for He cares for you affectionately and cares about you watchfully."*

The Holy Spirit says to you, "About this and that, which would bother you right now, do you not know that I will take that bother from you? Give the bother to Me. Allow Me to minister to you, for you have ministered to Me. What you have need of right now—consider it given. What you needed to know and understand—I have given you the wisdom. I have spoken to your heart but a moment ago. Write it down. Do not forget it."

"In a moment you will go about your day, but just right now, please listen to what I have to say. Do not be fearful for the things you will hear and see concerning family, cities and nations. Fear I did not give to you. Do not receive it; do not take it. Do not deal with it except to say, 'This far you have come and no more shall it be. For I am free from you, demon.'"

"Speak often of what My Son has done. Go and tell and share. Both by what you say and what you do, the world will know of Him. He is not a religion, nor a denomination. The world will know you by your love for one another, for Me, and for them."

DECLARATION: I declare over you that you receive the word of the Lord to you, and in Jesus' Name you are free from fear, cares, worry and anxiety. Give them to Him for He cares for you affectionately.

Move With Unction

The Holy Spirit puts things into you. They are eternal things and they are yours forever and ever. These divine deposits will take you into the coming of your Lord. They are just simple things, for the Holy Spirit is not complicated. He is so easy. If you know Him, He's not complicated. He is God, and I respect Him so.

You are the generation that prepares the way for the Lord.

When you know Him, you love Him. You become so comfortable with Him, and you trust Him. You must trust the voice of the Holy Spirit. You are not going to trust anyone you don't know. If you don't know Him, then you don't trust Him. That's just the way of it.

Jesus had so much success because He understood how to follow the unction of the Holy Spirit. I believe there was a lot more that He saw that He could do, but there wasn't the unction to do it. You need to understand this. You are the generation that prepares the way for the Lord. You are the people who go out and gather the harvest. The unction is not just for those who minister on the platform; all of us are to know Him.

The Apostle Paul taught on the nine gifts of the Holy Spirit in First Corinthians 12:8–11, and that is for all believers to experience. The gifts and manifestations of the Spirit are for you to move with as He would give you unction. You can know what to do. You can see and hear things in your prayer time. Don't run out and do it unless there is unction to do it. By unction I mean an *umph* to go and to do. You will know the difference. You may get it wrong a few times, but you will recognize when you do it right. Learn to move with Him, and to move with unction.

👑 **DECLARATION: I declare over you that you will be sensitive to the Holy Spirit and keen to His voice. You will follow Him in all you say and do, and yield to His unction for every move.**

The Bridal Call of the Christ

Church! Arise! Awaken, unto the bridal call of the Christ!"

Appointed times in the presence of the Lord will change your life forever! These are moments where time and destiny meet, and things planned from the foundation of the earth burst forth on your behalf. When something is about to be, God will send the prophets ahead to declare and decree, and carry a thing to the people. From city to city this is how it has been for me. I carry His heart, His sound and His words to you.

The Holy Spirit says of this day: "The time has come and surely is… Church! Arise! Awaken, unto the bridal call of the Christ! For such a day you have entered into; a day as no other before. Be it done unto you! Be it done unto the church universal according to My Word."

Speaking of the church universal, He means all the Body of Christ. It doesn't matter the denomination or "camp"; the Holy Spirit is speaking forth concerning *all* of God's sons and daughters throughout *all* nations. He's getting your attention. He is unfolding for you His ways and His plans. If you will follow them, they will change your life forever!

DECLARATION: I declare over you that you stand at attention! As part of the church universal, you arise and awaken unto this bridal call coming forth from Jesus Christ your Savior. He positions you to hear, to perceive and to receive, and I believe it will change your life forever.

Eternal Law

The Holy Spirit got my attention, and then He began to speak. "Line up your words with eternal law. You have been calling those things that are as though they were not. Sounds good, but not the law of Alpha and Omega."

...Live and have your being in the laws of Alpha and Omega.

With such verbiage and in such manner He spoke to me. It was so different from before. "The law of Alpha and Omega?" There are laws and eternal principles that your Father expects you to follow. You cannot follow the Christ with man's laws and man's ways. You must enter into the eternal laws and principles of the Christ—the Alpha and the Omega. You must do things His way if you want to partake of what He paid so rightly and majestically for by His royal blood. You have to live and have your being in the laws of Alpha and Omega.

There is a difference in "calling those things which be not as though they were," and "calling those things that are as though they were not." If you are doing the latter you are not following spiritual law, and it will have no effect upon natural things. You must use the laws of the unseen—the eternal realm—to bring change in the natural realm where your humanity abides.

DECLARATION: I declare over you that you line up your words with eternal law and call things that *be not* as though they were. You follow God's principles and operate in the realm of the spirit, and things change and align to eternal law in the natural realm.

Possessed of God

Anything you can see, you can change.

Your spirit man, the real you, has need of your earth suit—your body. That is why you have to tend to your temple. First Corinthians 6:19, declares, *"What? Know ye not that your body is the temple of the Holy Ghost which is in you, which ye have of God, and ye are not your own?"*

God the Holy Spirit has need of your temple, for He dwells *in* you! He possesses you spirit, soul and body. Do you truly believe that God Himself has your soul—your will, emotions and intellect? Do you believe and comprehend that the Supreme Being Himself inhabits your flesh? If you do, you will talk differently. You will think differently. You won't think like a mere mortal man. For immortal you already are! Your eternal life has already begun. You are a spirit, and your eternity was chosen by decision. Your eternal abode began when you received the Christ, and you moved into the laws and the principles of the realm that is the greater of all things. It is very different for you now.

Anything you can see, you can change. Anything of the five senses is subject to eternal law. Everything! Anything! What you see, feel and hear is the lesser of the greater inside of you. Greater is He in you! You see yourselves separated in a manner, but remember you are one. To think of yourself as merely a channel is lesser. You are possessed of God! The you that was, no longer is.

👑 **DECLARATION: I declare over you that you died, and your life is hidden with God in Christ. This life that you now live you live by faith in the Son of God who loved you and gave His life for you (Galatians 2:20). The greater One lives in you, causing you to operate in the greater rather than from your senses. He possesses you!**

The Time of Great Grace

Dear one, you've moved into a time of great grace! You have stepped over into a time that was prescribed, spoken of and fore-ordained. As it was with the early Church, it is for you. For was it not written of them that the apostles and disciples moved in *great power* with *great grace?* Is not your end—the latter day—to be greater than the former?

Those things that you believe and say, there shall be a performance of them coming forth now.

You have moved into a position of great grace, and by this grace there shall be a performance of things. Those things that you believe and say, there shall be a performance of them coming forth now. Not going to be, but is now. For a great grace has been released from the Father, through the Son, by the Spirit, out of the heavenlies. Out of the eternal, unseen realm it comes into this natural realm. Nothing is ever going to be the same. There shall be a performance of your words!

The Holy Spirit is telling you what to do. He's telling you how to say it. He is letting you know you are going to get what you've been saying. What are your words, dear one? What are you really saying? Your thoughts speak louder in the heavenlies than your actions in the earth. You come to Him in prayer and say to Him, and then you leave that place of prayer and your words change. It matters what you say. There will be a performance of what you have believed.

A sovereign thing has been done. There will now be an overflow of the increase that once was, because you've stepped into a great grace to perform it.

👑 **DECLARATION: I declare over you that greater is the grace to do, but greater too is the rate of return; therefore, line up your words to the Word of your Father, and say only what He would say. You will have exactly what you say and believe.**

The Weapon of Worship

The battle is in the spirit, and your weaponry is praise and worship.

A sound thunders throughout the land! It is the sound of the Church arising, and in one accord, worshipping the Lord. The power of praise and weapon of worship release a mighty wind from Heaven upon Earth. In an instant, strife, division, confusion and every evil work are swept away. Plans and schemes of the enemy are thwarted and held back.

Just as in King Jehoshaphat's day, when impending attacks were threatening from all sides, God Almighty had a plan for deliverance. *"Jehoshaphat stood and said, 'Hear me, O Judah, and ye inhabitants of Jerusalem; Believe in the Lord your God, so shall ye be established; believe his prophets, so shall ye prosper'"* (2 Chronicles 20:20b).

Singers and praisers were appointed to precede the army of God, to sing and declare the praise and mercy of the Lord. As they lifted their voices in praise to God, the Lord set ambushes confounding their enemies, who rose up against one another, and utterly destroyed each other. (See 2 Chronicles 2:20–22).

The weapons of your warfare are not carnal, dear one. The battle is in the spirit, and your weaponry is praise and worship! Know with great assurance, that when you lift your hands and voice in praise to your King, *the Lord* fights for you!

👑 DECLARATION: I declare over you that you will take up your weaponry in the spirit, and release the sound of praise and worship in the earth. Against every opposition, you let your voice of praise to God Almighty resound, for He will confound and destroy the enemy for you.

The Bookends of Life

The Holy Spirit visited me with a most demonstrative sound recently as I was passing from one room to another in my home. I heard what was like the sound of a horn blowing one long blast, followed by a long pause, and then another long blast. As you can imagine, I was surprised by this occurrence, and so I asked Him, "My Lord, what does this mean?"

... The sound comes to awaken you, to prepare you for what is up ahead, and to bring you courage!

I consulted with a dear friend who studies Hebrew, and who has prayed for me the last 20 years. What I learned is that this sound is the Tekiah, and it is the strong and powerful first blast the shofar makes to call the people to attention, to awaken us from spiritual slumber, and to prepare us for what is coming next.

In ancient times, the tribes knew to turn when they were gathered by this sound, because it signified that more was coming for them to hear. This sound I did hear was from Heaven, and it is known as "The Bookends of Life." It comes to awaken you, to prepare you for what is up ahead, and to bring you courage! Wow!

The Holy Spirit prepares you by the magnificence of His presence for what comes next both in the spirit and in the natural. It is through your declaration of His Word and by His Spirit that you will be able to stand bold through those things that come.

👑 **DECLARATION: I declare over you that you are prepared by His Word and Holy Spirit for what lies ahead. Your ear is turned to hear from Him, your heart is ready to receive, and your hands are ready to do.**

Enter Into the Fullness

It's not enough just to go up high in the things of God, you must enjoin yourself to God and enter into the fullness....

Revelation 4:1, in *The Amplified Bible,* says: *"After this I looked, and behold, a door standing open in heaven! And the first voice which I had heard addressing me like the calling of a war trumpet said, 'Come up here, and I will show you what must take place in the future.'"*

John the Revelator goes on to describe how the Holy Spirit's power came upon him to take him up into a place where he would know the future. The Spirit took him up, but then he had to go in. It's not enough just to go up high in the things of God, you must enjoin yourself to God and enter into the fullness, where you will see, know and receive direction for what is going to happen. The Holy Spirit is sounding an alarm as it were, calling you to a place where your attention is captured and held, for He has much to show and tell you of the things to come.

Dear one, many things are coming to their fullness, and it is so miraculous that you and I were anointed and appointed to be on Earth at this time! I believe God Almighty has gotten your attention. May you stay alert, watching, listening, and ready to courageously do all He has prepared and purposed!

DECLARATION: I declare over you that the Father will take you *up* and *into* His fullness, where you see, hear and know. In His presence you will receive all that you need to do what He has destined for you.

Faith in the Power

"And my language and my message were not set forth in persuasive (enticing and plausible) words of wisdom, but they were in demonstration of the Holy Spirit and power ...

For so established in the Word are you, that He trusts you with His power.

"So that your faith might not rest in the wisdom of men (human philosophy), but in the power of God."

—1 Corinthians 2:4–5, AMP

The Holy Spirit moves upon the Word of God deposited inside of you—the Word both written and spoken *of* you, and the Word spoken *by* you. He takes the faith that is so embedded in you—what has been written on the tablet of your heart—and He moves you across cities and nations. He takes you to people around the corner, and over the sea.

For so established in the Word are you, that He trusts you with His power. It is safe to give unto you the activation of all the anointings and giftings that were purposed inside of you.

It will not be your wisdom that you bring to the people He sends you to, for the world has had enough of man's wisdom. They are not interested in your carnal wisdom. Words will not entice. They will hear and respond to truth. Give them the Word of truth, so that their faith might not rest on man's wisdom, but on God's power!

👑 **DECLARATION: I declare over you that His Word in your heart and on your lips has built a foundation in you—a platform from which He launches you into places of destiny. It is not your wisdom, but His Word and the demonstration of it, that activates people's faith in His power.**

Activation of Anointings

God renews and activates, amplifies and enhances the giftings and anointings so purposed for you.

By the Spirit of grace, I activate in you what you received in days long ago. Healings and miracles you touched upon and knew. For in such a time as this, that stirs alive in you.

God renews and activates, amplifies and enhances the giftings and anointings so purposed for you.

The Lord trusts you. For what you have seen and touched upon too, the activation is now imparted for you to do. The knowing of things like never before. You will see and you will know and you will move accordingly. Nothing, absolutely nothing, will hold you back. Impart to those who come up alongside of you. They have got to have what you have, too.

DECLARATION: I declare over you that you will receive the activation of the giftings and anointings once imparted. They are stirred up and begin to flow out of you for this time of the end.

The Master is Passing By

The Holy Spirit is the manifestor of the works of Jesus Christ. He comes upon you to bring healing and deliverance, and to deposit change. Just like in the New Testament when Jesus walked the earth, God passes by.

Let Him touch you now as He passes by.

Remember along the road to Emmaus when Jesus joined the two men who were recounting all the happenings in Jerusalem concerning the Lord? They didn't recognize Jesus until He broke bread with them. *"Now it came to pass, as He sat at the table with them, that He took bread, blessed and broke it, and gave it to them. Then their eyes were opened and they knew Him; and He vanished from their sight. And they said to one another, 'Did not our heart burn within us while He talked with us on the road, and while He opened the Scriptures to us?' So they rose up that very hour and returned to Jerusalem, and found the eleven and those who were with them gathered together, 'The Lord is risen indeed, and has appeared to Simon!' And they told about the things that had happened on the road, and how He was known to them in the breaking of bread"* (Luke 24:30–35, NKJV).

Did we not know that was the Master? Did we not recognize the moment with Him?

Oh, dear one, the Master is passing by. Let Him touch you now as He passes by. Thinking will be different from this moment forward. Bodies will be different, because the Master passed by. He heals you. He delivers you. The change you desire has come through the only begotten Son.

👑 **DECLARATION: I declare over you that you will recognize this moment with God, and reach out in faith to receive from the Master as He passes by. The Lord touches your heart, your mind and your body. He heals you and makes you whole!**

Heavenly Place

Everything will be different for you when you pray from your position rather than from the temporal condition.

My heart overflows with thanksgiving for you and the gift that you are to your Father. I want you to know with great assurance, that you occupy a high place and position because of your faith in Jesus Christ. According to Ephesians 2:4–6, NKJV, *"...God, who is rich in mercy, because of His great love with which He loved us, even when we were dead in trespasses, made us alive together with Christ (by grace you have been saved), and raised us up together, and made us sit together in the heavenly places in Christ Jesus."*

Just as seasons change in the natural, the season is changing for you, the Church. I want to encourage you that though things all around you are changing, God does not change; and, who you are in Christ does not change. I want to affirm your position in Him so that you will stand fixed and immovable in your place of authority on the earth in this time.

You are a righteous one because of your belief in the Lord Jesus Christ. His blood, and your faith in its power, position you in the heavenly places with Him. At the Father's right hand the Son is seated, and you with Him there, where you see, say, pray, declare and decree how things on the earth ought to be. See yourself there with Him, and your perspective of events, situations and circumstances will change. Everything will be different for you when you pray from your *position* rather than from the temporal *condition*.

Remember that God's Word is true, and truth is *greater* than facts! Greater is He that is *in you* than he that is in the world!

🔱 **DECLARATION: I declare over you that you see, say and pray from your place and position of authority in the heavenlies, rather than from what you see, feel and experience in the natural realm. For the greater is in the unseen, and the greater One lives in you.**

The Voice of Faith

In this Thanksgiving season, I am stirred for you to praise and thank God for the life of faith He has destined for you to walk. You must *believe* that He is, you must *believe* that He is a rewarder of those who diligently seek Him, you must *believe* and speak, you must *believe* even when you do not see. Your faith

Your faith in the God of the impossible is the substance that makes all things possible!

in the God of the impossible is the substance that makes *all things* possible!

> **"As you therefore have received Christ Jesus the Lord, so walk in Him, rooted and built up in Him and established in the faith, as you have been taught, abounding in it with thanksgiving."**
> **—Colossians 2:6–7, NKJV**

The voice of thanksgiving is the voice of faith! In the face of faith-opposing circumstances, the power of praise and thanksgiving is a quickening force that dispels doubt, and brings into manifestation God's will on Earth as it is in Heaven.

What is it that is keeping you from walking in the fullness of your faith? Let your voice of thanksgiving sound above the forces that oppose. It is God's Word that stands: for He is the author and the *finisher* of your faith! I pray that as you abound with thanksgiving, the hand of God will move Heaven and Earth on your behalf! Join me now in lifting your voice to God with a heart of thanksgiving for Him and all He has done.

👑 **DECLARATION: I declare that you will lift your voice in thanksgiving to your Father, for He will do everything He said He would do. He keeps you, and brings you out, through and into all He has prepared for you to do.**

Give Thanks

Consider all the Father has done in your life, and think on His never-ending goodness and compassion toward you.

"Thank God in everything—no matter what the circumstances may be, *be thankful and give thanks*—for this is the will of God for you who are in Christ Jesus, the Revealer and Mediator of that will."

—1 Thessalonians 5:18, AMP

It is that heartwarming season when you gather around a festive table with family and friends in celebration of Thanksgiving. I am thankful that Father God has purposed for you to be building His Kingdom at this time in history. He has prepared you for such a time as this! I am thankful for the love of family and friends, whose lives are marked by and abounding with the fruit of the Spirit. I am thankful for our beloved America: a land born out of a love for liberty and godly pursuits. The Father holds this nation close to His heart and securely in His hand.

Consider all the Father has done in your life, and think on His never-ending goodness and compassion toward you. As the Scriptures exhort: *"...Be thankful and give thanks...."* Let His praises be found in your heart and on your lips, for the sound of thanksgiving is His will for you. Your heart will be lifted as His presence inhabits your praise, and melts away cares not meant for you to carry. A voice of thanksgiving is the sound of faith, and to your Father there is no sweeter sound. Thank You, God, for *You!*

DECLARATION: I declare over you that you will lift your heart and voice in praise and thanks to your Father. He is faithful and true, and there is absolutely nothing He cannot do.

Thankful for America

This month we celebrate a most meaningful event in our nation's history—Thanksgiving Day. It is a day set apart to preserve the remembrance of the Father's divine goodness, provision, and remarkable deliverance of the English Separatists who founded Plymouth Colony more than 390 years ago. In October 1621, this band of believers, better known as the Pilgrims, celebrated their first harvest with feasting, games and prayer.

"...Where the Spirit of the Lord is, there is liberty."—2 Corinthians 3:17

I admire the sacrifice, determination and faith the Pilgrims demonstrated. They were a people of purpose in search of a land of destiny. Their quest for freedom set them on a course across vast and icy waters in pursuit of a place of providential promise where their God-given liberty would be preserved. They would not compromise in their hunger and thirst for righteousness, and that tenacity helped lay the foundation of freedom that makes America so very different from every other nation. Ours is a nation built on the pursuit of religious freedom, *"...and where the Spirit of the Lord is, there is liberty"* (2 Corinthians 3:17).

The first Thanksgiving celebration was marked by a natural harvest, but I believe the seeds of faith the Pilgrims and the generations to follow have sown in the spiritual soil of our beloved land, are ripe and ready for a harvest of souls! I cannot think of anything more precious to our Father's heart than the gathering in of His children.

I pray you will know the depth of your Father's love for you as you gather with family and friends to commemorate the Thanksgiving holiday, and I declare over you a renewed passion for your nation, and for your place and purpose in it to burn within your heart!

DECLARATION: I declare over you, also, that you speak to the soil and to the seeds of faith planted long ago in your beloved land, and call them to come forth! "Be productive! Grow! Produce! Live and do not die!" You take your place in prayer over your nation, and stand in Christ's liberty that lives in you and makes you free.

A Heart of Thanksgiving

"O give thanks unto the Lord, for he is good: for his mercy endureth for ever."
—*Psalm 107:1*

As you celebrate the Thanksgiving holiday, may your heart be full of thanks to God. He is always so good! What stories you surely have to tell of His love and compassion toward you and your loved ones: testimonies of healings, protection, deliverance and provision.

I want to put you in remembrance of the goodness of God. His grace, favor and mercy are freely extended to you. The Father loves you! As you honor Him this Thanksgiving Day, do so from your heart and not as a tradition or ritual. I believe your heartfelt reverence and thanks will bring joy to your Father's heart.

DECLARATION: I declare over you that your heart will be filled with thanksgiving today, and you will bless the Father for all He's done: For giving you Jesus His Son and the promised Holy Spirit; for angelic ones who aid and assist; for wisdom and understanding of revelation; for seeings, knowings and authority to pray. He's given all you need in the natural and the spirit, and you are grateful.

A Thankful Heart

"Enter into his gates with thanksgiving, and into his courts with praise: be thankful unto him, and bless his name."

Thanksgiving is your faith in action, and its sound is pleasing to your Father.

—Psalm 100:4

The way to approach the Father about anything is with a thankful heart. Thanksgiving means a heart of faith is present. Faith believes that God is, that He is a rewarder, and that He is willing and able to do everything He said He would do. Thanksgiving is your faith in action, and its sound is pleasing to your Father.

When you come into the presence of Almighty God, thanking Him for His goodness and the means to come before Him, He takes notice. For you have access because of the blood of His Son! If Jesus hadn't died, you couldn't even enter into God's presence.

Requests are not the highest priority when you go to God. The love, adoration and fellowship with your Father are the reasons you seek His face. If you seek His face, you will always have what is in His hands. He is a good Father; see Him this way, and everything will change for you.

👑 **DECLARATION: I declare over you that you will see God as your dear Father. You come through the Holy blood of His Son to seek His face and spend time with Him. You give your love to the Father and thank Him for who He is today and forevermore.**

The Glory of God

Don't stay locked up in your humanity... God the Holy Spirit resides in you....

The Holy Spirit is the Spirit of glory, and He possesses you! Your humanity is like a cloak, and the closer you come to the end of this age, in the spirit the cloak will look like it is full of holes. The glory of God pierces through your humanity more and more as you come closer and closer to the catching away.

What do you think the glory is? How does the whole Earth get full of God's glory? *You* carry the glory of God! He has taken up permanent residence in you. Don't stay locked up in your humanity; God the Holy Spirit resides in you, and His glory will only get greater upon and through you.

 DECLARATION: I declare over you that you will be a carrier of God's glory in the earth. His glory pierces through your humanity to release His power and presence through you!

Awareness of the Power

I believe coming upon the Body of Christ is a greater *awareness of the power* that resides in each of you as believers in Jesus Christ. Because Jesus went to the Father, the works that He did, you will do also, and greater works than these will you do! (See John 14:12).

"Arise, shine, for your light has come! And the glory of the Lord is risen upon you."—Isaiah 60:1

The Prophet Isaiah writes to us of a great awakening. *"Arise, shine, for your light has come! And the glory of the Lord is risen upon you"* (Isaiah 60:1). Though Isaiah refers to Israel in this passage, you, the Church, are a type of Israel in the earth. His prophetic words transcend time, and define where you are right now in history.

"For behold, the darkness shall cover the earth, and deep darkness the people; But the Lord will arise over you, and His glory will be seen upon you. The Gentiles shall come to your light, and kings to the brightness of your rising" (Isaiah 60:2–3).

This glory—this manifested presence of God, with its recognizable brilliance—resides *in* you, and will be seen upon you to draw the nations to your Savior and Lord.

DECLARATION: I declare over you that you will know, understand, comprehend and awaken to the glory that resides on the inside of you. You will arise with and operate in the glorious manifestations of God in the earth!

Not Church as Usual

The Holy Spirit took up universal command in a mighty demonstration of power.

What a time in church history you have come into! I truly believe you are living in the last of the last days, the time of the end of the ages. It is a time of visitation of the Holy Spirit upon the people of the earth.

It is not life as usual for you. It was not life as usual for the early Church. They lived in a time of visitation of the Holy Spirit. Acts 2:1–4, tells how the Holy Spirit took up universal command in a mighty demonstration of power. The disciples yielded themselves unto the Spirit of God, and 3,000 people were born again in one day! It was a time of great demonstrations of the power of God. Signs, wonders and miracles are recorded all throughout the Book of Acts. The Book of Acts is a pattern for the Church today. This time in which you live is the culmination of all the ages. It is not life as usual—not church as usual—anymore.

I pray that it will be for you as it was for those in the early Church. It is my prayer that great grace, loving-kindness and favor will rest richly upon you, and that there will be no need among you, as Acts 4:33–34, *The Amplified Bible,* declares.

DECLARATION: I declare over you that God the Holy Spirit has command on this earth and in you. You stay yielded to Him, and a harvest of good fruit is produced. Power in demonstration as not even the early Church saw is destined to be, and it's coming through you!

Great Change Within

A transformation is taking place in your heart. God the Holy Spirit is drawing you into a depth of relationship with your beloved Savior that you have not known before. This place of intimacy is greatly important, for it will anchor you in Him in the midst of much change.

You are being made into new wineskins: suitable carriers of His power and presence.

Great change is taking place inwardly as the Holy Spirit makes adjustments in you. Your part is not to resist the seemingly hidden work of God in you, but to submit to His leadership in every aspect of your life. You are being made into new wineskins: suitable carriers of His power and presence. *"But new wine must be put into new wineskins, and both are preserved"* (Luke 5:38, NKJV).

Oh, how you need God's presence! God's presence will still you; His power will stir you. In His presence you will be changed, *"…into His image from glory to glory…!"* (See 2 Corinthians 3:18).

DECLARATION: I declare over you that you will submit to the heart changes your Father desires to make in you. Daily you will partake of His glorious presence that stills, stirs and changes you more and more into His image!

Greater Glory

"...If you believe, you will see the glory of God!"
—John 11:40

"The latter glory of this house (with its successor, to which Jesus came) shall be greater than the former, says the Lord of hosts; and in this place will I give peace and prosperity, says the Lord of hosts."
—Haggai 2:9, AMP

Greater glory is upon you, dear one! The former house Haggai spoke of in our opening passage refers to the temples of ancient times, where God's glory was manifested as a cloud that filled the place so that the priests could not stand to minister. In the desert place, the Israelites witnessed the manifested glory as a cloud by day and a fire by night. Such wondrous displays of His power they did see in that day! *Now,* in this time, God's temple is *you* and *me,* and the prophet said in the latter, *greater* will the manifestations be!

I believe you will see, know and experience things in God's manifested glory beyond any explanation. Encounters in His manifested presence will restore you into the ways and workings of the Holy Spirit so that you will know truth. Divine revelation will come upon all of your information so that you will rightly discern and make sound decisions concerning your life. From your place and position you shall see and take authority over principalities, powers, and rulers of the darkness of this world—entities that would try to rule over you, your body, your finances, your family, city, leaders and nation. Remember, in Christ they are no match for you! Greater glory is coming. Believe it! Expect it! For if you believe, you will see the glory of God!

DECLARATION: I declare over you that you will believe and receive the greater of God upon your life! You will expect encounters in His glory that cause you to see, know, understand and flow with the Holy Spirit. I declare and decree the way things are to be concerning you, your family, your city and your nation, and I believe the greater is upon you.

The Fullness of Time

To everything there is a season, and a time to every purpose under the heavens. And to every time there comes a fullness, when what has been conceived, must be born. The Father's purpose from the foundations of the world was to redeem His beloved Creation. By His divine design, a holy conception was planned; divinity joined with humanity to bring forth a work of the Spirit in the earth. Mary—a virgin—was found with child, and what was conceived in her was of the Holy Spirit! In the fullness of time, the fruit of this divine union—JESUS—was born, to take away the sins of the world.

In the secret place of waiting and incubating, the plan is matured, protected and perfected until the time of its revealing comes forth.

Think it not strange that when something of the Spirit must be birthed in the earth, it is the Father's nature to hide it away until the fullness of time. In the secret place of waiting and incubating, the plan is matured, protected and perfected until the time of its revealing comes forth. The divine purpose often remains blind to you unless you see as God does—with the eyes of faith. Man looks on the outward appearance, but God looks on the heart. Your Father's most precious work takes place on the inside where no man can see. He takes great pleasure in the humility of the hidden. Then, in His perfect timing, the unassuming, unseen unfolds, and His divine hand is displayed upon your destiny!

In this magnificent season, a revealing of the Christ in you is coming to its fullness. What has been conceived in you by the Spirit of God is coming to maturity. This season will bring forth the unveiling of many of God's purposes reserved for this hour, and the ushering in of His glory and power as you have not seen in the earth. No flesh can take the glory or claim this holy wonder, for it is a work of Almighty God.

DECLARATION: I declare over you that Almighty God, your Father, is preparing you for His holy purposes. His divine plan is unfolding in your life in His perfect way and time. At the fullness of time He will unveil and reveal His glorious power reserved for this hour.

Open Heavens

...When you see a door, walk through it!

It is a time where God is in the air! The very atmosphere is charged with His presence. It is as if you breathe Him in and out. I believe this is so because you are experiencing open heavens. Know this to be true son or daughter of the Most High: there are openings—portals—in regions of the earth that are closely guarded and sometimes fought over. These openings go straight into the third heaven, but must pass through the second heaven, which Satan—the Prince of the Power of the Air—occupies. (See Ephesians 2:2). That is why at times there are tremendous rumblings around certain geographic locations, and one can sense that change in the spirit realm almost like sensing the difference in pressure when flying in an airplane.

In Revelation 4:1, John speaks to us of a door. *"After this I looked, and behold, a door standing open in heaven!"* (Revelation 4:1, AMP). I want to encourage you that when you see a door, walk through it! If that door has been opened for you, it embraces you. The author of Hebrews writes that the worlds were formed—framed—by the very words of God! If something is framed, then go through it! There are openings around you every day, and as you fellowship with the Word and the Spirit of God, you will better see those openings. They are like dimensions to maneuver from one place to the next to bring together in one place and time what the Spirit of God wants to do in a split second! So walk on in and move with Him. There is movement in the spirit realm all the time. God the Holy Spirit and angelic ones are always on the move, all for purpose and the carrying out of assignments. Watch for the purpose in each and every moment He makes for you.

I carry in me a change—a shift in spiritual things. I stand underneath open heavens, and the Spirit of the Lord comes upon me to take me to a place and to come back again with a greater grace. From that place I impart this change and the greater to you!

👑 **DECLARATION: I declare over you that you stand under an open heaven. You will recognize the purpose in the moments God makes, and by faith you will go through the openings, doors and entrances framed and formed for you. In Jesus' Name you will receive this divine shift in the spirit, and the impartation of greater grace!**

God's Eternal Plan

Before time began, God had an eternal plan. From the counsel room of Heaven the Father looked out toward what was to be, and said, *"Let us make man in our own image."* So Heaven began by divine orchestration to prepare a way for the Word of God to become flesh, and to bring the revelation of Heaven to Earth.

May the gift of eternal life, wrapped in divine love, illuminate and fill your heart with the fullness of Him!

This revelation has brought forth a generation of people who are led by the Word and Spirit of God—a people of seeing and knowing. You are of that generation. And here you stand, in all that God has brought you into, on the very threshold of bursting through to the greatest manifestation of God's love and power upon Creation.

The blessed Father, Son and Holy Spirit gave everything that you might become one with Them. Oh, how we celebrate and worship our beloved Savior—God's extraordinary plan for all mankind. May the gift of eternal life, wrapped in divine love, illuminate and fill your heart with the fullness of Him!

👑 **DECLARATION: I declare over you that you are of the generation of revelation! By the Holy Spirit you see and know. You will walk in love, walk in the demonstration of God's power, and with the fullness of Him you are filled to overflowing.**

Angelic Visitation

Tremendous angelic visitation is upon you for this time!

All of creation is groaning with unprecedented intensity, while God the Holy Spirit moves upon His Church in preparation for this glorious time!

When a plan is ordained of God, then the Holy Spirit makes a way for it to be. That is the way it has been for me in my life and ministry. Each time you gather around the Name of Jesus, the Holy Spirit draws you, and makes a way for you to come and partake of the impartations He makes through the words, sounds and demonstrations of His Spirit. He is teaching and training you all the while to flow with Him in the hour that has come.

God the Holy Spirit has spoken much to me about angelic activity, and so I share with you what I believe I heard Him say: *"Tremendous angelic visitation is upon you for this time!"* The administration of angelic forces surrounding the inception of God's plans in the earth is His pattern in church history. The announcement of Jesus' birth, the warnings and messages delivered, the protection afforded by these heavenly ones, all point to movement in the spirit realm. You have the glorious privilege of living in this time, and operating with the mighty forces of Heaven at your disposal.

👑 **DECLARATION: I declare over you an anticipation of a great increase in angelic activity surrounding events that are yet to be, and you will receive the aid of these angelic ones sent to minister for *you*—an heir of salvation! (See Hebrews 1:14).**

Good News!

The message from the Church to the world has not changed in 2,000 years: "Fear not. For, behold, we bring good tidings of great joy to all the people; you have a Savior, and His name is Jesus Christ the Lord."

"Fear not: for, behold, I bring you good tidings of great joy, which shall be to all people."
—Luke 2:10

The word "gospel" means "good news." The Gospel of Jesus Christ certainly is good news, especially for those who don't know Him as Savior and Lord. As you hurry about this Christmas season, I encourage you to ask the Holy Spirit to put people in your path who need to hear the Good News. Then, when you are out and about, whether in the toy store, the shopping mall or grocery store, and the Holy Spirit says, "That one…," don't hesitate to speak Christmas greetings to the person He has shown you, and share the Good News!

DECLARATION: I declare over you that you will be ever mindful of the truth you have to share concerning the Christ. I declare that the Holy Spirit will lead you to those who need to hear the Good News, and with all boldness you will open your mouth to make known the mystery of the Gospel!

The Light of the World

May the joy of knowing Jesus light your heart, home and world this blessed season!

The Christmas season is a holy time. As you prepare to celebrate the birth of your magnificent Savior, I pray you experience a renewed revelation of His love. At the very center of your Father's heart is His Son. If you are in Christ and He is in you, then by the power of the Holy Spirit, the three are one.

This life of God in you is the light that lights the world. Jesus said of you, the carriers of His light and life, *"You are the light of the world... Let your light so shine before men, that they may see your good works and glorify your Father in heaven"* (Matthew 5:14; 16, NKJV). Never underestimate your influence; for greater is He that is *in you* than he that is in the world!

DECLARATION: I declare over you that you are a carrier of Christ's light, life and love. You are loved by your Father, for you are a son or daughter—a righteous one! His life and love illuminate you for the world to see and know His love through you.

Agree With God

W hat a joyous moment when Mary said "yes" to the Father's will for her life! In her agreement with God's holy plan, she made a way for Heaven's will for all humanity to be accomplished on Earth. Divinely aligned in her heart, her words of praise rang out in perfect harmony with the will and plan of God. Oh, what unfathomable power resulted: LOVE was born!

"My soul magnifies the Lord, and my spirit has rejoiced in God my Savior."
—Luke 1:46–47, NKJV

The same is true for you when you believe and agree with the Father's will and ways. When you are in one accord with His plan, there is no variance in you, and His power flows freely…magnificently unhindered. In all He asks you to do, your grace is great, your peace is perfect, His purposes prevail and the glory is His.

DECLARATION: I declare over you that you will be ever-mindful of the Father's will for you. I declare that you will lay aside your own plans and say "yes" to all that the Father has for you. Divine power and grace await you, and great glory awaits your King as you walk out Heaven's plans on Earth!

The Season of the Miraculous

...Everything about Jesus was miraculous; and He has not changed!

One night, some 2,000 years ago, Heaven reached out and touched Earth. Jesus' entrance into the world was surrounded by the miraculous. The virgin birth, the star, the angels announcing His arrival; all were miracles—divine interventions into the natural course of things.

During His life on the earth, everything about Jesus was miraculous, and He has not changed! He has such great compassion and love for the people of the world. It is His heart for the lost to be saved, the sick to be healed and the oppressed to be delivered. It delights Him when you, His son or daughter, enjoy all the blessings He provided for you.

You have entered into the season of the miraculous! I encourage you to meditate upon the compassion and love of Jesus toward you and your loved ones. Christ's compassion can be seen and felt. Take note that when the compassion and the love of Christ are in manifestation, the realm of the miraculous is opened unto you!

DECLARATION: I declare over you that as you meditate in God's Word concerning His love and compassion, you will flow in the manifestation of miracles. You will demonstrate compassion: divine love in action, and the realm of the miraculous will open for you.

Joy to the World

What joy Christmas brings to our hearts! It is a season of wonder...a season of miracles! A miracle is defined as: something wonderful; a supernatural event contrary to the established course of things.

Something wonderful of God took place on your behalf, and your established course was changed for all eternity!

Hallelujah! Jesus' birth was a miracle—a wonderful, supernatural event, that brought Heaven to Earth! Deity was conceived by humanity, and the Savior of the world was brought forth. Something wonderful of God took place on your behalf, and your established course was changed for all eternity!

DECLARATION: I declare over you that you will partake of the miracle life of God through the indwelling presence of eternity in your heart. He delivered you from darkness, and translated you into the Kingdom of light. What a miracle occurred when you received Jesus Christ, God's gift of salvation!

Something Wonderful of God

Whatever natural course needs to be shifted in your life, believe with all your heart that something wonderful of God—a miracle—is coming for you!

Christ's life was a demonstration of the miraculous. He never left anyone He touched the same. In all things, Jesus showed us the Father's will; and God's will is for a wonderful, miraculous life of supernatural events to happen for you! Healing miracles, miracles of provision, the drawing of that wayward child home to you and to Him, are the wonderful works He performs. In His great love, He demonstrates this miraculous, supernatural power from Heaven right here on Earth, and in earthen vessels.

Whatever natural course needs to be shifted in your life, believe with all your heart that something wonderful of God—a miracle—is coming for you!

As you celebrate this holy season and the miraculous first coming of Jesus, I pray that all the wonder that filled the shepherds, the wise men, Jesus' own earthly mother and father, and all those He touched throughout His life on Earth, would fill your heart with an expectation for miracles!

DECLARATION: I declare over you that an expectation for miracles is stirred! Right now I speak a supernatural shift in natural courses, and things change and rearrange in your life in Jesus' Name!

You're Almost There

I know in my heart that you have experienced but a foretaste of the healing power that is pressing up against you, ready to rush in and restore all things to wholeness—spirit, soul and body. Such an unction stirs in me for what is about to be. You're almost there! The manifestation of your miracle is right out in front of you. You are not going under; you are going over in Jesus' Name!

Healing power is pressing up against you, ready to rush in and restore all things to wholeness—spirit, soul and body.

When our daughter was in crisis, and my husband and I made the difficult decision to have her moved to another facility against the hospital's direction, we stepped out in faith and chartered a private plane to have her relocated. When you step out, a multitude of obstacles can present themselves that will so stretch and test your faith. Doubts, questions and reasonings will try to pull you off what you know in your heart to be true. In the face of contrary circumstances, you just have to stand and press on through.

During the flight, our daughter's breathing became extremely shallow, her heart rate began pounding out of control and her blood pressure was skyrocketing. No matter what the medical team did for her, she was not taking in enough oxygen. They said, "You're losing her!" We were suspended between what looked like life and death, and every second counted. My husband, Nick, crouched down to cradle his precious comatose daughter, and whispered in her ear, "Don't die, honey; we're almost there." God miraculously intervened, and we were granted clearance to land ahead of the commercial flights in front of us. A medical team and ambulance were waiting on the runway. God said, "Life and wholeness for her," and we believed Him.

I say to you today, 'Don't give up! Don't let whatever promise of God you are carrying in your heart, die. You're almost there!" His hand is outstretched toward you, ready to pull you on through if you will not lose heart or hope.

DECLARATION: I declare over you that you are but a breath away from the manifestation of your miracle. In the face of symptoms, circumstances and delays, you stand on God's Word and keep pressing through. You do not lose heart or hope, for your Father loves you and love never fails.

The Holy Ghost and Power

The Holy Spirit's demonstration is His power displayed and manifested.

I want to share with you about the great demonstrator of the works of Jesus Christ: God the Holy Spirit. He is the *power* of the Trinity! I want to stir in you an expectancy for His power to be demonstrated in *your* life. *"And my speech and my preaching was not with enticing words of man's wisdom, but in demonstration of the Spirit and of power: that your faith should not stand in the wisdom of men, but in the power of God"* (1 Corinthians 2:4–5).

Wisdom is not found in the words of men, but in the Holy Spirit's demonstrations and manifestations. His power is a substantive display: an act offering conclusive proof. Why? So that your faith—trust, hope, confidence—can stand firm, stable and fixed in God! The voices of men that would try to sway you this way and that, cannot entice, for they are void of one thing: power! The Holy Spirit's demonstration *is* His power displayed and manifested. He wants to move *in* you, *upon* you and *through* you to bless you and others, and to bring glory to Jesus Christ.

I believe as you purpose to raise your expectancy in the power of the Holy Spirit, He will manifest and demonstrate Himself to you in the most intimate, personal and powerful of ways. Look for Him. Listen for His voice. Wait. Watch. Trust in your hearing of Him, and then simply obey. Step out and follow what you see. What you hear Him say, you say.

DECLARATION: I declare over you that your faith stands in the demonstration and manifestation of God the Holy Spirit. You know His voice. You will recognize and obey His promptings. His power moves in and through you this day to bless others and to glorify Jesus Christ.

Speak of Him

In this blessed, holy season of hope for all the world, I encourage you to lift up the Christ so that all men will be drawn to Him.

Your sound has gone out to all the earth, and your words to the ends of the world.

As you go about your day and tend to the affairs of your life, let His Name be upon your lips, in your thoughts and stirring in your heart. Keep your ear turned toward Heaven in earnest expectation of His sound.

So many voices can be heard in the earth today, but His sound ascends above them all. Psalm 19:1, *The Amplified Bible,* reveals the unspoken testimony of the works of nature: *"The Heavens declare the glory of God; and the firmament shows and proclaims His handiwork."* And to all who give voice to His Word and demonstrate the works of Jesus Christ: *"Your sound has gone out to all the earth, and your words to the ends of the world"* (Romans 10:18, paraphrased). No matter how the world tries to silence the sound of the Son of God, Christmas is the one time where mankind is brought face-to-face with the reality of Jesus Christ and what He means personally, individually, to each and every heart.

This Christmas season, speak of Jesus to the ears that will hear. *"...Always be prepared to give an answer to everyone who asks you to give the reason for the hope that you have..."* (1 Peter 3:15). Even now, I believe the Holy Spirit is preparing for you divine encounters, and opening up doors of opportunity for you to walk through, providing places for you to speak His Name, and orchestrating occasions to bring eternal hope to hurting hearts. *"May the God of hope fill you with all joy and peace in believing, so that by the power of the Holy Spirit you may abound in hope"* (Romans 15:13).

👑 **DECLARATION: I declare over you open doors and opportunities abound for you to speak of Jesus Christ, your blessed hope. You hear His sound and proclaim it throughout the land, and Heaven and Earth are filled with His glory!**

Fruit in Season

"But when the fullness of the time was come, God sent forth his Son..."
—Galatians 4:4

God sent Jesus into the earth at just the right time. In the appointed season Christ came forth, and through His life and death secured a way for "whosoever will" to partake of eternal life.

How precious is the plan of God inside a man! It begins as a seed, seemingly so small, but a planting of the Lord always grows, and *in its season*, brings forth fruit.

I am so grateful for the plan God so masterfully crafted in Jesus. And, I am mindful of the plan He has fashioned inside of you. What is conceived in you is of the Holy Spirit, and at the right time, it will come forth. I know the waiting can seem long, but the Father's timing is perfect. The times and seasons are in His hand, and at the fullness of time, *all things* will come to fruition.

DECLARATION: I declare over you that your time of fullness is at hand! The Father brings forth the fruit of His life in yours, for the times and seasons are by His command. Fruit now comes forth in you for it is His plan.

An Awakening

A divine culmination of unprecedented glory and power is ready to burst forth in the earth! Can you sense the increase of God in and around you? The opposition grows, too; the darkness is great, but His grace does abound, and the light shines brighter upon and through you. Such an awakening is at hand—the arising of the Body of Christ to stand and command the will of God Almighty, and to thwart the plans of Satan and man.

Such an awakening is at hand—the arising of the Body of Christ to stand and command....

I want to encourage each and every one who is standing face-to-face with the forces of Hell working tirelessly to rob you of your identity and authority in the Christ. *Nothing* can separate you from God's great love for you! No matter what you may or may not feel, hear or see, know that His power is hard at work for your good and for His glory.

Out of the abundance of God's Word in your heart, let your lips give voice to the truth that overrules every fact. Remember that everything has ears, and must respond to your words filled with the substance of things hoped for, the evidence of things not seen. Do not grow weary in well doing, dear one, for in due season you will reap, if you do not lose heart! (See Galatians 6:9). It is harvest time! Financially, yes, but also in whatever area you are believing and thanking God for. It is time for *all things* to come to fruition!

DECLARATION: I declare over you that advancements and increase are coming upon every area of your life. Supernatural provision comes to you. Your every need—spiritual, relational and financial—is supplied in Jesus' mighty Name! You will believe and receive everything the Father has reserved for you. This is your time to shine for God's glory!

Time and Eternity

A great anticipation stirs and grows in your heart for the move of God—the move of love—that is coming!

As the Holy Spirit prepares to flood the earth with His final outpouring, the Church finds herself in a peculiar place. Caught between millenniums, you are a generation like no other. You have crossed out of the sixth millennium, but cannot yet move into the seventh, because biblically, the seventh millennium is the 1,000-year reign of the Body of Christ with Jesus. It is as though you are suspended between time and eternity.

Before you can move on into the next millennium, you know there must be a great harvesting of Earth's precious fruit. You are closer to that ingathering than ever before. A great anticipation stirs and grows in your heart for the move of God—the move of love—that is coming! There is no force more powerful than love to sweep humanity out of the kingdom of darkness and into the Kingdom of God.

Expect this divine power to move in and through you to touch the hurting with healing, the oppressed with joy, and the bound with liberty that only comes in Christ Jesus. He is coming, dear one; Jesus is coming soon!

DECLARATION: I declare over you that God ordained for you to be on Earth at just the right time. You will flow in precision with the Holy Spirit in the move of love flooding the earth. Healing power will flow through you. Delivering power will set people free. You have great expectancy for the eternal One in you to flow through your humanity in this most wonderful moment in time!

Divine Love

By inspiration of the Holy Spirit, the Apostle John eloquently writes of the proof of our position and identity as Christians. *"We know that we have passed from death unto life, because we love the brethren"* (1 John 3:14a).

"... The love of God is shed abroad in our hearts by the Holy Ghost which is given unto us."
—*Romans 5:5*

Divine love extended toward one another is the defining element of your faith in Jesus. Love is the fruit of your reborn spirit! God's love *in* you makes it possible for you to walk as Jesus did: in truth, grace, forgiveness, kindness, humility and love toward your brothers and sisters in Christ. Divine love is also a sign to those who don't yet know your beloved Savior. When someone is touched by love, he or she knows it is real, because love is an eternal substance. Love is a Person. Love is God Himself expressed through humanity!

When you repented of your sin and received Jesus Christ as your Savior, the love of God was shed abroad in your heart by the Holy Spirit. Eternal love abides in you at this very moment!

"But I don't 'feel' it, Mary Fran."

I know; faith has nothing to do with feelings.

I know there are situations and circumstances, family members and people at work or school or church, who challenge the demonstration of love, but if God says His love is in your heart, and it's the sign that you have passed from death to life, then by His power you can love the unlovely. Love is a divine thing, not a human thing. I have great faith in God's love in you, and by His power, you can do what He says you can do!

👑 **DECLARATION: I declare over you that God's love is alive in you enabling you to love the way He loves. Divine love flows freely from your life. It pours from your lips, is felt through your touch and consumes everyone you come in contact with. God's love in you causes every situation to turn around and succeed, because love never fails.**

Prayer of Consecration and Dedication

What the Father requires of you in this time is your heart.

My heart is filled with thanks for the place in time the Father has so graciously brought you to. He has prepared and preserved you for *this* time, like none other before it! What an awesome destiny you share—to prepare the way for the coming of the Lord! Forerunners you are, and just as Jesus' beloved cousin, John; you must decrease, that Christ may increase. You must bring low, make straight, declare and decree, *"Jesus is coming…prepare the way of the Lord!"*

In preparation for this time, you have been in a time of *transitioning* and *positioning*. What is occurring in the spirit realm is being felt in the natural, too. Movement and change are aligning you to His purposes now, so that you will be in place to ebb and flow with Him ever-so precisely.

What the Father requires of you in this time is *your heart*. Are you willing to "lay down your life"—*your* vision, *your* plan, the way you thought it would or should be—in exchange for His desires? Are you ready to say, "Father, not my will, but *Yours* be done?" His ways are so much higher, so much grander, so much more than you could ever ask or think!

Seek His face and His heart for your life as never before. I know He will answer your heart's cry to do His will alone, for He loves you just as He loves Jesus!

DECLARATION: I declare over you that you will make this decree a prayer of consecration and dedication to the will and plan of God for your life. "Father, I lay aside every weight and the selfish ambition in my heart. I ask you to make Your desires my desires. I say, 'Yes,' to You and Your plan, and I settle for nothing less than Your highest and best. Not my will, Father, but Yours be done, to the glory of Your Son."

Activate Angels

When Heaven came to Earth in the form of flesh, a way of salvation was granted for all by our gracious Father. Surrounding the arrival of His blessed gift to all humanity, was an abundance of angelic activity.

Your words are the key to the protection, deliverance, aid and assistance that angels provide....

Angelic activity is recorded in the Scriptures long before Jesus' birth, but a dramatic increase in the workings of angels marked the first coming of Christ. Visitations, announcements and instructions were delivered by heavenly messengers to Mary, the mother of our Lord; to Elizabeth, her cousin; to Zacharias; to Joseph and to shepherds in the fields. Angels came to announce and warn, to declare and prepare the earth for something wonderful of God!

These angelic ones who minister for you, the heirs of salvation, are sent from Heaven to carry out Kingdom business. (See Hebrews 1:14). You don't want to provoke angels as Zacharias did when Gabriel spoke to him about the coming of John the Baptist. Because of Zacharias' disagreement with the Word of the Lord, he couldn't speak until the plan of God manifested. Angels accompany and respond to the Word of God! Your words are the key to the protection, deliverance, aid and assistance that angels provide on your behalf! When you agree with the Word of God as Mary did, you activate angels to perform the Word you have spoken. According to Psalm 103:20, angels hearken or hear and obey the spoken Word of God! Angels are available in this present day to minister for you! Your part is to give earnest heed and not neglect the great gift God has given you through angelic assistance.

May you be filled with a greater awareness and expectation to activate the angels who stand ready and able to move Heaven and Earth for you at the sound of God's Word!

👑 **DECLARATION: I declare over you that you will give voice to God's Word and activate angels on your behalf! "Angelic ones, I commission you as the Word declares, to go and open doors, bring provision, protection, and cause situations and circumstances to align for Kingdom business and for blessing!" You give earnest heed to the great gift of angelic assistance, and you activate their workings in your life today!**

The King of Kings

God's glory— His manifested presence— illuminated the night, the earth He created, and the hearts of men!

When your Savior was born that holy night in a simple stable in Bethlehem, Heaven and Earth joined together in chorus, heralding the arrival of the King. Not just any king, but the King of kings, whose Kingdom has no end.

Angels, shepherds, earthly kings and ordinary men beheld His glory together. And together they worshipped the Christ Child, Heaven's gift of grace to the whole world.

God's glory shone bright that wonderful night, as God Himself was manifested on Earth in the form of human flesh. *"And the Word became flesh and dwelt among us, and we beheld His glory, the glory as of the only begotten of the Father, full of grace and truth"* (John 1:14).

God's glory—His manifested presence—illuminated the night, the earth He created, and the hearts of men! His glorious light shines upon you, oh righteous one! His indwelling presence is the light of the world. Christ in you, the hope of glory!

May Jesus light your heart and home anew this wondrous Christmas season!

DECLARATION: I declare over you that your heart is illuminated with the glory of God! You see and know as wisdom and revelation are opened unto you. What was concealed is now revealed, for the King of kings has come.

Nothing Shall be Impossible

What a beautiful time of year to express your heart to your Heavenly Father. Christmas is a season of warmth and wonder. It's a time to gather with loved ones, and to share in the joy of celebrating the hope of all the world. No greater gift could He give but Himself. Emmanuel—God with us!

Whatever the Holy Spirit has said to you, let it be to you according to His Word!

When God came to Earth as royal deity dressed in the humility of humanity, love came. Love is a force that nothing in this age or the ages to come can withstand. For with God—with love—*nothing shall be impossible!*

Father, Son and Holy Spirit came down to the Tower of Babel because the thinking and language of the people was such that nothing would be impossible for them. So God confounded their tongues, and languages were birthed for all peoples.

But when He visits you, the Holy Spirit speaks to you of His purposes, and with Him you agree. Then you decree a thing, and it shall be established. (See Job 22:28). Nothing shall be impossible for you if you believe and agree with God.

Whatever the Holy Spirit has said to you, let it be to you according to His Word! Perfect peace be upon you, and great grace, as you celebrate the Son, the Servant, the Savior this blessed season.

DECLARATION: I declare over you that the words of the Father are spirit and life to you. You humble yourself under His mighty hand and take your place as a son or daughter of God. All things shall be to you according to His Word, for with God, *nothing* shall be impossible!

The Church Glorious

You are not a people of fear, but a people of faith....

It is a time of unfolding events in the earth. In the midst of this time, God's people continue to gather and to call out in worship, lifting their hearts and lives in words, song and sound. All the while there's a knowing inside that soon and very soon, things as they have been known, will end.

You call out not in dread, for the Church glorious is empowered by the Holy Spirit. You continue on your march from place to place. Even during the events, you continue in your assignments, your destinies, and God's plan: to give every person an opportunity to hear the Name of God's beloved Son and receive what He has done for them. You will be about the plan as greater events unfold. You are not a people of fear, but a people of faith, and you continue on the move. You won't be stopped; you will build His Church, and the gates of Hell shall not prevail against it.

People of His light you are. As the darkness grows darker and events occur, the light of God will be greater through you unto all peoples. They will see and know that you are not believers who cower as the time of the end draws near. You are about "family business"; what is of your Father's heart. You will do all things by the instruction, leading and empowerment of God the Holy Spirit, for you are destined to be on the earth at this time of the end.

DECLARATION: I declare over you that you are gloriously empowered by His Spirit for this time. You will not cease to worship and call out to Him. You will march, you will build, you will see and you will know, and through you, His glory will be revealed.

Rejoice Exceedingly

I have such an expectation for you, dear one, and for the supernatural operations that surrounded Jesus' first coming to increase in your life as we draw ever-nearer to His return!

One encounter with Jesus Christ will change you....

Revisit with me Matthew chapters 1 and 2, and Luke chapter 2, and note the angelic activity, visitations, dreams, divine intervention and supernatural protection. Notice the manifestation of God's glory as Heaven came to Earth in the Person of Jesus Christ.

A holy hush stilled and silenced Earth in prelude to your Savior's appointed arrival. Yes, Jesus' birth marked the unfolding of Heaven's grand and glorious plan for all mankind. As this divine and prophetic event approached, the Father sent forth signs to summon the wisest of kings, and angels to announce to the lowliest of shepherds—for He is no respecter of persons. He heralds the cry: *"Whosoever will, let him come!"*

The shepherds came with haste to see this thing that had come to pass, which the Lord Himself had made known to them. What they witnessed they made widely known, and returned from their encounter with the Christ Child glorifying and praising God. The wise men gazed into the heavens at the bright and shining star—the sign of His coming—and they rejoiced with exceedingly great joy! When at last they saw the young Child and His mother, they fell down and worshipped Him, lavished costly gifts upon Him and returned home another way, their hearts forever changed by this Child of destiny they were warned to protect.

One encounter with Jesus Christ will change you, and in your heart you will conceive, carry and give birth to the plans that God ordained for you from the foundations of the world! In Jesus—God's precious gift to you—is everything your heart could desire. As you gather with family and friends today to celebrate the birth of your blessed Savior, may you rejoice exceedingly, worship wholeheartedly and look up expectantly for His glorious return!

👑 **DECLARATION: I declare over you that you agree with me in this prayer today. "Jesus, I worship You! I rejoice in You, my Savior. I glorify and magnify You this day. Thank You for divine encounters with You, my Lord, that change my heart and fill me with Your wonderful plans for my life. I love you!"**

Born for This Time

This is the time for the fulfillment of what you have believed!

Jesus is the Author and *the Finisher* of your faith, and so I believe that whatever it is you have trusted the Father for, *now* is its season of fulfillment! What dream or desire have you hidden in your heart? For whom have you prayed in the night season…trusting God for his or her salvation, healing or restoration? This is the time for the fulfillment of what you have believed!

The One who created you, and from the foundations of the world placed in you His plans for your life, now opens His hand to satisfy the deepest desires of your heart. (See Psalm 145:16). What seemed would never come to pass, *suddenly* springs forth, for, *"He who has begun a good work in you will complete it until the day of Jesus Christ"* (Philippians 1:6).

In Luke 4, after Jesus had read from the Book of the Prophet Isaiah to those gathered in the synagogue that Sabbath Day, He spoke to all whose eyes were fastened upon Him, saying, *"Today this Scripture is fulfilled in your hearing."* Jesus, God in the flesh, was the fulfillment of every prophetic Word written and spoken of Him. He is the Alpha and Omega, the Beginning and the End. He is our example of a man anointed by the Spirit of God—just like you and me.

There comes a day of fulfillment when the Word of God you have believed and decreed regarding your own life and those you have carried in prayer, will come to fruition. *"…Declare a thing, and it will be established for you; so light will shine on your ways"* (Job 22:28). God is watching over His Word to perform, complete and fulfill it! I believe God's fulfillment in your life will be a sign to those around you. At the height of chaos and confusion in the world, great clarity and peace will rest upon the ones who trust in God's Son. You were born for this time! Become what you have believed!

👑 **DECLARATION: I declare over you that all things you have believed are coming to their fullness. Just like Jesus, you are anointed by the Holy Spirit to accomplish all the Father has planned for you. It is your season of fulfillment! What you have believed, conceived and decreed now comes to fruition.**

Outpouring

A great expectation stirs in my heart for you, and for what is coming upon the earth! I believe you are experiencing a foretaste of what is to come even now as you gather around the Name of the Son.

"I will pour out My Spirit on all flesh...."
—*Joel 2:28*

This coming outpouring of power is for all! The Prophet Joel spoke of its coming in Joel 2:28, "I will pour out My Spirit on *all flesh*." All flesh means *all flesh!* Wherever God's Creation dwells, His Spirit will be poured out: in homes, in the grocery store, in the marketplace, in the halls of Washington, on movie sets, in school rooms and college campuses. I believe moving in the miraculous will be commonplace for the sons and daughters of the Most High in the time to come, if you will expect it and yield to the Holy Spirit as He moves.

The glory of God is beginning to fall in regions in sprinklings, but a deluge is on the way! You can be like Elijah, who prayed earnestly for the rain, and declared even before a cloud rose out of the sea, *"I hear the sound of an abundance of rain!"* Then he performed the will of the Father with speed and agility as a man anointed and empowered by the Spirit of the living God!

DECLARATION: I declare over you that you will expect a Holy-Ghost outpouring to flood you with the presence of God! You will run the race before you in the spirit and power of Elijah! You will flow in the miraculous, in healings, in signs, wonders, and in the mighty demonstrations of God that are destined for you!

The Fatherhood of God

"Behold, what manner of love the Father hath bestowed upon us, that we should be called the sons of God...."
—1 John 3:1

Something wonderful is happening to you concerning the Fatherhood of God! The Holy Spirit is impressing upon each and every one of you a revelation of the Fatherhood of the Creator Almighty that will so consume and inspire you, you will walk with God even through the hardest of times.

This tremendous, all-consuming understanding is going to transform you! It will change you to such a degree that you will be enabled to do *all* Father God has for you to do. Jesus was able to do what He did on the earth because He understood the Fatherhood of the Creator. Then, in John 14:12, Jesus said you would do what He did, and *greater works,* too!

God is going to take care of you! He has made a way to secure His sons and daughters in the earth. He understands your humanity very well, and He gives you understanding about what you need to do for *you* in the times we have come into. So, get ready, dear one! Make room in your heart for what has come: a revelation of your Father, and of *your place* in His heart!

👑 **DECLARATION: I declare over you that a revelation of God as your Father is opening unto you! You will receive a greater understanding of your place in the Father's heart, and it will empower you to be and to do all He has destined for you!**

Anointings Imparted

I mpartations are one of the greatest graces that my ministry carries. It is the Father's heart to impart some things specifically to you. I want you to take your hands and touch your eyes. Receive the anointing upon your eyes!

Impartations are one of the greatest graces that I carry....

Declare with me: "Father, I receive this anointing upon my spiritual eyes as You would so direct. I, too, will see and know. Thank You, Father, for anointing my eyes."

Now touch your lips and declare with me: "Father, I receive this anointing upon my lips. My lips will speak the Word of the Lord unto people as You would so direct me. I believe I am used of You in these last days. I agree with You that I have become a voice in the earth, and I am filled with You, filled with compassion, filled with Your Word that brings healings, deliverance, direction, comfort, and arrests souls to choose Jesus as their Savior and Lord."

Take your hands and lift them toward Heaven, and declare with me: "Father God, I receive the anointing now, this extraordinary anointing upon my hands. These hands will do the work of the ministry of Jesus Christ, Your only begotten Son. I receive this anointing, and by Your direction, I'll know who to go to. In Your Name, Lord, I will lay my hands on people and deliverance will come, healing will be, and the glory will be Yours."

DECLARATION: I declare over you the Father's anointing and appointing. These impartations made and declarations spoken over your life are to glorify Jesus Christ. You shall be a force within the army of God, endued with power that can stand Hell down. What you carry will rescue the souls of men into everlasting life.

Well Done!

... Where you've walked, now you'll run.

The Father says to you, dear one, "Well done. Well done sons and daughters of the Most High God." Hear the word of the Lord to you. The giftings that you have enjoyed shall be so enhanced by Him. My, how you will glorify Jesus and honor your Father's heart. The harvest will be won, and your great job will be done.

Suddenly, it shall be that you will be called out high in the sky. You will hear the sound of a trump, and my Lord shall stand there. The dead shall arise first, and you shall follow. Such a great cloud of witnesses are leaning in on you today, and in all the days and nights to come. You have been spoken of by generations past. You are the ones that have been so well spoken of and spoken into existence.

"Well done sons and daughters, well done. But you've only yet begun. Where you've walked, now you'll run. Well done; well done!"

DECLARATION: Declare this with me, "Thank You, Father, for Your encouragement to me. To know that I've pleased You blesses my heart and strengthens me to finish what You began, all for Your honor and glory, my Lord."

Do You Hear the Sound?

Sounds are coming down! Heavenly sounds are making their way down to Earth! Sounds, sounds...deep and bottomless...drawing out Creation's cry for our Creator. God the Holy Spirit beckons you, and from the depths of Him comes a cry that can only be answered by the deep in you.

God the Holy Spirit beckons you, and from the depths of Him comes a cry that can only be answered by the deep in you.

Do you hear the sound? Do you recognize His voice? His voice is as *the sound of many waters.* Sheep follow the voice of their shepherd alone, because *they know His voice.* Never will they follow a stranger, but will run away from him because they do not know the voice of strangers or recognize their call. (See John 10:4–5, AMP).

In Moses' time, a desperate cry arose from Earth to Heaven, and *the sound of divine deliverance* rang throughout the land of Egypt. Following the famine in Elijah's day, the prophet decreed he *"heard the sound of an abundance of rain."* In faith he declared and by faith he recognized the outpouring that was destined to fall upon the parched ground. After his declaration, he bowed in prayer and sent his servant to the sea to watch. Six times the servant saw nothing, but Elijah *heard the sound!* At last, the seventh time, a tiny wisp of cloud had formed. Blackness darkened the heavens, bringing a deluge of rain to water the earth and to cleanse a nation. When the Day of Pentecost had fully come, they were all with one accord in one place. And suddenly there came *a sound from heaven,* as of a rushing mighty wind that filled the whole house, and the people, too! (See Acts 2:1–2).

Sounds from Heaven are coming down! Do you hear the sound?

👑 **DECLARATION: Declare this with me, "The deep in me cries out to you O, God! I am watching and waiting and listening in faith. I have ears to hear what the Spirit is saying. According to First Corinthians 15:52, I declare that, *'In a moment, in the twinkling of an eye, at the last trump: for the trumpet shall sound, and the dead shall be raised incorruptible, and we shall be changed.'* You are coming! I hearken unto Heaven and await with ears to hear Your sound!"**

Prayer of Salvation

If you would please put your hand on your heart and give voice to these words:

"God, I ask Your Son, Jesus Christ, He who is God, He who is Savior, to be *my* Savior. Jesus, I receive Your life. I receive what You did for me. Your life, Your death, Your resurrection, Your forgiveness for my sins, I receive that now for me. Jesus, come into my life now. I declare You are my Savior. You are my Lord. No one else shall be lord over me! I receive forgiveness. I receive Your love. I receive my worth. I receive my esteem from You. I will no longer look to man for my worth or for my esteem. From this moment on I draw my worth from You. Jesus, teach me more about You. I receive Your love and I love You back. Amen."

PRAYER TO RECEIVE THE BAPTISM IN THE HOLY SPIRIT

If you desire the Person of the Holy Spirit to come upon you and fill you to overflowing with the presence and power of God according to Acts 2:4, then lift your hands toward Heaven and pray:

"God, my Father, I ask You in Jesus' Name to fill me with the Holy Spirit. Holy One, rise up within me and fill me to overflowing as I praise God. I fully expect to speak with other tongues as You give me utterance. Amen."

"Holy Spirit, I'm so thankful for who You are; the third Person of the Trinity. You are helper to me: the One who strengthens me, stands by me, advocates and intercedes on my behalf. You are teacher to me, and the revelator of the words and works of Jesus Christ. Please, Sir, open up the words of this book to me so that I might see, know, and understand the Fatherhood of God, the Savior, Jesus Christ, and You and Your giftings. Emboss upon my heart an understanding of the times so that I know what I ought to do, to arise and take my place and position as a righteous one, a son of God in the earth."

OTHER BOOKS BY DR. MARY FRANCES VARALLO

Walking Through a Miracle
Healing Scriptures
How to Keep Your Miracle
Jesus Christ—Savior, Healer, Deliverer and Holy Spirit Baptizer

ADDITIONAL PRODUCTS

CD's

The New You
The Person Holy Spirit
The Spirit's Compassion in Demonstration
Prayer, Authority and Forgiveness
Seven Golden Keys
It's the Time of Great Grace
I've Been Sent to Tell You
Arise
Breakthrough
Healing Scriptures (with musical accompaniment)
Adventures with God the Holy Spirit
The Power of Eternity in You

DVD's

Demonstrations of God
Miracles in the Atmosphere of Worship

For more information,
to order books and products,
or to contact
Mary Frances Varallo Ministries:

Website: www.MaryFrancesVaralloMinistries.com

Facebook: www.facebook.com/MaryFrancesVarallo

Twitter: www.twitter.com/RevMaryFrances

Mary Frances Varallo Ministries
4117 Hillsboro Pike
Suite 103-272
Nashville, TN 37215
615-383-1627
admin@mfvm.org